CURED

CURED

Salted, Spiced, Dried, Smoked, Potted, Pickled, Raw

LINDY WILDSMITH

PHOTOGRAPHY BY SIMON WHEELER

FEB 04 2011

kp krause publications
A division of F+W Media, Inc.

700 East State Street • Iola, WI 54990-0001
715-445-2214 • 888-457-2873
www.krausebooks.com

First published in North America in 2010 by
Krause Publications, a division of F+W Media, Inc.
700 East State Street
Iola, WI 54990-0001

To order books or other products call toll-free
1-800-258-0929 or visit us online at www.
krausebooks.com or www.Shop.Collect.com

Text copyright © 2010 Lindy Wildsmith
Photography, design and layout copyright
© 2010 Jacqui Small

This book has been produced by Jacqui Small
L.L.P., 7 Greenland Street, London, NW1 0ND

Library of Congress Control Number:
2009937527

ISBN 13: 978-1-4402-0512-5

ISBN 10: 1-4402-0512-4

Publisher Jacqui Small
Editorial Manager Kerenza Swift
Editor Abi Waters
Art Director Lawrence Morton
Production Peter Colley
Main photography Simon Wheeler

10 9 8 7 6 5 4 3 2 1

Printed and bound in China

CONTENTS

WHY CURE?

As we regress into our culinary pasts we cannot fail to come face to face with the curer's crafts: in the past curing, preserving, pickling, call it what you will, was as essential to life as breathing; preserved foods were the mainstay of everyone's diets from peasants to kings, and without them whole nations would have starved. When man discovered food lasted longer when hung near the fire, strung in the wind, buried in the sand, or laid in the sun to dry, it was no longer necessary to keep moving in search of food and the hunter-gatherer settled down near lakes or rivers. He started to make pots of clay in which he could cook and even evaporate seawater to make salt, which would draw the moisture out of flesh and therefore dry it and preserve it even longer. These became essential life skills and remained so for thousands of years.

Today with refrigerators, freezers and vacuum packaging there is no need to preserve meat or fish but we crave the unique tastes that develop in them as the chemical changes occur. The texture, the color and the taste intensifies, deepens and becomes richer. Much is muted regarding the fifth taste, that certain something, that quality of savoriness, something you can't quite put your finger on, the deliciousness, not sweet, sour, bitter or salty. The Japanese call it umami and equate it scientifically to MSG (monosodium glutamate), which exists naturally in our food. Parmesan has umami as do sun-dried tomatoes. The Japanese *dashi* is a stock that is the basis of much of their cooking and imparts this special quality to the food; it is made among other things with bonito flakes (dried tuna flakes).

So cured food has a special taste that we love but, I can hear you saying, we can go out and buy it, and so we can. There are more specialists than ever working across the world using age-old techniques enhanced by modern discoveries—smokehouses curing every kind of fish from the stealthy salmon to the humble but equally delicious mackerel, from a fillet of venison to a side of bacon; and plants where every fish from the tiny anchovy to the mighty tuna are salted and everything from a dainty scallop to a robust octopus are being pickled. There are caves where acorn-fed pigs hams are lovingly cared for to reach their maturity and farmhouse kitchens where confits, rillettes and potted titbits are still made as they were hundreds of years ago. At the end of the book I have included a comprehensive directory of the best of these products and where to buy them.

Preserving, be it fruit and vegetables, fish or meat, is an age-old process that has at its core something magical: turning base metals into gold, changing water into wine, arresting the march of bacteria. Okay, not quite as sexy as the first two but pretty extraordinary! It is a skill that can be dabbled in from time to time or delved into deep. It does not have to involve a great deal of time or expensive and complex equipment and it is a lot of fun. But you do need patience. Curing is not a

science, so there are no exact formula; it is a craft, so there are some rules. You can give as much of yourself to it as you like and the more you give the more pleasure you will get from it. Be warned: it is addictive; you will find you want to keep on experimenting with every kind of preservative and every kind of meat and fish. Like mastering jam making, once you have got it you want to flaunt it. It is a common misapprehension that preserving is a good way of using up inferior ingredients. This is not so! Use only quality fish and meat and preserve it with the best vinegars, oils, fats, wines, herbs, salts and spices there are. You will only get out what you put in.

There are many methods of preserving food, which have evolved in different ways in different countries depending on climate and ingredients. There is smoking, which is actually a threefold process involving salting, drying and smoking. Drying in its own right can be further divided into air drying, sun drying, wind drying and sand drying (burial). There is salting, by rubbing with salt, which is further divided into hard salting (salt cod), semi-salting (gravadlax), and light salting, which simply modifies the taste and texture but does not preserve it. Pickling involves immersion in brine or in acidic liquids. Fermentation cures with live cultures such as yogurt, bran and rice.

❀ THE CURER'S COMMANDMENTS

❀ Always use top-quality seasonal produce, sourced locally whenever possible. The present thinking on fish sustainability is to use as much variety as possible. Remember, produce is at its best and cheapest when in season.

❀ Experiment with smaller fish, smaller cuts of meat, and small quantities of fruit and vegetables until you have achieved results that please. When using smaller amounts than the recipe specifies remember to reduce the quantity of curing salt and spice otherwise it will end up far too salty.

❀ Follow the basic guidelines for each discipline, but don't be afraid to personalize rubs and marinades to make them your own. Vary vinegars, wines, oils, sugars, spices and herbs. Vary woods for smoking.

❀ Improvise with equipment you already own, before shelling out on a new kit.

❀ Let the seasons work for you. When dry curing meat such as hams, bacon and loins wait for the colder months. October to November is a great time as the animals are in their prime after a summer of plenty.

❀ You may prefer not to use curing salts or add saltpeter when curing meats and prefer to use sea or rock salt alone. You should be aware of three key facts: the cure will take longer, meats such as bacon and pastrami will not have that typical rosy glow but will be gray, and you are exposing yourself to more risk. Nitrates kill bacteria, salt arrests them.

❀ Careful wrapping and storage will make a difference to how long lightly home-cured food will keep. Vacuum packing will probably double its shelf life. To err on the side of caution keep cured food a week to 10 days. If not eaten within this time freeze after three days. Cured meats

and bacon will keep longer: if it smells and looks good, have a tiny taste and if it tastes good, eat it. See page 111 for the Parma ham test.

❀ Salt and health issues: cured meats and fish are full of flavor, have good texture, are more nourishing weight for weight than fresh, and are easily digestible, and consequently you eat less.

❀ Enjoy cured food as simply as possible with a drizzle of oil, a few drops of lemon juice, a dab of horseradish, a spoon of pickle, a grinding of spice, a few shavings of cheese, a swirl of sauce, and some decent bread.

❀ Leftovers make great tasting canapés; cut into slivers and stirred through a salad they make seriously good lunches.

❀ Don't rush things, this is truly slow food. Enjoy the culinary magic.

SPECIALIST EQUIPMENT

I urge you when taking your first steps into the world of curing not to even think about buying equipment that may well stand on the top shelf gathering dust for evermore. So many of the recipes in this book can be made by improvising with what you have at home. When you are just making small quantities for domestic use you can hot smoke in a steamer, slow cook overnight in a low oven, wrap sausages in caul fat (lace pig fat), take advantage of low winter temperatures or low oven temperatures instead of investing in dehumidifiers and temperature-controlled rooms, use muslin wraps instead of meat safes, and slice smoked fish and meat by hand.

Once you have found your feet you may well decide to grasp the curing baton firmly in your hand and run with it and if so there are certain pieces or equipment that really make a difference. If you are curing bacon, pancetta, cured loin of pork, venison, wild boar, pastrami and so on, a small domestic meat slicer will cut paper-thin slices that melt in your mouth, the like of which you will never achieve by hand slicing.

Once the curing is done, the meat or fish needs to be stored, as you may not want to eat it all at once, and a small vacpac machine will help lengthen the shelf life of cured meat and fish considerably without affecting the quality. Unlike freezing you can take the meat out, use what you want, and then vacpac it again without damage.

Hot smoking can be done in all sorts of simple ways without having to resort to buying a smoke box, but if you want to cold smoke that is a different kettle of fish. You will need the real thing or a great deal of ingenuity.

A slow cooker, that must-have kitchen aid from the 70s, makes confits and rillons to die for. You may already have one gathering dust so get it down and polish it up. And finally, if you want to make proper sausages, and you can have lots of fun doing so, you will need a sausage machine.

If you are a regular customer at your local butcher or deli you may, for a fee, get your sausages stuffed and your meat sliced. You may have a smoker nearby who will custom smoke. But please don't push your luck; talk to him first, say you are having a go at making such and such and would he mind—for a charge of course. Only ask if you are a regular customer and don't expect him to do it if he is busy or more than once.

See the directory on pages 284 to 285 for equipment suppliers.

There is the ancient form of the vacuum pack, covering food completely either with butter, olive oil, rendered fat, jelly or hard pastry crust, preventing the air from getting at it. Spicing involves rubbing mixtures of ground spices and herbs into the raw protein products; many of the spices and herbs we use every day to add flavor have antiseptic qualities—cinnamon, cloves, ginger, white mustard seed, aniseed, juniper, garlic, chili peppers, and herbs such as dill, thyme, bay, parsley, coriander seeds and tarragon help the preserving process. Nutmeg, mace and aniseed also help preserve the flavor of food. Finally, I come to the instant cure, the crudi, ceviche, sashimi, meat and fish dishes in which the proteins are altered by the addition of citrus juices, vinegars and spices. Not strictly a form of preservation but certainly a way of altering the flavor and texture of meat and fish that has become hugely popular.

It is not always easy to pigeon-hole a cured food. As I have already said, many of them involve more than one method, so I have grouped recipes under the cure that has most impact on the finished dish. Pastrami, therefore, is listed under spicing, gravadlax under salting and so on.

I have included guidelines for making many great cured specialties: the wonderful cured comestibles of the Swedish smorgasbord from gravadlax to herring rings. French potting from the farmhouse kitchen; the antipasti of Italy, amber bottarga from Sardinia and ruby red carne salada from Trento; smoked brisket and pulled pork beloved by barbeque devotees from the Southern states and the hunters' indispensable jerky, a spin-off from pemmican made by the Native Americans of North America; the migratory herring beloved in so many northern European countries; the German delicatessen dishes of *sauerbraten* spiced beef, liverwurst and rollmops; the iconic pastrami and corned beef of the New York Deli; salt cod and stockfish dishes; Spanish *escabeche*; *shimi saba* and *sashimi* from Japan; and lastly the delights of the British Provisioner—bacon, smoked salmon and ham, salt beef and potted meats. I also include some recipes for some of the classic pickles that should accompany them.

I have met many of the traditional practitioners of these crafts from as far afield as Britain, Scandinavia, northern Europe, Italy, Spain, Mexico, the USA, Robinson Crusoe Island, Japan and West Africa. I met some curers at the Terra Madre conference in Turin, that amazing melting pot of culinary diversity. I then went on to visit others in their own countries. I have searched out chefs who carry on these age-old traditions in their contemporary eateries, many of whom have generously shared their recipes with me. It is extraordinary to think that so many of the world's celebrated chefs are today dedicated to the traditional crafts of curing, giving them a new edge by using the most up-to-date equipment and technology. Rene Redsepi of Noma in Copenhagen smokes, salts, pickles and dries food for his restaurant. He also makes his own vinegars. Sweden's Magnus Ek of the Oaxen Krog restaurant in Stockholm boasts sandalwood-smoked trout, confit of pig's head terrine, and roe deer marinated with juniper berry, among many other innovative cured dishes. British real-food pioneer Mark Hix took up smoking two years ago. Today he smokes enough salmon in a smoker at the bottom of his garden to supply his four London restaurants.

The making of this book has been an amazing culinary journey. As in all journeys it has not been possible to include everything I had hoped and inevitably there will be some omissions. The more I have written and cooked the bigger the subject has become. This is first and foremost a cookery book for home cooks and consequently I have included lots and lots of recipes to complement the traditional flavors of cured food. I have created some delicious new contemporary ones, given a new twist to old favorites and included traditional dishes enjoyed by generations of enthusiasts.

You may well have bought this book simply because you love cured food but I hope you will be tempted at least to try some of the core recipes. Start by smoking a chicken on your stovetop at home or by making gravadlax or brining your own side pork; experiment using your favorite herbs and spices. It is amazing what you can produce at home without spending money on special equipment. Every bit of food you see in this book was prepared and photographed in my kitchen at home and almost every bit eaten and dare I say enjoyed by the team who helped produce this book. My thanks to them.

Clockwise from top left **Home-cured Swedish delicacies; Grinding a marinade in a mortar and pestle; Improvised hot smoking in the kitchen; Simple ingredients – salt, time and duck breast – go to make Lady Llanover's Salt Duck (see page 25).**

Salt cod (see page 52)

1 SALTED

BELOW THE SALT

Salting is a universal method of preserving, remaining the method of choice everywhere on earth where refrigeration is still not an option. It is the basis of most preserving processes, and is used to assist the drying process, particularly where climatic conditions are not ideal for air-drying. The effect of the salt is violently powerful, drawing the water out through the cell walls in tiny droplets by a process of osmosis. Water is thus removed from living microscopic bacteria, inhibiting their growth and ensuring that the food will remain unspoiled.

Anyone who has salted an eggplant before cooking it will have seen this process in action. The eggplant is sliced, sprinkled with salt, and a weight placed on top. Tiny droplets appear all over the cut surface and eventually these drain away.

The rule of thumb when preserving is to use the best-quality ingredients. In times of old, when it came to salting this was doubly true because salt was an essential and expensive commodity. Without salt, food could not be preserved and people could not exist without preserved food. Salt, therefore, played an important role in the economy of Europe. The Arabs were the first to recognize its potential as a revenue earner. The Normans copied the idea and governments everywhere were quick to cash in by imposing heavy taxes on it, just as governments do today with gasoline. The heavy taxation on salt eventually caused the decline in salt-preserved foods.

Because of the excessive cost of salt, it was highly prized and treated with reverence. Elaborate "salts" were crafted in silver and gold to display the salt on the table, its use limited to the nobility at the top of the table. In medieval times, when living was communal and everyone sat at the same table, the salt was offered only to important diners—those at the top of the table—and this is where the expression "below the salt" comes from in referring to people of lesser birth.

SALT OF AGES

Salt has been used to preserve food since time immemorial. It was mined as long ago as the Bronze Age and in the Iron Age seawater was boiled in shallow earthenware containers until water evaporated to leave sea salt. Babylonians and Egyptians pickled fish such as sturgeon, salmon and catfish, as well as poultry and geese. The Greeks made and traded salt fish around the Mediterranean. Romans set great store by it and their soldiers were given a salt allowance as part of their pay, which was known as a *salarium*, from which the word "salary" is derived.

During the Middle Ages the Church adopted what had once been a pagan tradition of fast or fish days—days when mortal man should practice self-denial by not eating meat, which was more expensive and considered more desirable than fish. To begin with, this was just one day a week, plus the 40 days of Lent leading up to Easter. Later on, for political and economic (by controlling food supplies) rather than religious reasons, more fish days were added to the Christian calendar, creating an even heavier demand for dried fish. Controlling and protecting the fishing industries was a major concern for leading maritime countries. Where there was fish and salt, there was ultimately power. Navies and armies survived on salt fish, voyages of discovery depended on it, and it played a central role in feeding most of Europe, as only small coastal communities had access to fresh fish.

In poor regions salt was extracted from seaweed. Acids found in nettles, burdock leaves, dill, parsley, white mustard seed, stinging nettles, and horseradish were all experimented with to take the place of salt. In Japan where there were no salt deposits they improvised and learned to make salt out of ground dried seaweed.

Ginger-cured gravadlax ready for draining and slicing (see page 56)

SALT OF THE EARTH

There are two ways of salting. One is dry salting or curing—rubbing salt into the flesh, once or several times over days or weeks; the more salt, the more rubbing, the longer the food lasts. For thicker pieces of meat, or meat or fish to be kept for a greater length of time, brining, wet salting or pickling is used instead. Salt is dissolved in boiling water, cooled, and the food submerged in it. Wet salting is more effective than dry salting, as brine has a penetrating effect upon animal tissue. The salt content of the brine mixes with the fluid in the flesh and works its way deep into the tissue.

Table salt contains additives to keep it free-flowing, which is not good for preserving. When it comes to meat that will later be served raw, a mixture of salt and a low concentrate of saltpeter, a nitrate, is used. Nitrates kill bacteria, while salt simply arrests them, so it is best to err on the side of caution when entering the wide world of cured meats and fish. Nitrates also help kick-start the sweating process and therefore speed up the curing process and lengthen the shelf life. However, nitrates are poisons and should be used sparingly. Due to the use of saltpeter in the making of explosives, it is increasingly difficult to obtain. Curing salt, which is salt ready mixed with saltpeter, is much easier to source and is available from mail order suppliers (see pages 284 to 285).

Natural sea salt is generally considered most suited to curing fish, in particular coarse sea salt because its action is slower and more thorough than fine sea salt. Much of the sea salt that is harvested is gathered mechanically and refined for industrial purposes. It is therefore essential to use best-quality hand-harvested sea salt. Rock salt was once a popular choice for curing, but natural sea salt is generally recommended, as it is consistent in quality. That said, many fine curers do use rock salt too. Sugar and all kinds of herbs and spices can be added to fish salt cures and this is where the home cook can enjoy experimenting without investing time or money in equipment. All you need is a large plastic, ceramic, glass or stainless steel container, a board, a weight, and a little time.

MAY YOUR PIG BE FAT

For hundreds of years, country people and indeed city people all over the world kept a pig. Come the autumn, the family pig would be fattened up and then slaughtered to give them a supply of fresh and preserved meat to see them through to the following spring. Each culture had its own traditions as to how this preserving was done, but what was common to all was the use of salt. The blood was drained from the pig's neck to make black pudding, its head severed, intestines removed and hung up to dry, and every single bit of it, from its tail to its bristles, used. The hams were rarely kept for home consumption, as they were a luxury. These would make good money, enough to allow the family to buy salt to preserve the bacon and pig meat to see them through the winter.

A fat pig meant a winter of abundance. Pickled pork (that is pork in brine) was a popular choice; when left in brine for a year or more, it melted in the mouth. Strips of meat—collars—were rolled and tied tightly and then immersed in brine. There was not a part of the pig that could not be pickled and enjoyed by the humblest to the mighty. Salt pork and bacon would have been high on a ship's provisions list of both the early settlers and later immigrants looking for a better life in North America and the colonies. Once thoroughly cured, pork will keep for up to two years and is capable of nourishing the longest of voyages.

Salt pork was also immensely popular in homes in the "colonies" and used in all kinds of dishes. The journeys made by the early settlers were long, arduous, and fraught with danger, and required just as much, if not more, careful provisioning than an Atlantic crossing. Bacon and salt pork would have been mainstays; any fresh game meat that fell into their hands and could not be consumed in the short term would have been preserved to last the journey.

These self-same long-life foodstuffs became the staple provision of the cowboys who roamed the prairies at round-up time. Chuck wagon cooks were relied upon to create decent food and the best of them were dab hands at spicing up cured meat into palatable chow, as well as curing and preserving fresh meat as and when it happened along. Profit-minded ranchers and trail bosses did not always provide fresh beef even though there was plenty of it, but rather more modest fare such as cornmeal, molasses, bacon (known as 'overland trout'), beans, and salt pork to keep the cowboys going. Pork and beans (see page 22) has become an iconic dish of cowboy cuisine.

PORK BRINING TODAY

This is commonly limited to hams, gammon and bacon joints, which are immersed in a brine solution for one week, wiped down, and hung for up to three weeks to mature. Some brine solution is injected close to the bone to help the salt penetrate the core of the meat. These hams are then boiled or partially boiled and roasted, glazed with sugar, before serving hot or cold. Using a brine (or pickle as it used to be called), a salt and water solution, is a quicker method of curing than dry salting, as it penetrates the meat faster and is therefore more suited to thicker cuts of meat. Many commercially produced hams are pre-cooked and pre-tenderized, injected with brine to speed up the salting process, and given less maturing and smoking time. Unsurprisingly, they lack any depth of flavor or texture, and have earned themselves in my view the label "plastic ham."

❀ BRINING GUIDELINES

❀ To find out how much brine you need, put your meat in the container you are going to use and add water, 4 cups (1 liter) at a time, until it is completely immersed. Pour off this water and measure it—this gives you the amount of brine needed.

❀ For 10½ pints (5 liters) water you will need 4 cups (900 g) curing salt (or 4 cups (900 g) sea salt and 1 teaspoon saltpeter mixed).

❀ Put 4 cups (1 liter) of the water in a large saucepan, add the necessary salts, and simmer until the salt dissolves. Stir in the remaining water and let cool.

❀ Put the meat in a noncorrosive container.

❀ Add the cooled brine and put a weight on the meat to make sure that it stays under the brine.

❀ Keep in the refrigerator, cool larder, or a cold cellar.

❀ Change the brine if it starts to smell.

❀ Rinse and dry the meat.

❀ Soak overnight in fresh water before cooking.

❀ Pork shoulder, side, head and hocks all brine well (see pages 20 to 21).

opposite left Side pork, pig's hocks and shoulder of pork ready for brining
opposite right The joints of meat are immersed in brine and weighted
below Boiled ham ready for glazing

A LESSON IN SALTING

Ebullient young chef Henry Herbert runs the kitchen at the Coach and Horses pub in London where they regularly cut, cure or cook every bit of a pig delivered from Somerset.

A whey-fed pig was due to be delivered and I was invited to be part of the welcoming committee. When I arrived the half pig was laid out ready for dissection. Henry had mapped out where to make the necessary incisions with a black marker pen. The only bit of this pig that was going to escape the chef's pleasure was the pork fillet, which to date Henry had been unsuccessful in curing, and also the kidney.

The animal was duly cut up and sorted: the bacon for salting; the ham for Wiltshire cure; the side pork, hocks and head for a brine bath (see below); the shoulder for slow roasting and mixing with side pork for sausages and hamburgers; and large hunks of fat to render down for rillettes.

HENRY HERBERT'S BRINE BATH

SERVES 26 TO 32

22 pounds (10 kg) ham, side pork, pig's head (see below), ears, hocks or lumps of pork skin

BRINE

30 pints (14 liters) water

11 cups (2.5 kg) curing salt or 11 cups (2.5 kg) coarse sea salt and 1 teaspoon saltpeter mixed, or according to the instructions

With experience, Henry has managed to rein in the temptation to over-complicate brines and marinades. His brine bath is man enough to take a whole ham. Half the quantity, or even less, is sufficient for most brining tasks. Choose a vessel that fits your refrigerator and the meat you want to brine. Then calculate how much brine you are going to need (see page 18).

Boil the brine ingredients together to dissolve the salt and then let cool.

Immerse the meat in the brine bath in an 8-gallon (30-liter) tub. Keep in the refrigerator, or cool larder if you are lucky enough to have one, for 5 to 10 days.

❦ **NOTE** Put a brined pig's hock or hunk of skin in meat and bean casseroles to give them extra flavor.

HENRY HERBERT'S BATH CHAP

SERVES 6 TO 8

½ pig's head, cleaned and prepared as explained in the recipe introduction (see page 18)

1 pig's tongue

Henry Herbert's Brine Bath (see above)

EQUIPMENT

Kitchen string

This recipes takes six to 11 days to complete. This is a traditional cured dish in which half a pig's head is rolled up around the tongue, tied up and cured in brine for 10 days, then cut into slices and fried.

To prepare the head, I watched Henry cut off the ear and blowtorch the whiskers. He then turned the half head over and flipped out the brain with the point of a knife. He took the head to the sink and gave it a good scrub in running cold water with a scourer, snout and all. Henry proceeded to cut the head flesh from the skull in one piece (if you know your local butcher well, you could ask if they could do this for you). He then cut out some glands that he said had an unpleasant texture and were harder than normal flesh—it is pretty obvious which bits these are as they look and feel different to the pig meat—and pulled away the blood clots.

Lay the head flesh, skin side down, place the tongue in the middle, and roll up tightly into a cone shape turning in the snout at the narrow end as you do so. Tie up tightly with string. Immerse in the brine bath for 5 to 10 days.

After this time, immerse the bath chap in a large pan of cold water, bring slowly to a boil, and then simmer for 6 hours. Let cool in its liquor.

Remove from the liquor and pat dry. Cover tightly with plastic wrap and refrigerate for 24 hours or longer as needed. Slice the bath chap: thickly for frying and thinly for cold cuts. It is great served with deep-fried crispy slivers of cured pig's ear and a dandelion leaf salad or fried with Pickled Cabbage (see page 238).

AUNTIE RACHEL'S BRAWN

**SERVES 6 TO 8 AS AN
APPETIZER OR 4 FOR LUNCH**

½ pig's head

Good pinch of freshly grated
nutmeg as desired

Finely grated zest of
½ orange (optional)

Sea salt and freshly ground
black pepper as desired

EQUIPMENT

Small loaf pan

This recipe takes three to six days to make. It was given to me by my friend Vee's Auntie Rachel with the opening instruction: "First clean the pig's snout." This had made me rather reluctant to try it. However, having overcome my squeamishness when I helped Chef Henry Herbert (see opposite), I was now ready to rock. Handling half a head is no different from handling any other piece of meat—honestly—and the meat is delicious. It does, however, help to ask your butcher to remove the eye first.

Clean the head, ears, nose and teeth and give it a scrub with a scourer under running water. Remove the whiskers—this can be done with a blowtorch. Take out the brains from their small protective pocket; fry them in butter for a delicious treat. Brine the head for 2 to 5 days (see Henry Herbert's Brine Bath opposite).

After this time, put the head in a large saucepan, cut side up, and cover with cold water. Bring gently to a boil and then gently simmer for 3 hours so that the water is hardly moving. Take the head from the saucepan and set on one side, cut side up. Put the pan back on the heat and boil until the liquid is reduced by half. Test a teaspoon of stock on a cold saucer to see if it turns to jelly.

Pick the meat from the bones while it is still hot. Discard any bits that look as if they do not have a soft texture. Put into a dish and season with salt, pepper and nutmeg to taste and add the orange zest, if using. Line the small loaf pan with plastic wrap, add the meat, and level out. Pour the reduced stock over the meat and let set. Transfer to the refrigerator overnight, turn out when cold, and cut into slices. Serve with salad or cut into cubes, put on wooden toothpicks and serve as finger food.

❧ **VARIATION** Italian brawn, or *testina*, is made in the same way, but rather than adding jelly, the warm meat is pressed and weighted for 2 days. Orange zest and garlic are added to the bits of meat.

left **Pig's head in brine**

SALT PORK

It is very difficult to give hard and fast rules about the quantity of brine you need because it depends very much on the size of the meat and the container you are going to put it in. I always try and keep the container size quite snug to the size of the meat and make sure the brine covers the meat completely.

❀ Start this recipe 1 to 2 weeks before you are going to need it.

❀ Firstly, work out how much water you will need. Put the meat in a suitable noncorrosive container. Add enough water to cover the meat. Pour off this water and measure it. This is how much brine you will need to make.

❀ Bring the measured water, about 8 cups (2 liters), to a boil in a large saucepan, add 1½ cups (350 g) of coarse sea salt and 1 teaspoon saltpeter or

1½ cups (350 g) curing salt (see page 16), and stir to dissolve. Let cool completely.

❀ Cover the pork with the brine and place a 2 to 3 kg (4½ to 6½ pound) weight on top of the meat. Keep in the refrigerator or cool larder for 1 to 2 weeks.

❀ Salt pork is delicious served with beans (see below), cabbage (see page 24), and mushy peas (see page 130).

PORK AND BEANS

SERVES 8

2½ cups (500 g) dried haricot or cannellini beans, soaked overnight in plenty of cold water

3¼ pound (1.5-kg) piece of salt pork rib or shoulder (see above), soaked overnight in fresh water. Alternatively, use a piece of butcher's cured ham

3 garlic cloves, peeled

1 small red chili

½ tablespoon thyme leaves

Butter, for greasing

2 tablespoons all-purpose flour

Finely chopped flat-leaf parsley, to serve

Sea salt as desired

TOMATO SAUCE (OPTIONAL)

1 tablespoon butter

1 onion, finely chopped

4 garlic cloves, finely chopped

(3) 14-ounce (400-g) cans whole peeled plum tomatoes, drained, seeded, and roughly chopped

You will need to start this recipe one to two weeks before you want to eat it.

For those of you who like your beans in tomato sauce, I have added an extra stage—sweating the beans in tomato cooked with garlic and onion. If you prefer your pork and beans white, then just omit the sauce ingredients and the related part of the method.

Drain the beans and rinse. Put the beans in a large saucepan and place the pork on top. Add the garlic, chili and thyme, cover with warm, not boiling, water, and gently bring to simmering point. Skim the surface of the water as necessary and cook on very low heat, so that the water hardly moves, for an hour.

After this time, take the pork out of the pan and set on one side. Drain the beans, reserving the cooking water. Preheat the oven to 300 to 325 F (160 C).

If you like your beans in tomato sauce, melt the butter in a large saucepan over medium heat. Add the finely chopped onion and garlic, and cook until lightly golden, say 5 minutes. Add the prepared tomatoes and cook until reduced down to a pulp, about 20 minutes, mashing with a potato masher every now and then until rich and creamy. Add salt to taste.

Rub a casserole dish generously with butter. Add the beans, the tomato sauce, if using, and the flour, stir well, and then add the salt pork. Top up with some of the cooking water from the beans. Bring to a simmer, skimming the surface of the water as necessary. Cover with a piece of parchment paper and the lid. Cook in the oven for 2 hours. Let rest for 20 minutes before serving.

Transfer the beans to a serving platter and scatter with chopped parsley. Slice the salt pork, arrange on top, and serve.

SALT PORK AND CABBAGE

SERVES 6 TO 8

3¼ pound (1.5-kg) piece of salt pork rib or shoulder (see page 22)

1 large carrot

1 large onion

1 leek

1 bay leaf

1 rosemary sprig

1 thyme sprig

CABBAGE

1 large onion, finely chopped

2 garlic cloves, finely chopped

1 head of cabbage, shredded

Good pinch of freshly grated nutmeg

A little stock

Sea salt and freshly ground black pepper as desired

Grapeseed oil, for frying

Salt pork and cabbage is the national dish of Ireland and should be served with boiled potatoes.

Soak the pork in cold water overnight, then throw away the soaking water.

Put the pork in a large saucepan, cover with fresh cold water, add the vegetables and herbs, and simmer very gently for 1 hour or until tender. Let stand for 20 minutes in the cooking water before serving.

To make the cabbage, put a wok or large skillet over a medium heat and cover the base with grapeseed oil. Add the onion and garlic and fry until soft, say 5 minutes. Add the cabbage, nutmeg and seasoning, and then stir-fry for 1 to 2 minutes. Reduce the heat and cook until tender, stirring occasionally. Add a little stock or water if the cabbage sticks or burns. Serve with chunks of salt pork, seasoned with black pepper.

SERVES 6 AS A STARTER

1 cup (225 g) coarse sea salt

1 duck, weighing approximately 6¼ pounds (2.8 kg), or a duck crown

Freshly ground black pepper as desired

This gorgeous recipe was developed by the doyenne of all British food writers, Elizabeth David, and Franco Taruschio from an original Welsh recipe. They took the dish under their wings and hatched a sensational cold-cured, ruby red duck breast. The ducks are salted while still on the bone and turned for three days. The brine is poured off and the ducks then cooked in a low oven in a water bath for one and a half hours. The flesh is soft, succulent, barely salty and aromatic. Serve thinly sliced with Pickled Raspberries (see page 236).

For this dish you only need the breasts and the duck carcass. Cut off the legs and wings and make confits (see page 196) or rillettes (see page 190).

Rub a thin layer of salt inside and outside the duck. Lay the duck, breast side down, on a layer of the remaining salt in a deep, noncorrosive dish and let it stand in the refrigerator or cool larder for 1½ days.

After this time, rub the remaining salt back into the inside and out of the duck, turn over on the other side, and let stand in the refrigerator or cool larder for 1½ days again.

Preheat the oven to 300 to 325 F (160 C). Pour off the brine that has formed and rinse the duck.

Transfer the duck to a deep ovenproof dish, cover with cold water, and put in a cold water bath—an ovenproof dish filled with boiling water to come halfway up the side of the deep dish. Cook in the oven for 1½ hours.

Drain the duck immediately and then let cool completely. Cut off the breasts, cover with plastic wrap, and refrigerate until required. The duck will keep for 10 to 12 days.

When ready to serve, cut into ½-inch (1-cm) thick slices, season with ground black pepper, and serve with Pickled Raspberries and baby salad leaves.

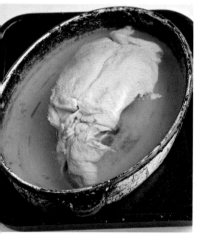

Above **The duck in its water bath ready for the oven**

HOME-CURED HAM OR COUNTRY HAM

SERVES 24 TO 30

21 pints (10 liters) water or half water and half ale or cider

18-pound (8-kg) locally sourced ham to home cure—explain to your butcher or supplier what you want it for; it will have to be special ordered

2¼ cups (500 g) curing salt or 2¼ cups (500 g) coarse sea salt and 2 tablespoons (50 g) saltpeter mixed

Scant 1 cup (200 g) demerara sugar

1 bouquet garni

2 teaspoons whole pickling spice

If you have not tried out your curing skills on a loin (see page 117), I would advise you to do so before trying a ham. I would also recommend that you read the introductory pages of this chapter (see pages 14 to 19) and those of the chapter on air-drying (see pages 100 to 131). Curing is learned by experimentation, but it is useful to know what the experts have to say first.

A refrigerated room is of course ideal, but few of us have access to such a facility. Nature's time for curing is late autumn/early winter, when temperatures have dropped. This is when pigs, before the introduction of refrigeration, were slaughtered and is the safest time to do home curing. The low temperatures will guarantee good results.

If you are thinking of seriously getting involved in curing hams, it is advisable to invest in a brine pump. A ham is a very thick piece of meat and it is essential that the brine penetrates to the very core, otherwise the meat will rot. A meat safe would be advisable, too. Otherwise, make sure you use a cool, airy place and that you hang the ham so that the air can circulate around it. You will need to wrap it in cheesecloth or dip in a thin layer of lard and black pepper (see page 110) to ward off the flies. And remember the ultimate Parma ham test (see page 111: your nose will tell you if the cure is good or bad).

This recipe will take two months to make.

Put half the liquid in a large saucepan with the remaining ingredients and bring gently to a boil. Simmer until the salt and sugar has dissolved. Let cool and then stir in the rest of the liquid. Stab the ham all over with a sharp knife or skewer to the very center of the meat. Fill the pump with brine and inject the brine into the thickest parts of the ham, in and around the bone.

Put the ham in a large, noncorrosive container and add the cooled brine to cover. Put a weight over the meat to ensure that it is completely immersed. If the ham is not completely immersed, you will need to make extra brine. Put the container in the refrigerator, cool larder, or a cold cellar and let stand for 3 weeks.

After that time, remove the ham from the brine, rinse and drain, wipe and dry it, then hang in a refrigerated room or meat safe. Alternatively, wrap in cheesecloth or immerse in a solution of lard and black pepper (see page 110), then hang in a cool, airy cellar or outhouse for 1 month. Either roast or boil the ham to serve (see page 29).

HENRY HERBERT'S WILTSHIRE CURED HAM

SERVES 26 TO 32

22-pound (10-kg) ham to home cure—explain to your butcher or supplier what you want it for; it will have to be ordered especially

Henry Herbert's Brine Bath (see page 20)

1½ cups (500 ml) molasses

6½ cups (1½ kg) coarse sea salt

1 tablespoon saltpeter

This recipe takes two months to complete.

Immerse the ham in the brine for 3 weeks (see page 18).

Remove the ham from the brine, wipe and dry it. Mix the molasses, salt, saltpeter and a splash of water together and massage the mixture into the ham. Let stand for a week, massaging it in every day.

After that time, rinse and drain the ham and then hang in a refrigerated room, or wrap in cheesecloth or immerse in a solution of lard and black pepper (see page 110), and hang in a cool, airy cellar or outhouse for 1 month.

Roast or boil the ham (see page 29).

CURING HAM. 1. The ham, ready to cure. 2. Stabbing the ham all over to allow the cure to penetrate. 3. Immersing the ham in brine. 4. The cured ham.

HOW TO COOK HAM

Even if you don't cure your own ham, buying a piece of ham from your butcher or local supplier and cooking it yourself is just as good. You can roast or boil it.

I like to boil ham, since I find it retains its moisture better, but roasted ham probably keeps longer, as it is drier. If you want to cook a whole ham, roasting is the simpler method because finding a pan big enough in which to immerse a whole ham is quite a task. The advantage of cooking a big piece of ham is that it gives you a hot or cold meal for lots of people; perfect for Christmas Eve with baked potatoes and pickles and subsequently plenty of fillings for sandwiches. A cooked ham will keep for a month in the refrigerator if wrapped well.

BOILED GLAZED HAM

SERVES 24 TO 30

18-pound (8-kg) cured uncooked ham joint

1 bay leaf or bouquet garni

Few cloves or juniper berries (optional)

1 carrot

1 celery stalk

1 onion

TO GLAZE

Dijon or other mustard of your choice

Demerara sugar

It is advisable to wrap the ham in foil once cooked and let stand for 20 minutes before serving.

Soak the ham in cold water overnight, then throw away the soaking water.

Put the ham in a large saucepan and cover with fresh cold water. Add the herbs, spices, if using, and vegetables to the water and bring slowly to a boil. Skim the surface of the water as scum rises to the top. Reduce the heat and simmer very gently so the water hardly moves for 40 minutes plus 20 minutes for every 2¼ pounds (1 kg) ham.

Let the ham stand in the cooking water for at least an hour or to cool completely.

Preheat the oven to 300 to 325 F (160 C). Take the ham out of the water and put in a roasting pan. Peel off the skin, then trim and score the fat in diamonds or squares. Spread the scored fat with mustard and coat with demerara sugar.

Bake the ham in the oven for about 20 to 30 minutes until golden. Keep an eye on the oven, as glazes can catch fire and burn easily. Serve hot with parsley sauce and mashed potatoes or in sandwiches with Green Tomato Pickle (see page 236).

ROASTED HONEY-GLAZED HAM

SERVES 24 TO 30

18-pound (8-kg) cured uncooked ham joint

TO GLAZE

Liquid honey

Dijon or other mustard of your choice

Lemon juice

When roasting ham, experiment with a roasting bag.

Preheat the oven to 300 to 325 F (160 C).

Cut the skin off the ham, taking care to leave an even layer of fat on the ham. Score the fat with a diamond pattern. If you prefer you can leave the skin on and trim afterward. Put the ham on a rack in a roasting pan. Add enough water to cover the base of the pan. Put in the hot oven and cook for 1 hour plus 20 minutes for every 1 pound (500 g) ham. Test by sticking a skewer into the thickest part of the ham. If the juices run clear, the ham is ready.

About 20 minutes before the cooking time is up, mix equal quantities of honey, mustard and lemon juice together. Coat the fat with the mixture using a pastry brush. Return the ham to the oven and roast for about 20 minutes until golden, but do watch it, as the glaze burns easily.

BOILED GLAZED HAM. 1. Removing the ham from the pan. 2. Transferring to a roasting pan, peeling off skin, scoring the fat and coating with mustard. 3. Patting with sugar. 4. The oven-ready ham. *opposite* The finished glazed ham

JAMBON PERSILLÉ

HAM AND PARSLEY TERRINE

SERVES 8 TO 12

3¼-pound (1.5-kg) gammon joint

Ham shank

Bouquet garni made from 1 celery stick with leaves, 2 parsley sprigs, 2 thyme sprigs, 1 bay leaf, 2 chervil sprigs (or use a good pinch of dried if fresh is unavailable), and 2 tarragon sprigs (or use a good pinch of dried if fresh is unavailable)

8 peppercorns

1¼-pint (750-ml) bottle of dry white wine

1 shallot, finely chopped

2 garlic cloves, finely chopped

2 tablespoons gelatin

2 cups (65 g) flat-leaf parsley (not including stalks) finely chopped, plus a few sprigs for decoration

EQUIPMENT

Terrine dish

This classic French dish comes from the Bourgogne and is served traditionally at Easter. It was originally prepared over two days with gently boiled ham, knuckle of veal, and calves feet aromatized with plenty of white wine, tarragon, chervil, bay, parsley and peppercorns.

The meats are cooked until they fairly fall off the bone and can either be shredded with a fork or chopped into various-size cubes. The meat is then either mixed or layered with lots of parsley and a cooled reduction of the cooking water, which jellifies when cold. The jambon persillé *is then transferred to a terrine to set and either served from the terrine or turned out.*

There are many versions, some more complicated than others. Jane Grigson in her book Charcuterie and French Pork Cookery *gives a simple version of the original recipe using calf's foot and veal hock. I have modified the recipe to be made with ham shank and gammon, which are easier to source. The ham shank bone produces wonderful soft, pink meat and excellent jelly, but is sadly not strong enough to set the terrine, so unless you use calf's foot it will be necessary to add gelatin to set the terrine. If you prefer you can just use gammon and again add gelatin.*

Soak the gammon and ham shank in cold water overnight, then throw away the soaking water. If time is short, immerse the meats in cold water and bring to a boil, then throw away the water and proceed as follows.

Add the bouquet garni of herbs and celery to the pan with the dried herbs, if using, and the peppercorns. Add 2¾ cups (650 ml) of the wine and then enough cold water to cover the meat. Bring gently to a boil and simmer so the water is barely moving. Cook for 45 minutes, then switch off the heat and let rest for 30 minutes. After this time transfer the meat to a carving dish, reserving the cooking liquor.

Return the pan containing the cooking liquor to the heat and boil on high until reduced by half. Strain and let cool.

Pour the remaining wine into a small pan, add the finely chopped shallot and garlic, and simmer until soft, say 10 minutes, then let cool.

Cut the meat from the shank in thin slices, discarding the fat and sinew, and then dice into small pieces. Cut the gammon into neat cubes, about ½ inch (1.5 cm), discarding any fat and skin.

When the cooking liquor has cooled, put a scant ½ cup (100 ml) in a bowl and sprinkle the gelatin on top. Wait for it to dissolve, then transfer to a microwave and cook for 30 seconds. Stir well and add to the rest of the cooking liquor. Whisk well and strain. Stir in the softened shallot and garlic and the chopped parsley.

Starting with a thin layer of the jelly, layer the finely chopped shank, the gammon cubes, and the jelly, finishing with jelly. Top with a few whole parsley leaves. Put the terrine in the refrigerator overnight to set and either serve from the terrine or turn out onto a plate.

BRINED ROAST SIDE PORK

SERVES 4

2¼ pounds (1 kg) side pork, off the bone

Henry Herbert's Brine Bath (see page 20)

Few cloves (optional)

8 sage leaves

1 rosemary sprig

3 garlic cloves, peeled

This recipe can take anywhere from 36 hours to a week to make, so plan ahead. Once you have your brining pot going in the refrigerator, there is nothing you won't want to put in it to try out the results. Slow-roast side pork is always good, but brining the pork first for anywhere from 24 hours to a week gives it a whole new melt-in-the-mouth texture and depth of flavor (see Salt Pork on page 22).

Restaurant chefs love brining side pork as, once brined, it keeps in the refrigerator almost indefinitely and they can cut off just as much or as little as they need to cook.

Cut the side pork from the rib bones (these can be marinated and roasted). Put the meat in the plain brine, weight, and refrigerate for anywhere from 24 hours to a week—the longer the better!

When the pork comes out of its brine, soak it in clean cold water overnight and then dry it thoroughly. If time allows, let the pork air dry for an hour or so. Score the rind in squares or diamonds and stud with a few cloves in a regular pattern, if liked.

Preheat the oven to 350 F (180 C). Finely chop the sage and rosemary leaves and the garlic, and massage all over the meat. Put on a rack in a roasting pan and add enough cold water to cover the base of the pan. Roast in the oven for 2 hours.

Take the pan out of the oven and let the side pork rest for 30 minutes. Transfer the meat to a serving dish. Cut the meat into squares and serve with applesauce and sweet potato mash or roast pumpkin wedges.

Home-curing bacon

The methodology of home-cured bacon is much the same as it has always been, involving salting, drying and smoking, but timings and quantities have evolved to suit conditions and taste. Drop traditional cured bacon into a hot skillet or place under a broiler and it immediately starts to sizzle, the fat turns translucent, and the lean puckers up, creating a sweet, melt-in-the-mouth experience. Much commercially produced bacon is pumped with salty water and when you put it in a hot skillet it leaches quantities of milky liquid and produces cardboard-like meat. Fortunately, if you do not have a suitable place for drying or maturing bacon, which is an essential part of the curing process, there are many wonderful artisan bacon products on the market. Start by asking your local butcher if he cures his own bacon—you will find that many do—or he may be able to recommend someone that does.

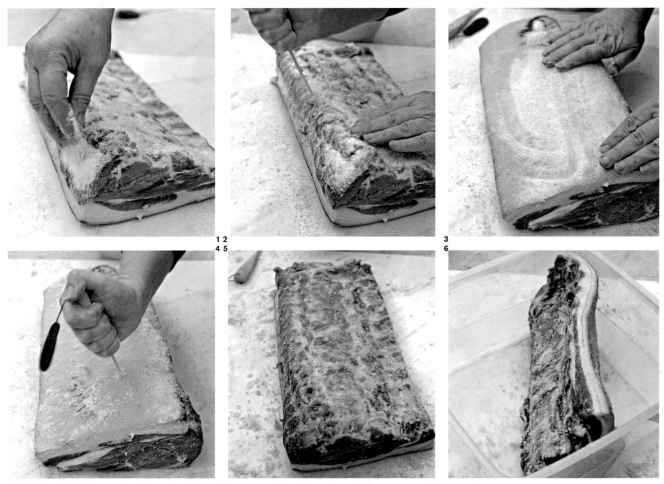

CURING BACON. 1. Rubbing the loin with cure. 2. Stabbing the thicker parts of the loin to allow the cure to penetrate. 3. Rubbing the rind with cure. 4. Stabbing the rind to allow the cure to penetrate. 5. The loin is now ready. 6. The loin transferred to a plastic container.

❧ BACON BASICS

❧ For every 2¼ pounds (1 kg) loin or side pork, mix 1½ tablespoons salt, ½ tablespoon demerara sugar and 1 teaspoon saltpeter. Alternatively, use 2 tablespoons curing salt.

❧ Rub the cure into the bacon on both sides. Pierce the thicker parts of the loin on both sides, including the rind, with a clean wooden skewer.

❧ Put it in a noncorrosive container and leave for 1 week in a cool larder or cold cellar.

❧ Wipe the loin clean and dry it thoroughly. Wrap it in cheesecloth to protect from flies and hang up for 2 to 3 weeks—the longer the better.

❧ For smoked bacon, cold smoke for 2 hours (see page 152).

WARMING BACON, LEEK AND GINGER SOUP

SERVES 4

2½-ounce (70-g) slice of streaky bacon, rind removed and cut into cubes

1 celery stalk, roughly chopped

1 carrot, roughly chopped

1 onion, roughly chopped

Splash of Marsala wine

3 leeks, cut into 1-inch (2-cm) rounds

1 large egg-size lump of fresh ginger root, peeled and finely chopped

3 cups (750 ml) vegetable stock or ham stock, if available

Sea salt and freshly ground black pepper as desired

Olive oil, for frying

Finely chopped parsley, to serve (optional)

On a cold winter's day nothing can compare with a bowl of homemade soup and a hunk of warm bread. This soup, made with lots of fresh ginger and a base of streaky bacon, beats them all.

Put a large saucepan over high heat and cover the base with olive oil. Add the streaky bacon cubes and the roughly chopped celery, carrot and onion and stir-fry until golden.

Add salt and pepper and the Marsala wine and cook until evaporated, then add the leeks and ginger. Reduce the heat to medium and continue to cook until the leeks start to soften. Add the stock and simmer for 30 minutes. Taste for seasoning.

Transfer to a blender and blend until smooth. Return to the pan, taste for seasoning, reheat. Scatter with finely chopped parsley, if using, and serve with hot crusty bread.

SCALLOP-STUFFED BACON ROLLS

SERVES 4

1½ cups (80 g) breadcrumbs

1 small onion, finely chopped

2 tablespoons parsley, finely chopped

6 good-size king scallops, shelled, cleaned (corals retained), and halved

6 thin slices of streaky bacon, rind removed and cut in half

4 tomatoes, halved, seeded, dried, and then turned upside down on paper towels to drain

Sea salt and freshly ground black pepper as desired

Olive oil, for oiling and drizzling

EQUIPMENT

4 skewers

This simple and delicious way of serving scallops was inspired by a visit to Orkney where the seafood is exceptional. Dipping the scallop and bacon in breadcrumbs is a canny way to make the scallop go further but make sure you don't overdo it.

Preheat the oven to 375 F (190 C).

Put the breadcrumbs, chopped onion and parsley, and salt and pepper in a bowl and mix together. Spread the crumb mixture out onto a large plate.

Dip the scallop pieces in the crumbs to coat. Dip both sides of the bacon slices in the crumbs, then roll each coated piece of scallop in a slice of bacon and thread three of these rolls onto each skewer. Oil a baking sheet, arrange the skewers on the tray, and drizzle with oil.

Fill the tomato halves with some of the crumb mixture, top with a piece of scallop coral, and sprinkle any remaining crumbs over and around the bacon rolls. Drizzle the tomato halves with a little olive oil and bake in the oven for 20 minutes. Serve at once with spinach or salad.

❈ **VARIATION** Use lambs' kidneys, oysters, soft dried figs or prunes instead of scallops.

PETIT SALÉ AU LENTILLES

SALTED SIDE PORK WITH LENTILS

SERVES 6

1¾ pounds (600 g) dry salted side pork, soaked overnight in fresh water (see below)

1 small dried sausage of your choice, stabbed with a skewer

1 ham hock

1 bouquet garni

1 teaspoon black peppercorns

⅓ cup (75 g) chopped bacon

1 large onion, finely chopped

6 garlic cloves, finely chopped

1¾ cups (350 g) lentils, soaked for 2 hours in cold water

1 bay leaf

2 tablespoons extra virgin olive oil

1 tablespoon white wine vinegar

2 tablespoons fresh herbs, say a mixture of thyme leaves and finely chopped parsley, plus extra thyme sprigs, to garnish

Sea salt as desired

Petit salé, *dry salted side pork, which is sold by charcutiers all over France, is easy to make at home (see below). This is a versatile, inexpensive, warming winter dish. It is sometimes also used as an ingredient for cassoulet. It takes one week to prepare.*

Put the salted side pork, sausage and ham hock in a pan, add the bouquet garni and the black peppercorns, and cover with water. Bring slowly to a boil and simmer gently for 40 minutes.

Fry the chopped bacon or lardons in a skillet until the fat starts to run, then add the onion and garlic and fry for 5 minutes. Add the drained lentils and stir for 5 minutes, add enough water to cover and a bay leaf, and simmer for 30 minutes or until tender.

Drain the lentils and add the extra virgin olive oil, white wine vinegar, and the chopped herbs. Season with salt to taste.

Lift the side pork, the hock and the sausage out of the cooking liquor. Cut in slices and arrange on top of the lentils. Garnish with a few sprigs of fresh thyme.

PETIT SALE: SALAISON Á SEC

FRENCH DRY SALTED SIDE PORK

SERVES 6 TO 8

½ tablespoon sugar

1 teaspoon crushed juniper berries

4 cloves

2 crushed bay leaves

2¼ pounds (1 kg) side pork with rind

SEL AROMATISÉ

2 star anise

1 teaspoon whole allspice

1 teaspoon cloves

2 bay leaves

Scant 1 cup (200 g) coarse sea salt

Sel aromatisé *is a basic ingredient in the French kitchen, which literally translated means aromatic salt. Make your own by grinding down some of your favorite spices and adding them to coarse sea salt. Use it to cure any meat, in this case side pork, or fish and seafood—I like to use it as a base for smoking oysters and other shellfish as it prevents them rocking about and imparts a subtle spice flavor.*

To make the *sel aromatisé*, grind the spices and the bay leaves together in a grinder or mortar and pestle and then mix with the coarse sea salt. Put in a screw top jar, seal and leave for a few days before use (it can then be used as you would regular coarse salt).

Mix the *sel aromatisé* with the sugar, spices and herbs. Take a handful and rub into the skin side of the side. Take another handful and rub into the flesh side and then rub the edges.

Scoop up the excess mixture and use it to make a thin layer to cover the base of a noncorrosive container.

Place the side pork flesh side down on the salt and then sprinkle the remaining salt mix over the top and sides.

Put a board and a weight on top and leave in a cool place for 4 days at least or for any length of time up to 2 months. Soak in fresh cold water overnight before cooking.

CORNED BEEF OR SALT BEEF: U.S. AND U.K. TRADITIONS

New York-style corned beef or salt beef is served in traditional Jewish delis across New York and London. Chunky cuts of salty, dark pink brisket are piled onto soft sliced rye bread and sandwiched with mustard and pickle.

Today there are more people with Irish ancestry in the USA than there are in Ireland itself. Corned beef (salt beef) and cabbage, the traditional St. Patrick's Day feast for all Irish immigrants, is said to have been the traditional Sunday feast back home. However, it is much more likely that they ate salt pork and cabbage (see page 24) before coming to the USA because beef would have been a luxury for the average family in Ireland.

The Irish would have salted beef rather than pork when they arrived in North America. Particularly large grains of salt, known as corns, were rubbed into the beef, hence it became known as corned beef rather than salt beef as it is called in the U.K. Confusing, because what we call pressed beef in North American is called corned beef in the U.K.

In well-off households in the England of yesteryear, salt beef was a popular choice. Huge pieces of beef weighing up to 22 pounds (10 kg) were pickled for three to four weeks, partially air dried and rubbed daily with ground allspice, crushed juniper berries, black pepper, minced shallots, dried bay leaves, saltpeter, garlic and salt. Today salt beef is generally made with pieces of brisket or thick flank weighing around 6½ pounds (3 kg). It is submerged in brine made with demerara sugar, sea salt and saltpeter, flavored with pepper, cloves, juniper berries, chili, bay and thyme and steeped for 10 days. It is then wiped dry and soaked overnight in fresh water before being boiled in a neat-fitting pot with carrots, onions, celery, herbs, including bay, and peppercorns, and enough water to cover, plus possibly a glass of beer or cider added, for 3½ to 4 hours. It is then left to rest for 20 minutes in its cooking liquid and transferred to a board directly before it is carved into thick slices oozing with juices.

LONDON'S BRICK LANE SALT BEEF

Most salt beef bars buy their brisket ready cured from a specialist company and therefore they define the art of perfect salt beef in the cooking rather than the curing. Sammy Minzly, the owner of the Brick Lane Bagel Factory, swears by Tipperary grass and hay-fed ox for his brisket. Sammy cooks his 6½-pound (3-kg) briskets for 3½ to 4 hours in barely simmering water with lots of bay leaves, one head of garlic, a handful of peppercorns, a whole carrot and an onion. He cooks around 25 a day, and as one succulent brisket is consumed, another is fished out of its cooking juices and loaded onto the counter for carving.

SERVES 8

3¼ to 4½ pound (1.5 to 2 kg) brisket

1 large onion

1 large carrot

6 garlic cloves, peeled

8 bay leaves

Handful of black peppercorns

SALT RUB

¾ cup (175 g) curing salt or ¾ cup (175 g) coarse sea salt and 2 teaspoons saltpeter mixed

⅓ cup (75 g) demerara sugar

3 garlic cloves, crushed

2 teaspoons whole pickling spice

2 crumbled bay leaves

1 teaspoon crushed black peppercorns

Franco and Ann Taruschio were the creators of that wonderful culinary institution The Walnut Tree at Llanddewi Skirrid near Abergavenny, South Wales. As Jan Morris said in the forward to their cookery book, Leaves from the Walnut Tree, *"They gave the place an atmosphere of mingled authority, festivity and relaxation." One New Year's Day, a minibus trawled around deserted London picking up the likes of Simon Hopkinson, Johnny Apple Junior, Bill Baker and Jeremy Lee to ferry them down to The Walnut Tree for a feast of Jewish melt-in-the mouth corned (salt) beef with beets and sticky salt cod and potatoes. One can only wonder at the quantity of alcohol consumed given the menu, the company and the occasion…*

This recipe takes up to 10 days to prepare, so plan ahead!

Mix all the salt rub ingredients together.

Pierce the meat all over with a fork and rub the salt mixture into the meat. Put in a clean noncorrosive container. Add enough water to cover the meat entirely. Place a plate on top and weigh down with something heavy. Cover with a cloth and keep in the refrigerator for 7 to 10 days (10 days is best).

Remove the meat from the brine and soak in fresh cold water overnight, then throw away the soaking water.

To cook, place the meat in a large saucepan with enough fresh cold water to cover and add the vegetables, garlic, bay leaves and peppercorns. Bring to a boil very gently, skim off the scum from the surface of the water, and simmer very gently so the water hardly moves, covered, for 3 to 4 hours, depending on the size of the piece of meat.

Leave the corned (salt) beef in the water to rest for at least 30 minutes before taking it out and carving. For cold corned (salt) beef, wrap it in parchment paper and press it by putting a plate and weight on top, then refrigerate. Serve with Pickled Gherkins (see page 245), mustard or Chrain (see page 234), and rye bread. It will keep a good week if well wrapped in the refrigerator.

❧ CORNED OR SALT BEEF GUIDELINES

❧ Choose the very best brisket from grass- and hay-fed animals.

❧ The best corned (salt) beef is made with a big, chunky, loose piece of brisket weighing 6½ pounds (3 kg) plus. If you want a smaller, family-size piece, ask your butcher for rolled brisket.

❧ Make a salt rub (see page 45), pierce the meat all over, and massage in the salt rub.

❧ Submerge the brisket in water, weight it and leave for 7 to 10 days, depending on the size of meat.

❧ Rinse the meat and soak in cold water overnight to remove the salt. Change the water before cooking.

❧ Simmer gently for 3 to 4 hours.

❧ Leave in the water until ready to carve.

❧ Serve in a rye bread sandwich with mustard and sliced gherkins or with Chrain (see page 234).

❧ It will keep for a week if well wrapped in the refrigerator.

1
2 3

PREPARING THE CORNED (SALT) BEEF. 1. Mixing the corned (salt) beef cure.
2. Piercing the meat with a fork. 3. Rubbing the cure into the meat.

4. The rubbed corned (salt) beef. 5. The beef placed in a plastic container and submerged in water.
6. Transferred to a pan to simmer gently. 7. Carve the corned (salt) beef once it has been drained.

PRESSED OR CORNED BEEF

SERVES 4 TO 6

14 ounces (400 g) corned (salt) beef (see page 45)

1 heaping tablespoon beef gelatin per 14 ounces (400 g) corned (salt) beef meat

4 tablespoons water per 1 heaping tablespoon beef gelatin

½ cup (100 g) beef drippings

EQUIPMENT

1-pound (500-g) loaf pan or mold lined with parchment paper

This takes the corned (salt) beef a step further.

When the corned (salt) beef is quite cold either grind or chop it finely (do not use a blender). Put in a bowl.

Sprinkle 1 heaping tablespoon beef gelatin into a small bowl with the water. Let dissolve without stirring, then put in a microwave oven for 30 seconds and stir. Strain and add the dissolved gelatin to the ground corned (salt) beef and stir well.

Press the mixture into the lined mold or loaf pan.

Heat the beef drippings gently in a pan. Insert a skewer here and there in the pressed (corned) beef and pour the melted drippings over the top to seal. Let cool and refrigerate overnight. Turn out the next day and slice. Serve with Chrain (see page 234) or Pickled Gherkins (see page 245). It will keep a good week in the refrigerator.

above Corned beef just out of the mold

PRESSED OR CORNED BEEF HASH

SERVES 2 TO 4

1 onion, finely chopped

2 garlic cloves, finely chopped (optional)

7 ounces (200 g) chopped Pressed or Corned Beef (see opposite), or any leftover meat or fish

1½ cups (350 g) roughly chopped or mashed cooked potatoes

Good shake of Worcestershire sauce

Sea salt and freshly ground black pepper as desired

Olive oil, for drizzling

Sunflower oil or melted butter, for frying

A quick and scrummy way to serve any leftovers. Hash can also be made with chopped leftover corned (salt) beef, ham, lamb, salt cod or other fish—in fact, any leftover meat and fish. The basic mixture of roughly mashed or chopped cooked potatoes and finely chopped onion and garlic can be shaped into cakes and fried in a pan or cooked in the oven in a roasting pan. The choice is yours.

Heat a skillet over medium heat, cover the base with sunflower oil or melted butter, and fry the finely chopped onion and garlic, if using, until transparent.

Add the chopped pressed or corned beef, roughly chopped or mashed potatoes, plenty of Worcestershire sauce, and salt and pepper to taste and mix together. Fry for 5 minutes, or until the base has browned, then drizzle olive oil over the top.

Transfer the skillet to a preheated hot broiler and cook until brown and crispy on top. Serve drizzled with extra Worcestershire sauce and topped with fried eggs and Chrain (see page 234) or Plum Chutney (see page 233).

Salt cod: the king of commodities

The Vikings navigated the coast of Portugal to trade goods and ideas. They took home with them Portuguese princesses to marry Danish kings and, more importantly, vast quantities of salt to preserve their cod. When the Vikings stopped coming, the canny Portuguese, having no cod of their own, sailed the seas as far as Newfoundland to fish it. By the 16th century they took with them, as the Vikings had taught them, their *fiel amigo*, their "good friend" or *bacalhau* (salt cod) as it is generally called, to Africa, North and South America, and the East Indies.

Salting dehydrates the fish, thus reducing its size and weight, making it an ideal ship's victual; it also increases its nutritional value. Consequently, a little salt fish could keep a ship's crew going for months on end, and because it was nourishing, cheap, and kept indefinitely, it became embedded in food cultures everywhere.

Newfoundland and the Eastern Seaboard owe their existence to the salt cod industry. Hundreds of boats came from Europe as early as A.D. 1500 to catch the abundant shoals of cod that hovered around its coast. The long journey home meant that fish once salted needed to be strung up to dry on the Newfoundland beaches before being shipped, thus creating settlements along the coast.

The first settlers in the Maritime Provinces would not have been able to survive without salt cod and smoked herring, as both the climate and the soil they found there were poor and inadequate for agriculture. The fact that Atlantic cod could be transformed into a durable protein meant that it became a valuable trading commodity.

By the time of the slave trade, the east coast of North America produced large quantities of its own salt cod. The trade in salt fish stimulated the infamous trade triangle between Britain, the Northern colonies, and West Indian plantations, and supported the expansion of trade routes around the world. Sue Shephard in her book on preserving entitled *Pickled, Potted and Canned* relates that the French ports of La Rochelle and Le Havre dominated the salt cod trade in the 16th and 17th centuries, and that England, too, played an important role in the development of the industry.

Salt cod became a staple of Caribbean and West African cooking, although as the food of slaves and servants it was snubbed by the middle classes for a long time. Every island and territory has its own specialty. West Indian salt fish is more delicate, more cod-like than Portuguese *bacalhau*, which has a very intense flavor.

Today cod is imported from Norway and Iceland for salting in Portugal. Edite Vieira, author of *The Taste of Portugal*, will only eat salt cod made in Portugal; she says the flavor, texture and color are superior to all others. She must have a point, since why else does it feature so heavily still in their excellent cuisine. It is said that the Portuguese have a different recipe for their *fiel amigo* for every day of the year.

LIGHTLY SALTED COD

SERVES 12 AS AN APPETIZER

1 tablespoon coarse sea salt

¾ tablespoon granulated sugar

2¼ pounds (1 kg) thick whiting or farmed cod

This is a useful recipe for prolonging the life of any white fish if you are not able to use it straight away. Serve thick loins as a starter sliced very thinly with a drizzle of olive oil and black pepper or Chrain (see page 234) or even Pickled Gooseberries (see page 234). Use as you would fresh fish: try making fish cakes (see page 130) or broil and serve with roast beets or poach and serve with an egg and spinach. Curing the fish makes the flesh firmer and thick pieces of fish would work well in a fish stew in a light tomato sauce or try the recipe for Corfiot Stockfish Stew (see page 129).

Mix the salt and sugar and rub into the fish. Put in a large thick plastic bag and seal. Alternatively, lay it in a long, shallow dish and cover with plastic wrap. Leave in the refrigerator or a cool larder for 12 hours, turning from time to time.

Wipe the fish down and let dry on a rack where the air can circulate around it in the refrigerator. Cover with plastic wrap and use as required. It will keep for a week or longer in the refrigerator.

❧ **VARIATION** After drying, brush with oil and hot smoke (see page 138) for 20 minutes with fennel pollen or finely chopped fennel fronds sprinkled on top.

left Lightly salted cod rubbed with salt and sugar
opposite Thinly sliced lightly salted cod

SALT COD AND PARSNIP GRATIN

SERVES 6 TO 8

1½ pounds (750 g) salt cod, well soaked (see below)

1 cup (250 ml) milk

1 cup (250 ml) water

1½ pounds (750 g) parsnips

3 large free-range eggs

Good bunch of parsley

1½ tablespoons unsalted butter

1 heaping tablespoon all-purpose flour

Scant ½ cup (100 ml) heavy cream

1 good teaspoon mustard

2 tablespoons fresh breadcrumbs

Freshly ground black pepper as desired

Use Rowley Leigh's recipe in the box below to make your own salt cod. Alternatively, you can buy it from specialist fishmongers and delicatessens.

Rinse the well-soaked salt cod and poach it in the milk and water for 10 minutes. Drain the fish, reserving the cooking liquid, and flake the meat into a gratin dish, taking care to remove any bones. Taste and if the cod is still chewy and salty immerse it in cold milk and let stand overnight or for 12 hours. Discard the milk.

Wash the parsnips and steam them for about 20 to 25 minutes or until tender. Peel away their skins and cut into ½-inch (1-cm) slices. Add to the gratin dish.

Meanwhile, hard-cook the eggs and then peel and cut into quarters. Add to the gratin dish. Wash and chop the parsley and mix with the parsnip, egg and fish in the dish.

Preheat the oven to 425 F (220 C). Melt the butter in a saucepan. Add the flour and stir over a low heat with a wooden spoon for 1 minute. Pour in a little of the cooking liquid from the cod to make a smooth paste before pouring in the rest and whisking constantly until it comes to a simmer and forms a smooth sauce. Add the cream and mustard, season with plenty of ground black pepper, and simmer gently for 10 minutes before pouring over the mixture in the dish.

Bake in the oven for 10 minutes. After this time, sprinkle the breadcrumbs over the surface and bake for another 5 to 10 minutes until golden brown. Serve straight away.

HOMEMADE SALT COD

I met Rowley Leigh, the chef proprietor of Le Café Anglais and much-lauded food writer, currently of the *Financial Times*, on a press trip to the Parma Ham Festival while researching this book. He very generously asked me if I needed any recipes…

He advised, "If salting your own fish, use 2¼ pounds (1 kg) of rock salt to 2¼ pounds (1 kg) of fish, laying the fish on a bed of the salt and then covering with the remainder. If salted for 24 hours, the fish will need rinsing for five minutes under cold water; if salted for a week, it will need soaking overnight. Time and great care should be taken in the soaking and washing of salt cod. Soak for 24 hours in cold water, changed three or four times; using milk can speed up the process."

SERVES 8

14 ounces (400 g) salt cod (see opposite)

1 potato, cooked in its skin and peeled (optional)

Milk, for poaching

1 bay leaf

5 tablespoons olive oil

3 garlic cloves, finely chopped

3 shallots, finely chopped

¾ cup (200 ml) heavy cream

Juice of ½ lemon, plus extra to taste

Good pinch of freshly ground black pepper

Sea salt (optional) as desired

Salt cod is soaked, poached and processed into a heavenly creamy concoction, served on croutons. If a more subtle flavor is required, add mashed potato to this mixture.

The day before making the brandade, soak the salt cod in 3 to 4 changes of cold water over a period of 24 hours. Cook the potato, if using, in a microwave oven for 10 minutes, then peel and cut into chunks.

Rinse the salt cod well and put in a saucepan, cover with 1 inch (2.5 cm) of milk, add the bay leaf and bring to simmering point. Remove from the heat, cover, and let stand for 20 minutes. The fish should flake easily. Drain and flake the fish. Taste the fish at this stage and if it is still unpalatable soak in milk overnight or for 12 hours more.

Put a small sauté pan over medium heat, add the olive oil and finely chopped garlic and shallot, and cook until soft. Add the cream and heat through. Put the cod, and the potato if using, in a blender fitted with the plastic blade and blend the salt cod with the potato until chunky. Add the garlic, shallot and cream and process to a smooth purée. Add the lemon juice and black pepper, then taste, adding extra lemon juice and salt if necessary. Serve with homemade crostini (see page 184).

OTHER SALT FISH STAPLES

Salt cod was not the only fish to feed the power and prosperity of nations. Herring and other migratory shoals of fish arrived in seasonal gluts around the northern shores of Europe and North America. There is a hub of northern countries including Scandinavia, Poland, the Baltic states, the Netherlands, Belgium, northern Germany, and the British Isles that all enjoy this same culinary heritage. Many of these countries also share an important seafaring history, and in order to travel the globe, it was necessary to take enough victuals to last for the ship's journey, where such salted fish stocks proved an invaluable asset. Salted herring and anchovy were also mainstays in North America.

The Dutch are still passionate about herring today. One of the first things you will spot on the roadside are brightly colored carts selling them; the national street food of Holland. Simply pick them up by the tail, tip your head back, and lower them into your mouth whole. Glug! These are the *Hollandse nieuwe* (young herring), usually caught in May or June when they are really plump. The occasion is celebrated with Vlaggetjesdag, little flag day, when the first catch is sold at auction. The first load of fish to be landed is always given to the Queen of the Netherlands. The fish are gutted (all but the pancreas is removed), matured, and salted in barrels. They are dark brown and very salty, and need to be soaked very well before use.

ALASKAN SALT SALMON

Native North Americans did not originally know about salting, but in Alaska salt fish (salmon) became a staple item. When Russian immigrants first arrived they found salmon in plenty, and had brought with them their own traditions of pickling. Salt fish is still as popular here today, either boiled with potatoes and onions for soup or baked to fill *piroski*—deep-fried parcels. Leftovers go into hash or fish patties.

Fillet the salmon. Place a layer of rock salt in a noncorrosive container. Lay the fish fillets on top, skin side up, and cover with more salt, then cover with a board and a weight. Leave for six weeks and then drain off the water. Make a 100 percent brine solution, so that an uncooked egg will float in it. Pour this over the fish until covered. If keeping long term, pour the brine away in early spring, make fresh brine and submerge once more. Salt salmon will keep indefinitely when properly cured.

Today, salmon is more likely to be lightly cured in a spiced salt and sugar mix for 24 hours, then lightly smoked.

BEET-CURED SALMON

SERVES 12

2¼ pounds (1 kg) organically farmed salmon side, skin on, off the bone and scaled (your fishmonger would be able to do this)

MARINADE

1 cup (240 g) demerara sugar

1 cup (240 g) coarse sea salt

1½ tablespoons crushed black peppercorns

1 heaping tablespoon crushed juniper berries

5 tablespoons (80 ml) dark rum

3 cups (150 g) dill, including stalks, chopped

Zest of 3 lemons, pared with a potato peeler

2 pounds 4 ounces (1 kg) raw peeled beets, grated

Will Holland worked with Alan Murchison at L'Ortolan before taking on La Bécasse in Ludlow where he runs a well-ordered kitchen and his young team with a remarkably polished and yet friendly manner for such a young man. Will has a wealth of cured dishes on his menu such as gravadlax, confits of duck, and smoked rabbit loin.

Lay the salmon, skin side down, in a large, noncorrosive container. Run a knife the length of the salmon from the tail end, "combing" up the pin bones. Remove the bones with a pair of tweezers.

Mix all the marinade ingredients together and spread on top of the salmon. Massage twice a day for 4 days, drawing the marinade back from the flesh and then massaging it in again. Drain off the excess fluid before massaging. Cover the salmon with plastic wrap and then lay another piece of plastic wrap over the top of the container. Store in a refrigerator or cool larder.

After the 4 days, scrape off the marinade and discard. Wipe the fish with paper towels. The beet must only penetrate the top of the salmon to give it that, as Will calls it, "tequila sunrise look." It will keep a good week if well wrapped in the refrigerator.

CLASSIC GRAVADLAX

SERVES 8

2¼-pound (1-kg) salmon side, scaled, off the bone, skin on (ask your fishmonger to prepare the fish)

2 tablespoons coarse sea salt

2 teaspoons freshly ground black pepper

2 tablespoons golden superfine sugar or liquid honey

1 cup (50 g) dill, plus extra, finely chopped, to garnish

½ teaspoon ground cinnamon

DILL SAUCE

5 tablespoons Dijon mustard

1½ tablespoons red wine vinegar

1 tablespoon superfine sugar

¾ cup (175 ml) olive or vegetable oil

1 cup (50 g) dill, finely chopped

Sea salt as desired

❀ FOUR SEASONS VARIATIONS

❀ In summer—1 cup (50 g) elderflowers, juice and zest of 1 lemon, cut into wedges, and 2 tablespoons thyme leaves.

❀ In autumn—1 cup (50 g) peeled and grated fresh ginger root and 2 teaspoons Chinese five spice powder.

❀ In winter—the juice and zest of 2 oranges, cut into wedges, and 2 teaspoons ground cinnamon.

Gravlaks, gravlax, gravalax or gravadlax—take your pick; my spell check does not like any of them—literally means buried salmon. Since medieval times and possibly earlier, salmon, herring and other oily fish, even shark, were buried in holes in the ground and covered with birch bark and stones. This caused the fish to ferment, creating a soft flesh and a sour taste. Long-term burial preserved the fish through the long winters for consumption when the snow was on the ground and food was scarce. It was actually a very smelly product, quite unlike the one we know and love. Smelly salmon is now known as rakefisk *in Norway and* surfisk *in Sweden. Modern-day gravadlax is buried in salt rather than in the ground, or better described as dry cured and is not fermented.*

Marinating salmon to make your own gravadlax is very simple and rewarding. Dill-flavored gravadlax is the classic version, but you can personalize the recipe by choosing your own herbs, spices and flavorings according to season. Try, for instance, orange and cinnamon at Christmas, and if you have access to wild salmon and common hedgerows in early summer, as I do in Herefordshire, a combination of salmon and elderflowers is sublime (see Variations below).

Freeze the prepared salmon for 2 days. Take out and let thaw. Check carefully for bones by running your fingers along the salmon flesh and pull out the bones using a pair of tweezers.

Mix the salt, pepper, sugar, dill and cinnamon together and rub into the flesh. Lay the salmon, skin side down, inside a large, thick plastic bag. Seal the bag and let stand in the refrigerator or cool larder for 24 to 48 hours, as time allows, turning the bag from time to time. Alternatively, lay it in a long, shallow dish, cover with plastic wrap and leave for 24 to 48 hours in the refrigerator. Pour off the leached liquid from time to time from the dish or bag.

After this time, wipe away any excess cure. Sprinkle lightly with the chopped dill and slice thinly when ready to serve.

To make the sauce, put all the ingredients in a screw-top jar, screw on the lid, and shake well. Serve the gravadlax with the sauce and bread and butter or boiled potatoes and green salad leaves.

❀ INSIDER KNOW-HOW

❀ It is traditional to use more sugar than salt—use equal parts sugar and salt for a firmer consistency.

❀ Bash the dill in a bag before using to enhance the aroma.

❀ The longer the period of marination, the firmer the flesh and the less raw it will be.

❀ Rub the salmon with the cure and let stand at room temperature to speed up the process and avoid hard surfaces forming on the salmon.

❀ Bags of dill freeze well. Use from frozen by simply crushing the dill bag with a rolling pin and the herbs will disintegrate as if chopped finely.

opposite **The cured gravadlax**
below **Thinly sliced gravadlax served with boiled potatoes and dill sauce**

Drawers from my spice cupboard *clockwise from top left*
Black peppercorns, mustard seeds, nutmeg and mace, star
anise, cinnamon bark, juniper berries and cloves

²SPICED &
MARINATED

"DRY" MARINATING: THERE'S THE RUB

Today we use spices and herbs as flavorings, but in the past they were also used for their preserving qualities. Spiced meat and fish, even when raw, keep longer than fresh. Spices, like salt, were expensive, essential commodities because of their medicinal, antiseptic and preserving powers.

A rub constitutes a dry mixture of vegetables such as celery, carrots, onion, garlic and/or ginger, herbs, spices, and sugar, mixed together and ground down into a paste either in a blender or using a mortar and pestle. The paste is then rubbed into meat, poultry, game and fish, which is weighted and left to stand for hours, days or weeks according to the recipe. The resultant product is then either smoked, roasted, boiled or barbecued, or eaten raw. Classic pastrami, for example, is rubbed with a paste made of spices, bay and garlic, weighted for one to three weeks, during which time it is massaged daily, then dried and smoked (see page 72). Some recipes, such as Rinaldo Dalsasso's Carne Salada (see page 78), call for the best cuts, but in these cases the meat is either served in its raw cured state or lightly smoked. Tough cuts are further slow cooked or smoked, or both. Fish, poultry and game all respond well to spicing, but generally speaking do not need to stay in the cure for any length of time, as the flesh is much more tender than meat.

In the past huge pieces of meat were preserved with spice rubs. The original recipe for Melton Hunt Beef in *The Art and Mystery of Curing, Preserving and Potting all kinds of Meats, Game and Fish*, published in 1864, called for a piece of boned beef weighing 30 pounds (13.6 kilograms). The meat was hung to dry, then rubbed with juniper berries, allspice, black pepper, bay leaves, shallots, sea salt and sugar for a week, turned every other day, and then rubbed with a pickle of rock salt, saltpeter and garlic every day for 10 days. If not needed straight away the meat was tied up, coated in dry bran or pollard, and smoked for a week with beech chips, oak lops (small branches and twigs), and fern. Otherwise it was baked, cooled for 48 hours, and then sliced.

There are similar recipes for manageable pieces of meat that have been around for hundreds of years. Spiced Christmas Silverside, for example, is rubbed with demerara sugar, salt, allspice and juniper berries for seven days and then wiped clean and cooked slowly in a cast-iron pot. In days gone by when there was no refrigeration, such cures were the only ways of keeping meat fresh.

"WET" MARINATING

Sauerbraten is a delicious way of spicing meat that has been a tradition in Germany for hundreds of years and is still a popular dish in every home in the country. Spices are mixed with vinegar to make a marinade in which the meat sits for several days before being cooked (see page 80). This and other traditional recipes were also methods of tenderizing otherwise tough cuts of meat and, it has to be said, disguising the taste of overly strong game and meat.

Marinating spiced tuna loin (see page 77)

Besides vinegar, liquid marinades can combine spices and herbs with wine, beer, cider and yogurt, in which the meat is submerged and left to cure. And it is not meat alone that can benefit from wet marinating. Sicilian chef-patron Andrea Alí told me how during World War II when food was scarce mountain farmers hid their homemade cheeses in barrels of *vinacce* (grappa brew) to mature. When the cheeses were eventually brought to light, they discovered they had created a new-tasting cheese.

SPICED SAUSAGE-MAKING TRADITIONS

As the imperial armies of Rome marched across Gaul, Britain and Germany they carried with them strange strings of highly spiced fresh, dried, or smoked pouches of meat. This portable nourishing food was a convenient way of preserving and packaging small bits of meat for leaner months. By the Middle Ages sausage-making was popular all over Europe, as the airtight intestines, used as skins, protected the meat from airborne bacteria. The use of black pepper protected the meat from bacterial growth.

Apicius, the Roman gourmet, includes a recipe for *lucanica* sausage in his recipe book using pepper, cumin, rue, savory, parsley, mixed herbs, laurel berries and liquamen (a Roman condiment) to flavor ground meat, to which he added whole peppercorns, plenty of fat, and pine nuts inserted into the intestine. *Salsiccia Lucanica* is a specialty of Basilicata in southern Italy and also around Milan. Both regions lay claim to their origin. In Greece, today, a sausage known as *loukaniko* is still popular, flavored with red wine and ground coriander. Spiced sausages are, in fact, produced not only all over Europe but also in many parts of the world.

Every wave of immigration that broke onto North American shores brought with it a new ethnic cuisine that has shaped the tastes of the present-day nation. Recipes were handed down and tweaked from generation to generation making them uniquely American. This is exemplified by the variety and popularity of homemade spiced fresh, semi-dried and dried sausages made there.

REAL "BARBEQUE"

A couple of years ago I was sitting in a pub in Dublin with a group of students from South Carolina when a poster advertising a local barbecue caught their eye. They asked me searchingly what barbecue was over there. I replied a bit of anything—sausages, ribs, chicken, but I could tell this was not the answer they were looking for. Curious, I asked a few questions and discovered that "barbeque" in South Carolina and in the Southern states is quite different to a barbecue.

Lake E. High, President of the South Carolina Barbeque Association, explains: "Unfortunately, most Americans who live outside of the South in general, and North and South Carolina in particular, use it ('Barbeque') as a verb or, if they use it as a noun, use it incorrectly. Midwesterners or Yankees will say to friends, 'I'm going to barbeque some hamburgers tonight.' Or they will say, 'Let's put some brats on the barbeque and break out some beer.' And while everyone will be having a great time sitting around in the smoke, the use of the word in that way is incorrect. That neighbor is going to grill some hamburgers, not barbeque them. The cooker he is going to cook them on should be called a grill, not a barbeque." Having established that what we know as a barbecue is not "barbeque" at all but broiling, I then needed to find out what "barbeque" is in the South. I got in touch with Lake High and Andre Pope, senior judge on the South Carolina Barbeque circuit, who were amazingly helpful.

Simply put, a South Carolina "barbeque" is a whole shoulder of pork, also known as Boston butt, slowly cooked on the bone over low heat in the smoke until it falls apart. It is more smoked than cooked; more roasted than grilled. In place of the ubiquitous smokehouses that were used in the past throughout the state, today they use what they call a pit (see pages 285 to 285 for a Web site with further information). But I used a smoker very successfully (see also pages 284 to 285).

If you cook beef, chicken or pork ribs this same way, they are referred to as barbecued beef, barbecued chicken or barbecued ribs. They also make "barbeque" with lamb, turkey, goat, and even possum in the Southern states.

Chilies, garlic, Muscovado sugar, bay, peppercorns and spices ready to make a rub

"BARBEQUE" AND SMOKING

It was the Spanish who first introduced the pig into the Americas and to the Native Americans. Way back in the 1500s, the Spanish conquistadors came to what is now South Carolina and named their first colony Santa Elena. It was there that the white man first learned to prepare proper "barbeque," when the Native Americans introduced the Spanish to the concept of true slow cooking with smoke. So the Spanish supplied the pig, the Native Americans showed them how to cook it, and that is when authentic "barbeque" was first eaten.

Early illustrations of "barbeque" were described as "Indians smoking meat," but the heat source is much hotter than it would be in a true smoking process. In smoking, the meat being smoked is cut away from the bone or animal rather than being smoked whole. Smoking is such a slow process that the interior of a whole animal would go rotten before the smoke had a chance to penetrate the meat. In "barbeque" the hog is often cooked whole for a big celebration.

There is, however, a very fine line between smoking and "barbeque." Smokehouses, which were common on every farm in South Carolina up until the 1940s, used a fair amount of smoke but only a very low heat over a long period of time in order to preserve the meat. In "barbeque," temperature plays a larger role, requiring a heat of 210 to 260 F (100 to 125 C) for 7 to 10 hours depending on the size of the meat being cooked.

It is interesting to note that it was the first Scottish settlers with their ancient tradition of smoking fish who were instrumental in introducing the first vinegar and pepper basting and finishing sauce. Back then, this "barbeque" would have been used to preserve rather than simply cook the meat, with the vinegar acting as a natural antiseptic, the pepper keeping off the flies, and the salt in the dry rub arresting the spread of bacteria.

SOUTH CAROLINA "BARBEQUE" OR PULLED PORK

Pulled pork is the traditional "barbeque" associated with the Southern states of America and served up for big family get-togethers and celebrations such as the fourth of July. Large pieces of shoulder of pork, or Boston butt, are dry rub marinated and cooked slowly in a smoker or pit (see page 68), mopped, and injected with a vinegar finishing sauce (see page 69) until the meat is so soft and melting that it falls to pieces. It is served piled around a bowl of homemade barbecue sauce for dipping.

Every family has its very own recipe and there is rampant competition as to whose is best. "Barbeque" festivals are held all over the Southern states to select a "barbeque" champion for the year. Carolina favors a spicy sweet cure, while Texas is hot on chili. Tennessee prefers to leave out the sugar and goes for a more savory rub. Combinations of seven or eight ingredients such as cayenne, black pepper, chili and paprika, together with onion, celery and garlic salt, and sugar are combined by the cupful and then used at will through the "barbeque" season. I have it on good authority that the avid South Carolina "barbeque" devotee adjusts the spice combinations to suit their taste and to create their very own personalized recipe. So this is your opportunity to add your own favorite spices.

Be warned that the South Carolina "barbeque" is not the barbecue that most of us are familiar with (see page 64). If you don't have a pit or a smoker (see pages 284 to 285)—I used a Bradley smoker, which is easy to control—this recipe can be adapted to cook in a domestic oven, although you won't have that gorgeous smoky finish.

1

2

"BARBEQUE" PREP. 1. Applying the dry rub to the pork. 2. Injecting the pork, after "standing," with mop sauce. 3. Smoking the pork. 4. Mopping the pork with the mop sauce. 5. The pork is ready to be pulled apart.

3 4
5

GEORGIA-STYLE BARBECUED BEEF

SERVES 15 TO 20

11-pound (5-kg) point end of brisket on the bone with fat cap (ask your butcher to prepare it)

Dijon or other mustard of your choice, for coating

Hickory or oak wood chippings or briquettes, for 2 hours' smoking

MOP SAUCE

2 cups (500 ml) white wine vinegar

1 tablespoon sugar

1 tablespoon sea salt

2½ teaspoons crushed red pepper flakes

2½ teaspoons ground black pepper

DRY RUB

2 tablespoons sugar

4 tablespoons sea salt

2 teaspoons ground black pepper

2 teaspoons paprika

1 teaspoon cayenne pepper

2 teaspoons garlic granules

½ teaspoon ground cumin

1 teaspoon onion granules

1 teaspoon ground ginger

2 teaspoons crushed red pepper flakes

MUSTARD BARBECUE SAUCE

1 cup (225 ml) Kraft yellow mustard or other mustard of your choice

½ cup (75 ml) Karo syrup (dark if you have it)

½ cup (75 ml) tomato ketchup

⅓ cup (75 ml) white wine vinegar

¼ tablespoon finely chopped dill

¼ tablespoon ground allspice

¼ tablespoon hot sauce

½ teaspoon freshly ground black pepper

½ tablespoon liquid smoke

¾ tablespoon sorghum or molasses (the sorghum seems to add something it needs)

Sea salt as desired

Before starting this recipe, please read the instructions for the South Carolina "Barbeque" or Pulled Pork (see page 68). If you don't have a pit or a suitable smoker to make this in, you can use a domestic oven; although you won't have the amazing smoky flavor, you will have a deliciously spicy, melt-in-the-mouth piece of brisket.

Make the mop sauce a day ahead. Pour the vinegar into a large saucepan and bring to a boil. Reduce the heat and stir in the sugar until completely dissolved. Add the salt, crushed red pepper flakes and black pepper and stir. Boil for 3 to 5 minutes. Remove from the heat and let cool. Pour into your "mop bucket" sauce container and let stand for 6 to 8 hours. Shake before using.

Mix the rub ingredients together in a bowl. Coat the brisket in mustard and then roll in the rub mixture.

Preheat the smoker or oven to 175 to 195 F (80 to 90 C). If your oven temperature does not go this low, set the oven at its lowest setting and leave the door ajar. Prepare enough wood chippings or briquettes to smoke the beef for 2 hours. Fill a bowl with water and place on the base of the smoker or oven and refill during cooking, as the water evaporates. Place the beef on a rack in the smoker or oven as far away from the heat source as possible. Close the damper of the smoker, if using, and cook for 8 hours.

To ensure that the meat is cooked to your liking, push a meat thermometer into the center of the meat after it has been in the oven for a few hours. The temperature should reach 140 F (60 C) when the meat is red inside, 160 F (70 C) when pink, and 170 F (75 C) when cooked through. One hour before the cooking time is up, baste the beef with the mop sauce. When the cooking time is up, baste the meat once more, then wrap in foil and rest for 30 minutes before carving.

Combine all the ingredients for the barbecue sauce in a small saucepan and simmer for 30 minutes. Serve the beef in rolls or with salad, the barbecue sauce, Chrain (see page 234) and Pickled Walnuts (see page 243).

below The rubbed brisket ready for the oven **opposite** Barbecued beef sandwich

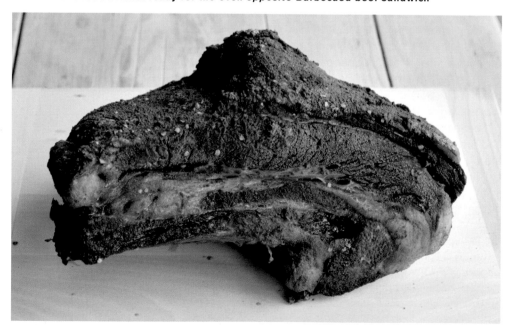

PASTRAMI OF BEEF

SERVES 12

2 bay leaves

6 garlic cloves, peeled

1 medium-strength red chili

1 tablespoon black peppercorns

1 tablespoon white peppercorns

1 tablespoon coriander seeds

1 tablespoon mustard seeds

1 tablespoon paprika

1 tablespoon ground cinnamon

1 tablespoon ground ginger

5 tablespoons rock salt and 1 teaspoon saltpeter, mixed, (optional) or 5 tablespoons curing salt (see page 16)—I use Weschenfelder's Supracure (see pages 284 to 285) as it makes glorious pastrami

3 tablespoons unrefined cane sugar

2¼ to 4½ pounds (1 to 2 kg) lean beef brisket, trimmed as necessary (see opposite), top rump or bottom round

❧ **NOTE** If you do not want to use nitrates in this recipe, use the pastrami spice mixture but replace the rock salt mixture or curing salt with coarse sea salt.

Pastrami is an icon among cold meats, star of the city deli and as such a difficult act to recreate at home. Deli pastrami, crafted by experts from specially selected Angus beef butchered specifically for the job, has a certain shape, texture and color, all of which are hard to replicate at home.

It is therefore important to keep an open mind about how your homemade pastrami is going to look and taste. Firstly, you may wish to avoid using additives or manufactured curing salt, which contains small amounts of nitrates, sticking with a simple salt and sugar cure spiced up to suit. This will give you great results, but your pastrami will not have the characteristic pink coloring; the meat will be gray.

The cut of the meat will also be different unless you are lucky enough to use a specialist butcher who makes his own pastrami. Do not expect the wide rectangular or rounded slices we are used to. You will have to ask your butcher to cut you a flat piece of brisket, possibly with a fat cap that will then need trimming; the majority of butchers will not be familiar with what you want, so it will need to be special ordered and expect to do a bit of explaining.

Ask the butcher to cut lengthwise a big piece of thick flank. Tell him you need a large "sheet" of brisket approximately 1½ to 2½ inches (4 to 6 cm) thick, 8 inches (20 cm) wide and 12 inches (30 cm) long. The whole brisket as used for corned (salt) beef or "barbeque" is not suitable and neither is a rolled piece of brisket. Alternatively, ask for a piece of top rump or bottom round, which will give a rounder piece of meat. This is not the traditional pastrami, but many specialists now use these alternative cuts and they may prove easier to source. Trim the meat so that it is an even shape.

Crush the herbs and whole spices together with the ground spices, salt and sugar either in a mortar and pestle or a blender and rub the resultant paste into the beef thoroughly. This should take 10 minutes. Wrap the meat in a heavy-duty freezer bag, seal, and set in the refrigerator with a weight on top for 1 to 3 weeks, as time and mood allows. Massage the meat twice daily.

After this time open the bag, pour off any liquid that may have formed, and rub the spices back into the meat to form a crust. Add extra rub if necessary. Hang the meat in a cool, airy place for 24 hours or unwrap and let drain on a rack set over a dish in the refrigerator.

Preheat your pit or smoker and apply enough wood chippings or briquettes to smoke for 1½ hours. Place the beef on a rack in the pit or smoker or oven (place the rack in a roasting pan) as far away from the heat source as possible.

Wrap closely in foil, put in a vacuum pack or roasting bag, and cook in a water bath—immerse in cold water in an ovenproof dish and set this in a shallow ovenproof dish half-filled with cold water—in a low oven at 300 to 325 F (160 C) until it reaches an internal temperature of 170 F (75 C). Alternatively, immerse the roasting bag in water, bring gently to a boil, and simmer for 1 hour. Let rest for 20 minutes.

If eating hot, transfer to a carving dish, slice, and serve with rye bread or potatoes, roasted baby beets and dill pickles, and/or Chrain (see page 234). If not eating hot, take the meat out of its wrappings while still hot, cover tightly with plastic wrap and let cool overnight at room temperature. Refrigerate and slice paper thin when needed.

above and above right **Traditional pastrami of brisket hot in the smoker and soft and rosy cold-cut pastrami from top round**

THE NEW YORK CITY DELI

The word "delicatessen" comes from the German *delikatessen*, meaning "delicacies to eat." During the 1840s there was a tidal wave of German emigration to the USA and specifically to New York City. Many of these people set up humble shops selling their native pickled meats, smoked fish, and homemade specialties. Hamburgers, meat loaf, cold cuts, dill pickles, herring in cream sauce and rye bread, liverwurst and wieners, much of what we now think of as typical New York City deli fare, originally came from Germany.

During the course of 2,000 years of history, Jewish cooks have created many rich culinary traditions, encompassing a wealth of tastes and reflecting the traditions of their communities worldwide. So it is with cured meat, fish and pickles. There are certain dishes such as salt beef, or corned beef as it is known in the USA, and pastrami that are specifically associated with Jewish food rather than the country of origin. Pastrami (*pastirma* in Turkey and *pasturma* in the Balkans) originated possibly in the Levant or the Balkans where each household killed animals in the autumn. The meat was cut into long strips, brined, and hung up on drafty walls to dry. In Armenia they made pastrami from beef seasoned with garlic and

cumin. Lamb, calf, goat and young water buffalo were also preserved this way.

Jewish delis in New York, keeping kosher, differed from other delis in as much as they sold beef products rather than pork and dairy produce. The vast North American prairie grew cattle that produced beef at an affordable price, and brisket, a long, thin strip of tough meat threaded with fat, was within the means of the immigrant Jewish population. It was also a cut of beef permitted by their prescribed diet and this is why they started making pastrami with beef rather than the meats they had used at home.

The pastrami-on-rye sandwich so loved of New York delis was popularized by immigrant Romanian Jews who had the job of brewing the alcohol (a task forbidden to others) and salting the meats served with it to increase the thirsts of the customers.

Pastrami as we know it today is basically spiced salt (corned) beef taken a step further by hot smoking for several hours. What distinguishes a run-of-the-mill pastrami from a good one is the choice of rub, which may include ginger, chili, garlic, cinnamon, paprika, bay, cloves, peppercorns, allspice, red wine vinegar, onion, coriander, mace, juniper berries and cardamom.

PREPARING THE PASTRAMI. 1. The spiced rub ground in a mortar and pestle. 2. Massaging the rub into the brisket. 3. The meat in a plastic bag to marinate. 4. Weights (juice cartons) placed on top and left in a cold place for 1 to 3 weeks.

The cured pastrami set on a rack to dry.

PASTRAMI, EGGPLANT AND FETA SALAD

SERVES 4 AS AN APPETIZER

1 large eggplant, cut into rounds ½ to 1 inch (1 to 2 cm) thick

5½ ounces (150 g) pastrami, thinly sliced

1 garlic clove, halved

3 tablespoons extra virgin olive oil, plus extra for drizzling

2 cups (75 g) mixed salad leaves

½ cup (75 g) green beans, halved, lightly cooked in salted water, plunged into iced water to cool, drained and dried

12 mixed olives

2 tomatoes, cut in half, seeded, upturned on towels to drain and then diced

1½ tablespoons white wine vinegar

½ cup (50 g) feta cheese, crumbled

Sea salt and freshly ground black pepper as desired

Pastrami is delicious hot or cold, great in salads and sandwiches. This recipe makes a good lunch dish or appetizer. It is essential to get your griddle pan white hot before putting anything on it. That way the food sears quickly without the use of oil, leaving it succulent on the inside.

Put a cast-iron ridged griddle pan over maximum heat for 30 minutes or until white hot. Put the eggplant slices on the hot griddle pan and sear on each side until stripy—this should only take a minute or two and will leave the inside soft and succulent.

Arrange the pastrami slices on a large platter. When the eggplant slices come off the griddle pan, rub with garlic, drizzle with olive oil, and arrange on top of the pastrami, leaving a border of pastrami uncovered.

Put the salad leaves in a bowl with the green beans, olives and diced tomato. Add the olive oil, white wine vinegar, salt and pepper, and mix well.

Pile the salad on top of the pastrami and eggplant and then top with the feta. Alternatively, arrange in single servings. Serve at once.

SERVES 4

2 teaspoons coriander seeds

1 tablespoon coarse sea salt

½ tablespoon golden granulated sugar

1 teaspoon crushed black pepper

1¼ pounds (600 g) tuna loin

Extra virgin olive oil, for drizzling

Slices of lemon, to serve

A few years ago I bought a gas grill, which has become an extention of my kitchen. On summer evenings I cook everything on it. In winter I griddle on it rather than filling my kitchen with smoke. Simply put the griddle pan on the lit barbecue and wait until it becomes white hot.

Crush the coriander seeds with the salt, sugar and black pepper in a blender or mortar and pestle and rub into the tuna loin.

Transfer to a deep dish, cover, and let stand in the refrigerator overnight or for a few hours.

Pour off any excess liquid that may have leached out. Let dry on a rack for 1 hour then cut into 4 equal-sized steaks.

Put a cast-iron ridged griddle pan over maximum heat for half an hour or until white hot. Put the tuna steaks on the hot griddle pan and sear on each side until stripy—this should not take longer than a minute or two and will leave the inside soft and succulent. Transfer to a hot plate, drizzle with olive oil, and serve at once with slices of lemon.

below and bottom **The tuna steaks raw and cooked on the griddle pan**

❀ **VARIATION**   Serve the spiced loin cut into paper-thin slices raw as an appetizer with baby salad leaves and Pickled Gooseberries (see page 234) or Mirabelles (see page 233).

CARNE SALADA

SERVES 20

1 small carrot, finely chopped

2 bay leaves, torn

4 garlic cloves, halved

12 juniper berries, crushed

12 black peppercorns

1 tablespoon ground black pepper

⅔ cup (150 g) sea salt

2¼-pound (1-kg) piece of beef topside, trimmed of all fat

CARPACCIO TRENTINO STYLE

Carne salada is a centuries-old tradition originating in the pure mountain air of the Trentino Dolomites. The best-quality cuts of beef are dry marinated for three weeks in a mixture of salt, herbs and spices. The resultant meat is ruby red, aromatic, and melts in the mouth. Trentino chef Rinaldo Dalsasso is a devotee of the curer's craft. This and the Smoked Lake Garda Trout (see page 154) are two of his signature dishes that he brought to London for a Trentino food and wine matching. It is cut into paper-thin slices as an appetizer or cut into ½ to 1-inch (1 to 2-cm) thick slices, broiled or grilled with olive oil, preferably from Lake Garda, and served with borlotti beans and sage.

Carne salada is very simple to make and differs from bresaola in as much as it resembles raw meat, while bresaola is more like prosciutto. For bresaola, beef is marinated in red and white wine, sea salt, herbs and spices for seven to ten days and then air dried for two to three weeks or until it feels hard to the touch.

Mix all the ingredients except the beef together and put in a large noncorrosive container. Add the joint of beef and turn until it is well coated in the salt mixture. Put a weight on top, refrigerate and turn every 2 days for 3 weeks.

After this time, dry well and hand-slice thinly or use a slicing machine for paper-thin results.

below left and right The marinated carne salada and the cured meat sliced paper thin

SERVES 6

7 ounces (200 g) Carne Salada (see opposite) or bresaola (see pages 284 to 285 for recommended producers), thinly sliced

1 to 2 large crisp apples, cut into matchstick strips and immersed in salt water until ready to serve

2 tablespoons Parmesan shavings or Grana Trentino

Extra virgin olive oil, for drizzling

Freshly ground black pepper as desired

Carne salada is also delicious served with arugula and cherry tomatoes or porcini mushrooms, according to the season.

Divide the Carne Salada between four plates.

Drain the apple julienne, dry, and then scatter on top of the meat with the Parmesan shavings on top. Drizzle with olive oil and season with black pepper.

FRIEDRICHS RHEINISCHER SAUERBRATEN

FRIEDRICH'S MARINATED SPICED MEAT WITH POTATO DUMPLINGS

SERVES 4

1 large onion

1 large carrot

1 piece of celeriac, weighing 3½ ounces (100 g)

1 cup (250 ml) red wine vinegar and 2 cups (500 ml) water or ⅔ cup (150 ml) red wine vinegar and 2½ cups (600 ml) red wine

1 bay leaf

4 cloves

1 teaspoon black peppercorns

4 juniper berries, crushed

1¾-pound (750-g) piece of beef topside, silverside or top rump, or pork, lamb, venison wild boar, or turkey joint

3 tablespoons clarified butter (see page 172)

1 cup (250 ml) water

2 tablespoons cornstarch, or use crumbled gingerbread or pumpernickel

2 tablespoons raisins

1 tablespoon blanched split almonds

2 tablespoons white Rhine wine

Good pinch of sugar

3 tablespoons sour cream (optional)

Sea salt and freshly ground black pepper as desired

Swedish Red Cabbage (see page 82), to serve

POTATO DUMPLINGS

1 pound (500 g) potatoes

1 egg, lightly beaten

1½ cups (250 g) all-purpose flour

Generous pinch of freshly grated nutmeg

Rheinischer Sauerbraten is a very popular and traditional spiced meat dish from the Rhineland of Germany that was originally made with horsemeat. This recipe was given to me by my friend Annegret, whose mother and father, Friedrich, ran their own grocers in Essen. On Sundays they both busied themselves at home in the kitchen and sauerbraten *was a favorite Sunday lunch treat. Her father took charge of marinating the* sauerbraten *while her mother prepared the spices, added the final touches, and made the dumplings and red cabbage or salad to serve with it.*

German wine is generally undervalued, so treat yourself to a dry red wine from the up and coming vineyards of the Ahr valley or some Graucr Burgunder *(German for Pinot Grigio) from Palatinate or Baden to serve with your* sauerbraten.

Dice the onion, carrot and celeriac and then bring to a boil in the vinegar and water or wine with the bay leaf, cloves, peppercorns and juniper berries in a saucepan. Let cool.

Put the meat in a large, noncorrosive bowl, pour over the cooled marinade, and refrigerate for 2 to 3 days. After this time, take the meat out, dry it, and season with salt and pepper. Strain the marinade and reserve the marinade and the vegetables.

Heat a large skillet over medium heat and add the clarified butter. As soon as the butter melts, add the meat and fry all over until brown. Set the meat on one side. Add the drained vegetables to the hot fat and fry until browned. Put the meat back into the pan containing the vegetables, then add the water and 1 cup (250 ml) of the strained marinade. Cover with a lid and braise gently on low to medium heat for 2 hours. After this time, take the meat out and let rest in a warm place for 20 minutes.

While the meat is braising, make the dumplings. Boil the potatoes in their skins (how long they take depends on size) in a saucepan of salted water until tender, then drain. Peel them while they are still warm and pass them immediately through a potato ricer or mouli-legume.

Add the egg, flour, nutmeg, and salt and pepper and mix well. Form into 1-inch (2-cm) balls, drop into a saucepan of boiling salted water, and cook, uncovered. When the dumplings rise to the surface (this will only take a few minutes), remove with a slotted spoon and arrange on a serving dish.

To thicken the meat juices, some traditional recipes suggest crumbling in gingerbread or pumpernickel, but otherwise simply whisk in the cornstarch. Finally, add the raisins, almonds, wine, sugar and sour cream and simmer gently for 5 minutes.

Serve the meat sliced with the hot sauce, dumplings and Swedish Red Cabbage.

PREPARING THE SAUERBRATEN.
1. Marinating the meat with vegetables and spices.
2. The braised spiced sauerbraten.
3. Sliced sauerbraten with dumplings and red cabbage.

1 2
3

SWEDISH TJÄLKNÖL

FROSTED SPICED WILD BOAR WITH CHANTERELLE SAUCE

This recipe was introduced to me by my Swedish friend Susanne who likes nothing better than to gather all her friends and family around her Scandinavian style in the open air, with picnics, floral wreaths and songs. She prepared it for a sailing expedition along with pickled herring, salads and hard bread.

Before the introduction of refrigeration every Swedish home had an outdoor underground larder dug out in the frozen ground. Fresh food such as meat, game and fish were stored there during the winter in freezing temperatures until required. Brining was used to preserve meat and fish too and is still popular today. It would therefore follow that the tjälknöl *was a traditional Swedish way of preserving meat.*

However, Swedish food writer Berit Lyregård told me differently. This method of slow cooking frozen meat in the oven and afterward putting it in brine became popular in the 1970s. The story goes that a hunter's wife forgot a piece of wild meat she wanted to thaw in the oven overnight and the following day put it in brine to soften it so they could eat it. But the result was a very tender piece of meat, with a nice taste of salt and spices; the method caught on and is ever popular.

In Sweden elk, reindeer, venison, bear, hare, beaver and wild boar are all popular game meats and can be prepared this way, as can beef, lamb and pork.

Serve carved with boiled potatoes, chanterelle sauce, and pickled cabbage as a main course, sliced paper thin on open sandwiches, or as a plated appetizer with pickles.

Put the frozen meat joint on a trivet or rack in a roasting pan in the lower part of the oven for approximately 10 hours at a temperature of 170 to 210 F (75 to 100 C)—if your oven temperature does not go this low, set at its lowest setting and leave the door ajar. The cooking time will vary according to how you like your meat cooked. When the meat has been cooking for about 3 hours, push a meat thermometer into the middle of the joint. It will read 140 F (60 C) when the meat is red inside, 160 F (70 C) when pink and 170 F (75 C) when cooked through.

While the meat is cooking, boil the water in a saucepan with the brine ingredients for 3 to 4 minutes and then let cool a little.

When the meat is ready, put it in a noncorrosive dish or plastic bag and immerse in the brine in a cool place for 5 hours. After this time, wipe the meat dry and let stand for 30 minutes.

While the meat is standing, melt the butter for the sauce in a saucepan, add the finely chopped onion, and fry over low heat until soft but not browned. Add the mushrooms and stir-fry for a few minutes. Add the stock and simmer for 20 minutes, then stir in the cream and simmer, shaking the pan now and then for 10 minutes, until the sauce has thickened and the mushrooms are tender. Taste for seasoning, adding salt and black pepper as necessary.

Put the shredded cabbage in a saucepan with the water and salt and bring to a boil. Stir in the brown sugar and caraway seeds and simmer for 10 minutes or until tender. Drain well. Transfer to a bowl and toss the cabbage in the vinegar and butter until thoroughly coated. Serve the meat thinly sliced with chanterelle sauce and red cabbage, and with mashed potatoes. Alternatively, serve as cold cuts with horseradish and Pickled Gherkins (see page 245) or Chrain (see page 234). For a sensational appetizer cut the meat paper thin on a meat slicer.

SERVES 6 TO 8

2¼ pounds to 3¼ pounds (1 to 1.5 kg) lean wild boar or venison such as haunch, beef or pork that has been previously frozen (use cheaper, tougher rather than prime cuts)

BRINE

4 cups (1 liter) water

⅓ cup (100 g) sea salt

1 teaspoon sugar

½ teaspoon crushed black peppercorns

1 bay leaf

15 juniper berries, crushed (use a few sprigs of thyme leaves instead if using pork)

CHANTERELLE SAUCE

2 tablespoons butter

1 red onion, finely chopped

5 cups (400 g) chanterelles or other mushrooms, sliced

¾ cup (200 ml) vegetable or chicken stock

1¼ cups (300 ml) heavy cream

Sea salt and freshly ground black pepper as desired

SWEDISH RED CABBAGE

1 medium head of red cabbage, shredded

4 cups (1 liter) water

1 teaspoon salt, or as desired

⅔ cup (125 g) brown sugar

1 tablespoon caraway seeds

½ cup (125 ml) red wine vinegar

3 tablespoons butter

SPICED BUTTERFLY OF LAMB. *far left* The marinade ingredients. *left* Smoothing the spiced marinade into the meat. *above* Smoothing the saffron-yogurt marinade onto the lamb.

SPICED BUTTERFLY OF LAMB

SERVES 6 TO 8

3½- to 5½-pound (1.5 to 2.5-kg) leg of lamb, boned and split (ask your butcher to prepare it)

SPICE MARINADE

5 garlic cloves, crushed

1 egg-size piece of fresh ginger root, peeled and finely grated

½ teaspoon cumin seeds, crushed

½ teaspoon ground cinnamon

½ teaspoon cardamom seeds, crushed

¼ teaspoon ground cloves

3 teaspoons coarse sea salt

½ teaspoon ground black pepper

1 teaspoon ground turmeric

2 tablespoons lemon juice

YOGURT MARINADE

½ teaspoon saffron strands or ¼ teaspoon powdered saffron soaked in 1 tablespoon hot water for 10 minutes

1 cup (250 ml) natural yogurt

2 tablespoons blanched almonds

1 tablespoon liquid honey

A leg of lamb is boned and split open, skinned and the excess fat removed. It is then spiced and submerged in yogurt for several days before being roasted.

Remove the skin and any excess fat from the lamb. Stab the lamb 5 or 6 times with the sharp point of a knife.

Put all the spice marinade ingredients together in a mortar and crush with a pestle. Smooth the paste all over the lamb, pressing the paste into the slits. Put the lamb in a large bowl.

For the yogurt marinade, put the soaked saffron, yogurt, almonds and honey in a blender and blend until smooth. Spoon the mixture over the lamb. Cover the bowl with plastic wrap and let marinate in the refrigerator for 2 days.

Preheat the oven to 425 F (220 C). Transfer the lamb to a roasting dish with a lid and roast in the oven for 30 minutes, then reduce the heat to 350 F (180 C) and cook for another 30 minutes or until the lamb is cooked through. Uncover the roasting dish and let cool to room temperature. Serve with flatbread.

SERVES 4 TO 6

2 pheasants

2 tablespoons muscovado sugar

2 teaspoons coarse salt

Good pinch of ground cumin

Good pinch of mixed spice

Pinch of ground cloves

Good pinch of ground cinnamon

1 teaspoon crushed juniper berries

1 teaspoon ground black pepper

4 medium to large cooking apples

20 slices of pancetta or bacon

½ cup (100 g) hard pork back fat, cut into ½-inch (1-cm) pieces (optional)

2 cups (500 ml) pear cider

This dish can be adapted to cook other game birds or rabbit. Many butchers sell game birds skinned rather than plucked. Wrapping the game pieces in thin slices of bacon or pancetta helps keep the meat moist.

Pull the pheasants apart in two pieces, separating the crown and legs. Put the pieces in a deep bowl. Mix the sugar, salt and spices and rub into the pheasant. Cover with parchment paper, put a weight on top, and leave in a cool place overnight.

After this time, pour off any water that may have collected and discard. Joint each pheasant into ten small pieces. Cut off the breast meat and cut each breast into two equal pieces, cut off the wings and leave whole. Cut off the legs and divide into two drumsticks and two thighs.

Core the apples, leaving the skin on, and cut into rounds, ½ to ¾ inch (1 to 1.5 cm) thick and arrange in a single layer in one or two shallow ovenproof dishes. Wrap each piece of pheasant in a thin slice of pancetta or bacon and put one on each apple round. Top with a square of back fat, if using.

Cover the base of the dish with pear cider and transfer to a preheated oven at 400 F (200 C) and roast for 20 to 30 minutes until golden brown. If you like your pheasant breast pink, remove the breast pieces after 10 or 15 minutes.

Arrange the apple and pheasant piles on a serving dish and keep warm. Add the remaining pear cider to the roasting dish, scrape up the pan juices, and mix well. Set over high heat on the cooktop and boil until reduced by half. Taste for seasoning. Pour over the pheasant and serve with roast potatoes and a seasonal vegetable.

HOMEMADE CHORIZO SAUSAGE

**MAKES 9 POUNDS (4 KG)
SAUSAGES**

2 tablespoons smoked
paprika

Scant ½ cup (100 ml)
Spanish white wine

4½ pounds (2 kg) side pork,
ground or finely chopped

4½ pounds (2 kg) loin
of pork, ground or finely
chopped

Small head of garlic, peeled
and minced or finely chopped

1 tablespoon dried oregano

5 tablespoons coarse sea
salt or curing salts if drying

EQUIPMENT

15 feet (5 meters) sausage
casings

You can adapt these quantities to taste. If you don't want to make your own but you do appreciate an authentic product, you can buy chorizo from La Carniceria de Julian online (see pages 284 to 285).

Mix the smoked paprika and the white wine together. Put the meat, garlic, oregano and salt in a bowl and mix together roughly, then add the paprika mixture and mix until all the ingredients are well distributed.

Let the mixture stand in a cool place to cure for a few days, then stuff the mixture into the casings with the help of a sausage machine and tie the sausages by hand.

Cook from fresh and freeze what you can't use. Alternatively, hang the sausage strings in a dry, cold, airy place for 3 weeks.

If you don't have access to a sausage machine, make patties with the mixture and fry or grill, or make *crépinettes* (see page 94). Use the sausages within 1 month.

HABAS CON CHORIZO

SERVES 4

1 cup (200 g) fava beans
(podded weight)

1 onion, finely chopped

1 to 2 small dried chorizo, cut
into small cubes

Good handful of flat-leaf
parsley, chopped

Sea salt and freshly ground
black pepper or chilli flakes
as desired

Olive oil, for frying

FAVA BEANS WITH CHORIZO

Serve warm or cold as an accompaniment or an appetizer.

Plunge the beans in a saucepan of salted boiling water and cook until tender, say 5 to 10 minutes, and then drain.

Heat a skillet over medium heat, add a little oil and the chopped onion, and fry for 2 minutes, then add the chorizo cubes and continue to cook until the onion is soft.

Take the pan off the heat. Scrape up the onion and chorizo and put to one side, then prop the pan up so that the excess fat will drain away from the onion. Let stand for 10 minutes and then drain off the excess fat.

Add the beans and half the chopped parsley to the onions and chorizo and mix well. Taste and add salt and black pepper or chilli flakes as necessary. Transfer to a serving dish and scatter the remaining chopped parsley over the top.

❈ **SAUSAGE MEAT TOP TIPS**

❈ If you don't have a meat grinder, freeze cubes of meat for 1 to 2 hours before chopping in a blender.

❈ If you don't have the necessary equipment to stuff sausages into casings, wrap sausage-meat in plastic wrap where boiling is required for liverwurst or foil for sausages to be baked.

❈ Make hamburgers with the mixture to grill or fry.

❈ Make *crépinettes* (see page 94).

❈ Make croquettes by forming the meat mixture into balls, coating in beaten egg and rolling in breadcrumbs. Fry in sunflower oil.

LIVERWURST OR LEBERWURST

PORK AND PIG'S LIVER SAUSAGE

**MAKES 2 POUNDS 4 OUNCES
(1 KG) SAUSAGES**

1¾ pounds (800 g) lean
shoulder or side pork

1 tablespoon lard

2 cups (300 g) onion, finely
chopped

7 ounces (200 g) fresh pig's
liver

½ teaspoon sugar (any kind)

½ teaspoon sea salt, or to
taste

1 teaspoon paprika

½ teaspoon ground white
pepper

½ teaspoon ground coriander

Good pinch each of ground
nutmeg, cloves and
cardamom

Good pinch of dried
marjoram

EQUIPMENT

3 to 6 feet (1 to 2 meters)
sausage casings or (2)
18-ounce (500-ml) oiled loaf
pans or terrines

Liverwurst is an anglicization of the German word Leberwurst, *literally meaning liver sausage; it is made with ground side pork or shoulder and approximately 20 percent pig's liver. In North America it is served in rye bread sandwiches with red onions and mustard.*

First of all grind the meat. If you are using a blender rather than a meat grinder, it helps to cut the meat into cubes and freeze for 1 to 2 hours beforehand to prevent the meat forming a mush. Alternatively, if you prefer to cook the meat first, simmer the pork whole in a large saucepan of lightly salted water for 90 minutes, let cool completely and chill, then grind finely.

Melt the lard in a skillet. Add the chopped onion and fry over low heat until soft but not colored. Chop the liver and add to the fried onion and cook through. Add the sugar, salt, spices and marjoram and mix thoroughly. Let cool a little and then add to the ground meat.

Transfer the mixture to a blender and reduce to a smooth purée. Pack the mixture into sausage casings and tie them with string in 8 to 12-inch (20 to 30-cm) lengths, leaving 2½ to 3½ inches (6 to 8 cm) at the end of each length empty, to allow for expansion. Otherwise, try rolling in plastic wrap to make the same-size sausage shapes. Simmer in a saucepan of water for 45 minutes, then dip them in cold water to keep the fat from settling at the bottom.

Alternatively, preheat the oven to 300 F (150 C). Pack the mixture into the oiled loaf pans or terrines and cover tightly with foil. Transfer to a roasting pan filled with 1 to 2 inches (2.5 to 5 cm) of boiling water and bake for about 2 hours until the meat is cooked but not browned (a meat thermometer should read 175 F (80 C)). Refrigerate for 1 to 2 days before using. It will keep a good week if well wrapped in the refrigerator.

opposite Liverwurst on toast
with sliced red onion and
mustard *right* Liverwurst just
out of the loaf pan

CRÉPINETTES AUX MARRONS

SAUSAGES WITH CHESTNUTS

MAKES 1¾ POUNDS (750 G) CRÉPINETTES

2 cups (250 g) chestnuts or 1 cup (150 g) pre-cooked and peeled chestnuts

1 pound (500 g) lean shoulder of pork or equal quantities of pork and veal or pork, veal and game or poultry, ground

1¼ cups (250 g) hard pork back fat, cut into small pieces

½ teaspoon coarsely ground black pepper

1 teaspoon dried sage or thyme

Good pinch each of ground cinnamon, cloves, nutmeg and cumin

½ teaspoon sea salt

1 large sheet of caul fat (lace pig fat)

A smear of vegetable oil, for roasting or frying (optional)

Crépinettes are the French solution to homemade sausages without going to the trouble of stuffing sausage casings. They are made with a classic sausage-meat mixture, but you can use any other sausage-meat recipe in the same way. Handfuls of the mixture are enveloped in pieces of caul fat.

The mixture can be modified to your taste; experiment with other nuts such as walnuts or pistachios, and add truffles and apples in autumn and fresh herbs in summer. You can of course use this recipe to make classic sausages if you prefer.

Preheat the oven to 400 F (200 C). Cut a small cross in the chestnuts with a sharp knife and put in a roasting pan. Roast in oven for 10 minutes. While the chestnuts are cooking, grind the meat.

Leave the chestnuts to cool a little, then peel and chop roughly. Mix the meat, diced fat and spices together and then stir in the cooled chestnuts.

Lay the caul out on a board and cut into 5-inch (10-cm) squares. Lay a piece of caul on the palm of your hand, put a handful of the sausage-meat mixture in the middle, and use your fingers to close the caul around the mixture, creating a sausage shape so that the caul edges overlap and seal. Repeat with the remaining mixture.

Fry, broil or bake the packets until golden brown as for sausages.

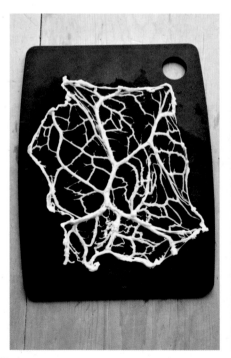

above left and above right **A large piece of caul fat and the sausages wrapped and ready to cook**

❀VARIATIONS

A few other sausage variations to use with the basic quantities in the *crépinettes* recipe:

❀ Bologna summer sausage—ground beef with mustard seeds, garlic, smoked cayenne, and crushed red pepper, refrigerated for 3 days, shaped into logs, cooked at a low temperature for 8 hours, wrapped in plastic wrap and refrigerated.

❀ Creole sausages—a fresh sausage made with coarsely ground pork, cayenne pepper, paprika, black pepper, and crushed bay leaf. The sausages are broiled.

❀ Andouille—a cajun sausage of pork, garlic, black pepper, cayenne pepper and thyme mixed together and made into sausages. Smoked over pecan or hickory wood or sugar cane until almost black.

❀ Texas hotlinks—pork and beef ground with red and black peppers, paprika, garlic, bay leaves, aniseed, mustard, coriander and thyme, then smoked or broiled.

THE WALNUT TREE

This restaurant in Wales has long been a place of culinary pilgrimage. After its founders Franco and Ann Taruschio sold it 10 years ago it lost its way. Chef patron Shaun Hill took it on and put it right back on the map. I watched as head chef Roger Brook made the black pudding.

Shaun says "black pudding partners lots of things well. Bacon and apple fritter are traditional. We serve it with sautéed kidneys and a parsley and wholegrain mustard sauce—pan juices, crème fraîche, mustard, then a squeeze of lemon, salt and pepper and lots of roughly chopped parsley."

When I made it I found it went really well with all kinds of things, from a cooked breakfast to goat's cheese.

right Ingredients for black pudding

BLACK PUDDING

MAKES 2¼ POUNDS (1 KG)

1 cup (100 g) dried pig's blood

1⅔ cups (400 ml) milk

1 cup (160 g) onions, chopped

1 teaspoon chopped garlic

3 apples, peeled, cored and chopped

1 teaspoon ground cinnamon

1 teaspoon ground coriander

1 teaspoon cumin seeds

1 teaspoon smoked paprika

½ cup (160 g) pork fat, diced

⅓ cup (30 g) rolled oats

⅔ cup (30 g) breadcrumbs

Sea salt and freshly ground black pepper as desired

Pork or duck fat, enough to cover the base of the pan, plus extra for greasing

EQUIPMENT

3 to 6 feet (1 to 2 meters) large diameter sausage casings (optional)

Black pudding sausages are very delicate and can easily break before, during or after cooking. This method of cooking the pudding in the oven in a roasting pan solves the problem and makes great homemade black pudding without any effort.

Unless you keep and slaughter your own pigs you can no longer buy fresh pig's blood, but it is very easy to buy dried blood from a specialist supplier (see pages 284 to 285).

Put the dried pig's blood in a large bowl, stir in the milk, and let stand.

Cook the onions and garlic in the pork or duck fat over low heat, and when soft and golden, add the apple and cook until the latter softens. Stir in the spices, the diced pork fat, rolled oats and breadcrumbs, and then mix in the blood and milk mixture and season with salt and black pepper. Stir well and then transfer to a blender and blend to a coarse consistency. Preheat the oven to 225 F (110 C).

Transfer the mixture to a greased roasting pan set in a water bath—an ovenproof dish filled with boiling water to come halfway up the side of the roasting pan—and cook for 50 minutes or until it loses its "wobble." The black pudding can be cut into squares or spooned to serve. Keep in the refrigerator for up to 1 week.

Alternatively, pour the mixture, with the help of a funnel, into sausage casings tied at one end. Make a large coil, transfer to a saucepan of barely simmering water, and cook for 20 minutes. Immerse in cold water.

MAKING THE BLACK PUDDING. 1. Put the dry ingredients in a large bowl with the cooked onions, garlic and apple.
2. Add the dried blood and milk mixture. 3. Stir well before processing. 4. Put in a loaf pan and cook in a water bath.

Fried egg, bacon and black pudding

BLACK PUDDING CANAPÉS

❄ Using 5 ounces (150 g) black pudding, make 24 quenelles (2 teaspoons each). Wrap each quenelle in a piece of pancetta (see page 109) and arrange on an oiled baking sheet.

❄ Bake for 10 minutes in a preheated oven at 400 F (200 C). Let cool.

❄ When ready to serve put the black pudding quenelles onto 24 canapé bases (see page 164) and reheat in a hot oven before serving.

❄ Alternatively, put a dainty dollop of black pudding on a canapé base, top with a tiny roll of pancetta, arrange on a baking sheet and put in the preheated oven to heat through for about 5 minutes.

SHIFTING SANDS OF TIME

For our ancestors, the question of preserving food was a question of survival. They instinctively knew how to use the elements to halt the process of food decay. In northern climates they used cold air or ice to preserve fish, while in the intense heat of the Middle East excess meat and fish were laid in the sand or hung on rooftops to dry. Drying has been used as a method of preserving around the globe since history began, and is still used today. The same basic principles of drying were practiced the world over, but they were refined as people traveled and connected with other civilizations. This gave them the opportunity to see how others overcame the problem of food deterioration and to learn new techniques. These skills were then passed down through the generations.

It is very hard to differentiate between the various curing techniques because most cured foods undergo more than one process, many involving both salting and drying. The drying process is an important stage in most modern curing methods. Following brining, salting and spicing, large pieces of meat and fish, sausages and salami are generally hung or laid out to dry, to age, to mature or to cure—call it what you will—before being cooked, smoked or eaten raw. Depending on the product and the type of cure, the drying period can be short, such as in the case of gravadlax (see page 56), or long, in the case of Parma ham (see page 110), but it is nonetheless an essential part of the preserving process, since drying serves to kill bacteria.

Dried meat and fish are higher in nutritional value, as the protein and minerals are more concentrated and therefore more valuable weight for weight than their fresh counterparts. This made them essential victuals for any kind of extended journey, campaign or exploration.

Until the introduction of refrigeration, man relied on dried meat and fish, biscuits and dried fruit to see him through times when food was scarce. As long ago as 12000 B.C., Egyptian tribes are known to have dried poultry and fish in the hot desert sun. Interestingly, the same Egyptian word was used for preserving fish by salting and drying as was used for the process of embalming mummies. In 10000 B.C. the Japanese were making pots and jars in which to store the food that they hunted, fished and gathered, drying meat, fish and shellfish. The Babylonians in 1690 B.C. reportedly made a paste from pounded dry fish to put in soup.

STRUNG UP TO DRY

Some form of hard preserved meat, game or fish has sustained and assured the survival of indigenous tribes the world over, and was subsequently adopted by the canny settler determined to survive. Air drying was the easiest method of preserving, and is still practiced in tribal cultures, where meat is generally cut into strips and fish either gutted and filleted or left whole and strung up in the wind or sun to dry. In many cases, the fried meat fibers were then transferred to the fireside to smoke. Often the meat was pre-prepared to speed up the removal of moisture. Where salt was not available, it was beaten, squeezed, weighted, or even jumped on to break down the fibers. These techniques continue to be used in many parts of the world. Many of them have become sacrosanct symbols of home and country to expatriates around the globe.

In South America, Native Americans made sun-dried venison and buffalo, which today is known as "tassajo." Strips of meat are dipped in maize flour, dried in the sun and wind, and then rolled into balls for ease of transportation.

"Pemmican" was devised by North American native tribes in order to nourish them as they moved around their majestic terrain. Thinly sliced meat from wild animals too large to eat all at once, such as venison, bear, buffalo and whale, was either hung up to dry over the camp fire or in the sun or wind, depending on where they were and the time of year. It was then pounded to a powder flavored with berries and preserved with fat. Pemmican has been handed down from generation to generation and is still popular today as a high-protein snack, and as a source of meat on trips where fresh meat is not available or where weight may be a factor. Today it is known as jerky in the USA, and family recipes are closely guarded secrets.

North American native tribes also had access to masses of chum and sockeye salmon, which were good for preserving, as they were low in fat. They did not know about salting, so the salmon was air dried and smoked. Surplus fish were filleted, cut into strips, scored deeply, and hung on racks to air dry. To speed the process up, they built wood fires below them. The fish were then turned, rubbed and squeezed to encourage the process. This is how salmon, haddock and herring were originally smoked in Scotland, producing a smoked product very different from the one we know today.

In parts of Africa, fish is still sun or wind dried and hard smoked until almost burned. Large, open-ended oil drums covered with a mesh at one end are set over a charcoal fire, on to which wet wood shavings are scattered at the ember stage, producing a dense smoke.

In order to survive, the first Dutch settlers in the South African Cape learned the age-old craft of drying game meat from the native Bantu people. Today it is made from beef as well as game meat and is enjoying popularity beyond the country's boundaries. Biltong, as it is known, is being produced in the U.K. as a gourmet food and is on sale at the delicatessen counter at Fortnum & Mason in Piccadilly, London, and more prosaic outlets.

Drying is an ancient form of curing and one that is still used worldwide. However, in our modern world, where health and safety rules and we can no longer wait for the seasons, most specialist cured meats are made in temperature-controlled and dehumidified rooms. By curing foods ourselves and waiting for the seasons to change we can use the elements just as our forefathers did.

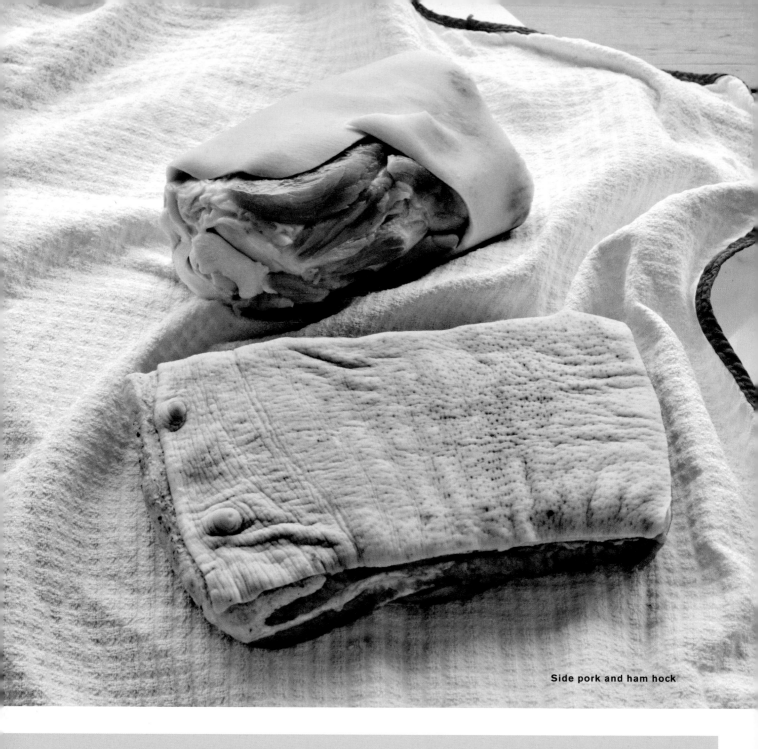

Side pork and ham hock

YE OLDE VIRGINIA HAM

The tradition of curing hams was introduced to America from Europe with the first settlers. Virginia, a very lean ham, dry salted and aged, and Kentucky, dry salted and smoked over hickory and apple wood, are two such worthies.

"Swine, Poultry and other domestic Animals brought from England augmented the abundant natural Supply (of fish and game). The Hogs, one contemporary Writer said swarmed like Vermin upon the Earth and were permitted to run as they liked and find their own Support in the woods.

From these Hogs, the Virginians produced one of their most famous Foodstuffs and their most popular standing Dish. Whatever else appeared upon the Table, Ham Bacon or Jowl were always there.

To eat ye Ham in Perfection steep it in half Milk and half Water for thirty-six Hours, and then having brought the Water to a boil put ye Ham therein and let it simmer, not boil, for 4 or 5 Hours according to Size or ye ham—for simmering brings ye Salt out and boiling drives it in." [c.1674]

The Williamsburg Art of Cookery

REGIONAL HAMS

The taste and texture of a finished ham depends on so many things: the climate and country; the breed of pig; its lifestyle and feed; the curing method; and the length of time that it is hung to dry or mature. Generally speaking, in warmer, drier climates the ham is dry cured and therefore eaten raw. In damper, cooler climes the ham is pickled in brine and dried and cooked before eating (see page 26).

Air-dried hams developed as a luxury item in Roman times when hogs roamed the forests of Europe, grazing on acorns and chestnuts. The hams of Gaul, Iberia, Corsica and the Rhineland were all renowned. Today very few pigs are left to run wild, but wonderful hams are still being produced in these areas.

The French *Jambon de Bayonne* made around Orthez in the southwest of the country has a smoky flavor and brown exterior; *Jambon de campagne* is the generic name given to cooked hams made all over France. *Jamón Ibérico*, made from the wild red Iberian pig that is left to roam in woodlands to eat acorns in southern and western Spain, is salted, dried and matured. I recently tasted *Bellota Negra* for the first time, which melts in the mouth as if it were richly flavored ham ice cream. The pigs have a pedigree akin to that of a racehorse, which may explain its high price tag. There is also a lesser product, but still delicious—the *Jambón Serrano*, mountain ham that is dry salted and matured.

Westfälische Schinken or Westphalian ham, a notable German cure, is cut from native pigs, the blood massaged out, dry salted and then marinated for weeks, during which time it is taken out, washed and marinated again, then dried and smoked at a low temperature over beechwood sawdust mixed with juniper twigs and berries. It is traditionally served in spring with white asparagus and bread and butter. Finally, the duke of hams, *prosciutto di Parma*, is dry salted, wiped down and hung in a carefully ventilated chamber and turned. All these hams are served thinly sliced, in their cured state.

In Scandinavia the native elk and reindeer found in the forests are dry cured and smoked. In the past, bears, too, were considered fit for the table, smoked bear tongue being a delicacy. In fact, in Germany the tradition of Westphalian hams originally came from the curing of bears' ham rather than pigs' ham.

Traditional English "York" ham refers to the curing method: dry salting, smoking and maturing for several months. Then there is Bradenham ham, originating from Wiltshire: a sweet, delicate variety with a black outside, cured in molasses with juniper berries and spices. Some air drying was practiced in Britain too, although not as commonly as salting, due to the damp climate. Goat hams and mutton hams were cured in Wales and called rock venison. Air-dried Carmarthen ham is still made in the old farmhouse way today by pork curer Albert Reese and his wife Ann, which has gained enormously in popularity with the resurgence of interest in traditional food in Wales. It is rumoured that the Romans learned to make air-dried ham in Carmarthen and took the recipe back to Italy! Small beef hams and venison hams were cured in Scotland, and in Cumbria they smoked mutton hams, which were known as "macons." Veal, goose and badger were all given the same treatment. Today, with the current financial problems associated with traditional farming and the consequent upsurge of interest in old culinary traditions and rare breeds, many farmers and producers are turning to these long-forgotten comestibles and have found niche markets for them.

CRAFTING YOUR OWN CURING

Most of these cured wonders are today made by professionals, but in the past when every family kept a pig and every bit of the pig was used it was a household affair, so there is no reason why anyone can't pursue the craft on a domestic basis. Curing techniques have been developed over centuries using a process of trial and error, taste, a combination of natural drying, smoking and heating processes, and the use of natural chemicals such as salt, sugar, spices, herbs, acids, oils and yeasts. Anyone wanting to try their hand at home curing would be well advised to keep this in mind. Learning through experience and exercising patience and common sense are the key

❧ **THE HOME-CURER'S CODE**

❧ Coarse sea salt is best to use.

❧ In damper climes nitrate is necessary to make the meat safe; it kills bacteria.

❧ Ascorbic acid (vitamin C powder) acts as a catalyst, helping curing salt work efficiently, and heightens the reddening of the meat.

❧ Color is an indication that the curing process has taken well.

❧ Sugar acts as food for fermentation.

❧ Hanging pulls salt through the meat muscle.

❧ Smell will indicate the quality of the cure.

❧ Cut off a tiny bit of the cured meat to taste as the ultimate test before diving in.

❧ **NOTE** It is possible to cure using only salt and time but to ensure consistent results in northern climes it is advisable to use nitrates as they do in Germany.

ingredients rather than a list of foodstuffs. Which is why in this chapter I shall explain how the experts in the field do their curing and leave it to you to develop your own craft, because this is how they learned theirs.

The French, Italians, Spanish and Germans are the leading players in the curing field with their world-famous hams, salami and sausages, so if you rear your own pigs and are thinking of embarking on charcuterie in a serious way, study of their methodologies will be rewarding. In Germany more nitrates are used than in the Mediterranean and anyone living in northern climates would be wise to keep this in mind. You don't necessarily need a Mediterranean climate to achieve the right results—although it helps—but what you do need is pure, dry air and good-quality meat, along with time and commitment, as curing doesn't happen overnight.

AIR-DRIED SPECIALTIES

In days gone by, goose was the poor man's pig and all the products that we associate with the pig were once also made with goose. In the northern Italian region of Friuli in the heart of the countryside is a family-run *agriturismo* that conjures up a way of life "once upon a time" in a farmhouse in those parts. At Casale Cjanor they have a large flock of geese and in November they kill 50 or 60 a week to produce delicious goose specialties such as liver pâté, salami and their phenomenal *prosciutto di oca*, cured goose breast. The entire goose breast is rubbed with a mix of 75 percent salt and 25 percent sugar, weighted and left overnight. The breast is then folded and rolled in crushed black peppercorns, tied, and hung for five or six months.

In Gargano in Puglia, shepherds traditionally made sun-dried *muscisca* from mutton and goat's meat probably since Roman times. The meat was cured with garlic, chili, pepper and wild fennel. Today it is made commercially with strips of veal flavored with herbs.

The Italian *alimentari* or grocer is a treasure house of air-dried specialties: cured meats and sausages hang in such profusion that they create a canopy, as rich as any cathedral *baldachino* (canopy). To experience Italian *salumeria* (salami) at its finest in a single visit, next time you are in Milan make a short detour from the Duomo and call in at Peck in the Via Spadari; enter, breathe the fragrance, open your eyes and see, and you will think you have stepped through the portals of heaven... this is probably the most food-inspiring emporium you are ever likely to visit anywhere in the world. As well as the many different types of hams mentioned later in the chapter, there are salamis such as the peppery *spianata*; soft salami (immature) like *ciauscolo di Visso*; mortadella, a cooked meat cure; *coppa*, *culatello*, *capocollo* and *lonza* from various parts of the pig; and *testino*, the Italian version of brawn, made with the cheeks, ears and tongue. Curing is not limited to the pig: wild boar, beef, venison and sometimes even goat and sheep are made into hams, salami and other delicacies according to region. Although cures vary, they all must be hung to dry.

The art of *prosciutto di Parma* or Parma ham

There are many wonderful dry-cured hams made all over Italy, such as *prosciutto di Carpegna*, *di Modena*, *di Norcia*, *di San Daniele*, *il Toscano* and *il Veneto Berico Euganeo*, and in many other parts of the world, but it is perhaps *prosciutto di Parma* that is most universally known and respected as a gourmet product of quality. Parma ham production bears close scrutiny for anyone tempted to try curing their own.

Parma ham has a long and noble pedigree. The Roman statesman Cato the Censor (234 B.C. to 149 B.C.) made reference to a tasty curing of pork legs through abundant salting: "The legs were left to dry, greased with a little oil and could age without spoiling. This process resulted in a delicious meat which could be eaten over a period of time while maintaining its flavor." And later, in 5 B.C., preserved salted pork legs from the Etruscan Po River Valley were traded with the rest of Italy and Greece.

PORK LEG, SALT, SEA BREEZE AND TIME

The raw meat for making Parma ham comes fresh from the accredited breeding farms via the slaughterhouses that are scattered over 11 regions between Lombardy and Latium. The pigs are fed on a mixture of Parmesan whey (Parmesan cheese is also made in the area) mixed with dried feed. They are slaughtered at nine months and the trimmed hams are fire-branded with an identification code name. The legs are cooled for 24 hours and then trimmed to the classic rounded chicken drumstick shape, at which stage 24 percent of fat and muscle is discarded.

There are 180 recognized producers of *prosciutto di Parma* and they are to be found only in a designated area in the hills around Parma. One of these production houses, Stefano Borchini's Slega *prosciuttificio* in Langhirano, produces 1,100 hams every week. On arrival they are checked to see if they have the look of a genuine Parma ham, and any ham that does not come up to these high aesthetic standards will end its journey there and then.

❀ The femur head must be intact and gently rising out of the flesh, not proud of it.

❀ The angle of the cut of the ham must have a gentle rise.

❀ There should be an even amount of fat around the red meat; not too much, not too little.

❀ There should be only so much marbling.

❀ There should be no excess blood clotting on the leg.

❀ There should be no veining on the skin.

❀ The meat should have a low water content: a high water content impedes the maturing process.

Parma ham is made with the best pork, coarse sea salt and the breeze—the windows on every story of the production house are flung open when the air is dry to let in the gentle sea breeze that rolls in over the Parma hills

from Liguria. This then permeates the hams and helps give them their distinctive flavor. Add to that time, expert eyes, hands and true passion. Stefano can recognize his own Parma hams in a blind tasting and even knows which part of the ham the tasting has been cut from, as salt levels vary within the ham.

Five days after slaughter, the pork is salted for the first time. The curer tips out salt onto a white table. He adds about 4 cups (1 liter) of tap water to one side of the mound and gently massages it into the salt. He takes hold of a ready-trimmed ham and brushes the skin loosely with the wet salt. A handful of dry salt is then pressed onto the surface of the red meat and swept deftly across the large muscle in one long, firm caress. Wet salt is pressed into the exposed vein. Lots more dry salt is pressed into the dip around the femur head to fill it. Salt is then sprinkled lightly over the red meat surfaces that have not already been salted. This whole process is carried out quickly.

The all-important metal seal bearing the production house's initials and the curing start date is attached. The salted ham is transferred to a cold room at a temperature that is high enough to allow the salt to permeate the whole ham, but cold enough to prevent the spread of bacteria; Stefano keeps his at 34 to 41 F (1 to 5 C).

After four days, any salt left on the ham is discarded and the salting process is repeated, and lasts 15 to 16 days, after which time the meat has become darker in color and slimmer. The total salting time is three weeks at Slega, but varies between production houses. The ham is then tested scientifically to see if enough salt has been absorbed. Any remaining salt is brushed away and the surface quickly dehydrated to destroy any remaining bacteria.

The drying process then follows to draw the moisture from the ham and kill any lingering bacteria. The salt goes in and water comes out in a process of osmosis, causing the rate of humidity in the room to rise. If the temperature is too high, the process must be halted. When the humidity in the ham is the same as the humidity in the room, the ham is ready. This process is measured electronically, but the ultimate test is the smell. If the ham smells bad, it means, as Stefano describes it, that "the bacteria have had kids" and it has gone off. There are no preservatives other than salt in Parma ham. The salting and drying process takes a total of three months, after which time there should be a 16 percent weight loss.

The hams are transferred at this point to a dry cold room where they stay for 70 days. Before World War I when there was no refrigeration, Parma ham production only took place in winter. At five or six months, the "open" end of the hams are coated with a mixture of pork fat, salt and pepper, and possibly rice flour, known as "sugna," to keep the outer layer of meat soft and stop it drying out faster than the inner layers. The fat acts as a seal, while the pepper prevents fly contamination. The windows are opened and closed, allowing the air to permeate the hams for six or seven months "while they sleep," and after this time the meat is greased again.

After 12 months the hams are transferred to the cellar and an inspector is called to carry out the ultimate test. He inserts a pointed instrument made of highly porous horse bone, the *gocia*, about 1 inch (2 cm) deep into the ham near to the bone, into the muscle, into the vein, and into the fat, five times in all. After each incision he waves the *gocia* under his nose, breathing in the fragrance. If it smells sweet, it is good; if it smells bad, the ham is destroyed. He must test 12 hams at random, and if they don't all pass the test, he takes another 12 and another 12 until they all do. The hams that have been passed are hot-branded with the distinctive Parma ham Ducal Crown. All hams are tested at 12 months; those that are destined to be hung for longer—24 or 36 months—to mature are not tested again.

❧ NUTRITIONAL SEAL OF APPROVAL

❧ In recent years many of us have reduced our meat and fat consumption in the interests of a healthy diet. Pork is incorrectly viewed as high in saturated fat; it is in fact higher in monounsaturated fat. Recent scientific research has endorsed the nutritional value of Parma ham. During the curing, proteins are cracked and predigested by enzymes present in the muscle. The result is an increase in free amino acids, giving the cured ham excellent digestibility, while its delicate umami flavor speaks for itself.

Row upon row of Parma hams strung up to dry

TAGLIOLINI AL PROSCIUTTO DI PARMA

TAGLIOLINI WITH PARMA HAM

SERVES 4

11 ounces (300 g) cherry tomatoes

10 ounces (280 g) Parma ham, cut into slivers and chilled

5 tablespoons white wine

Scant ½ cup (100 g) butter

Small bunch of basil leaves

11 ounces (300 g) homemade tagliolini (made with 5 yolks and 2 eggs per 2¾ cups (330 g) flour) or good-quality handmade dried tagliolini

Sea salt as desired

Olive oil, for frying

Freshly grated Parmesan cheese, to serve

This is a simple and delicious dish to make but it is essential to have the wok hot before you start and to work quickly. Chill the sliced Parma ham before adding it to the pan to stop it sticking together in a lump. The pasta and the sauce should be ready at the same time. Mix it all together and serve at once so that all the flavors remain fresh.

Bring a large saucepan of water to the boil. Add salt.

Heat a wok over medium heat and add enough olive oil to cover the base. Add the cherry tomatoes and stir-fry for a few minutes. Add the Parma ham, and when it becomes transparent, add the wine and cook until evaporated. Add the butter, mixing all the while, and the basil leaves. Turn off the heat.

Cook the pasta in the boiling water until tender. This will only take a few minutes.

Strain the pasta, add to the wok, and mix well. Serve at once with freshly grated Parmesan cheese.

PARMA HAM MENU

During the annual Parma Ham Festival, restaurants in and around Parma offer special tasting menus based on Parma ham. Masticabrodo is a restaurant near Torrechiara in the hills outside Parma, run by chef patron Francesco Bigliardi and his charming front-of-house wife Ide.

Before lunch, a small group of food writers and I watched as Francesco made tortelloni stuffed with pumpkin and amaretti biscuits and the dishes that we would be eating for lunch. Prior to our arrival he had made the pasta with 14 egg yolks and 7 eggs to every 2¼ pounds (1 kg) of flour, which was that amazing corn-fed yellow that only Italian eggs give. I lived near here in Bologna when I first arrived in Italy in the 1960s, a time when we all tucked into cream and butter without thinking twice, but to see Francesco happily spoon great dollops of butter (the original recipe contained 7 ounces [200 g]) onto the pasta made me draw breath. Then I relaxed and marveled that nothing has changed here and I was about to tuck into the kind of Sunday lunch that has been enjoyed by generations of these warm-hearted, friendly people.

The butter is bought from a farm nearby, as is the ricotta Francesco uses. It is so easy to forget, now that we can buy ricotta in our supermarkets, what real fresh ricotta tastes like, particularly when it is still warm, and butter for that matter. We ate it slathered between leaves of puff pastry and rose pink Parma ham, followed by a plate of pasta the likes of which I had not eaten since the last time I was in Emilia-Romagna; I had forgotten the joyous rich taste of unadulterated butter. The pork with herb-infused cream that came next melted away in my mouth.

SERVES 4

4 sage sprigs

2 thyme sprigs

2 rosemary sprigs

2 garlic cloves, sliced

Scant ½ cup (100 ml) extra virgin olive oil

2 pork tenderloins

1 cup (100 g) Parmesan cheese, grated

4 slices of Parma ham

All-purpose flour seasoned with salt and pepper as desired

Scant ½ cup (100 ml) cognac

⅔ cup (150 ml) stock

¾ cup (200 ml) heavy cream (optional)

Sea salt and freshly ground black pepper as desired

EQUIPMENT

8 wooden toothpicks

PORK TENDERLOIN STUFFED WITH PARMESAN AND PARMA HAM

This is a great recipe to impress friends and family. It can be prepared to the stage when the stock is added in advance and simmered and finished when ready to serve.

Put two sage sprigs, the other herbs and the garlic in a shallow dish and cover with olive oil. Let infuse in a warm place in the kitchen for an hour or so.

Trim and then cut the pork tenderloins in half, discarding the ragged ends, creating four equal portions. Cut each tenderloin piece through the middle lengthwise, but do not cut into two; open out flat to make a single slice of meat.

Sprinkle with some of the Parmesan cheese and freshly ground black pepper, lay a slice of Parma ham on the top of each, sprinkle with more Parmesan cheese and more black pepper, and put a sage leaf on top. Roll up each piece of pork, dip in seasoned flour and shake off the excess, and then secure with two wooden toothpicks.

Heat a skillet, and when hot, add some of the infused oil and the meat and brown quickly all over. Add the cognac and cook until evaporated, then add the remaining oil, herbs and garlic, and the stock. Reduce the heat and cook for 7 minutes.

Transfer the meat to a dish to rest. Pull out the toothpicks and discard. Add the cream, if using, to the pan and simmer gently for 5 minutes. Strain and serve poured over the meat. Serve with celeriac mash.

STUFFING THE PORK. 1. Cutting the pork. **2.** Opened out and sprinkled with Parmesan. **3.** Topped with a slice of ham, sage leaf, and Parmesan. **4.** Rolling up the stuffed pieces. **5.** Rolling in seasoned flour. **.6** Secured with two wooden toothpicks.

MAKES 3¼ POUNDS (1.5 KG)

Scant ½ cup (100 g) demerara sugar

⅓ cup (80 g) curing salt or ¼ cup (60 g) coarse sea salt and 1 tablespoon saltpeter mixed

½ teaspoon ascorbic acid (vitamin C powder)

1 loin of pork, about 4½ pounds (2 kg), from a traditional breed cross that gives good marbling, skinned, boned and most of the fat trimmed off. Don't throw away the bones—these are the spare ribs; marinate as per Jerky (see page 118) and roast for 1 hour at 400 F (200 C)

1 tablespoon sweet paprika

1 teaspoon finely chopped rosemary

Trealy is an idyllic hill farm overlooking rolling Welsh countryside where they produce artisan-made charcuterie from locally bred Saddleback and Gloucester Old Spot crossed with a Large White or Yorkshire pig.

If you are thinking of keeping your own pigs, they should be fed an 18 percent protein pellet feed augmented by household vegetable waste such as cabbage and cauliflower, but no citrus fruits. This feed should be integrated with corn and barley during the last six weeks. Finally, the meat should be well hung after slaughter.

Look at the shape of the loins and choose a loin with the bulk of the fat on the back, and most importantly, check that there is good marbling in the meat. Trim off the bulk of the fat, leaving just a little on the back.

Before embarking on this recipe, read the previous sections of this chapter carefully and remember the Parma ham test (see page 111): if the meat smells sweet, it is good; if it smells rancid or of ammonia, it is bad. It's as simple as that! This will take six to eight weeks to make.

Mix the sugar, curing salt and ascorbic acid together. Put the loin in a noncorrosive container and rub the mixture into the meat. Put in the refrigerator or a cool place for 4 days. After 2 days, pour off any blood or moisture that may have accumulated and redistribute the cure, massaging it into the meat.

After another 4 days, wipe off the cure and dry the meat well. Make a paste with the sweet paprika, finely chopped rosemary, and a tiny amount of water, and rub this into the meat. Return to the refrigerator for 24 hours, but make sure that the air is able to circulate around the meat by standing it on a rack set over a dish. Take anything out of the refrigerator that might create humidity, such as fruit and vegetables.

After this time, wrap the meat in cheesecloth and hang in a cool larder or outhouse where there is a good air flow for 40 to 50 days; use a fan to aid the circulation of air. If a fine, white powdery mold settles on the meat, there is no problem; simply wipe it off. If there is a light green mold and a good smell, wipe the mold off the meat and cut off a tiny bit of the meat to taste. It will keep for 1 month.

left Loin of pork rubbed with salt
opposite Thinly sliced loin of pork

MAKING JERKY

Jerky, the name deriving from the Spanish word *charque*, evolved from the Native American "pemmican" (see page 103) as a way of preserving meat that could not be eaten fresh while out on long and arduous hunting trips.

Thin slices of meat were cut and wind dried on the move. Today it is made by hunting enthusiasts as a way of preserving their quarry, but also to take on long hunting expeditions to eat as a snack to keep them going.

Traditionally, jerky is made from venison, moose, elk and antelope (even bears and prairie dogs too in the past), but beef is good and wild boar is also well worth trying. Be sure to use very lean cuts of meat and to trim off any sinew before processing the meat. Game meat is highly suited to the process, as it is very lean.

Marinating is not essential—the strips of meat can simply be dry salted and spiced before undergoing the drying process—but it allows you to put your own stamp on the product and makes it more interesting as well as more tender. I used my favorite spare rib marinade for this recipe which is deliciously umami.

Jerky can be dried in an oven, but if you are a serious hunter and want to make it regularly, it would be worth buying a dehydrator, as it is more efficient. The meat will lose about a quarter to a third of its weight when it is dried. Jerky may also be rehydrated and cooked.

When properly dried it will bend slightly before snapping; if not thoroughly dry it will go moldy. Store in an airtight container or plastic bags. Jerky can also be smoked. For detailed recipes and equipment suppliers, visit three men with nothing better to do at www.3men.com.

ASIAN VENISON JERKY

MAKES 1 POUND (500 G)

2¼ pounds (1 kg) venison, wild boar meat or other premium cuts of beef

MARINADE

Scant ⅓ cup (140 ml) tamari

½ cup (120 ml) Chinese rice wine

1 tablespoon freshly ground black pepper

2 teaspoons coarse sea salt

2 teaspoons Chinese five spice powder

2 teaspoons garlic granules

If you have never tasted jerky it is quite a strange experience; it's like eating one of those very hard sweets, which is almost like a gob stopper in your mouth and then suddenly it becomes all soft and chewy. I think it is a man thing! Simon Wheeler (the photographer on this book) loves jerky and when he and Lawrence Morton (the designer on this book) left my home to travel back to London after the shoot they took to the road, just like those North American hunters, with a bag of jerky in their pockets to keep them going on the trek home...

Cut the meat along the grain into ¼-inch (5-mm) thick strips 6 inches (15 cm) long. Put the marinade ingredients into a noncorrosive container and add the strips of meat. Cover and let stand in the refrigerator for several hours or overnight.

After this time, drain the meat thoroughly and dry on paper towels. Cover with plastic wrap and beat the meat with a mallet or wooden rolling pin to tenderize, making sure that the strips of meat are all the same thinness.

Preheat the oven to its lowest temperature. Spread the meat strips out on racks, taking care not to allow the pieces to touch. Set the racks over baking sheets lined with foil, put in the oven, and cook for 24 hours. The meat will darken as it cooks. When it is ready, it should bend slightly before breaking.

❧ **MARINATING MAXIM** Always fit marinade timing to suit you; longer or shorter periods of time won't change the recipe drastically but will make things easier for you. This rule does not apply to curing times, however.

❄ JERKY-MAKING GUIDELINES

- ❄ Only use lean cuts of meat. Trim all sinew and fat.

- ❄ 2¼ pounds (1 kg) meat will make 1 pound (500 g) jerky.

- ❄ Partially freeze the meat to aid slicing.

- ❄ Cut meat across the grain into thin strips ¼ inch (5 mm) thick and 6 inches (15 cm) long.

- ❄ Beat meat out evenly using a mallet or wooden rolling pin.

- ❄ Marinate for extra flavor or simply dry spice and salt.

- ❄ Dry meat using a clean drying cloth or paper towels.

- ❄ Spread slices out on racks set over a baking sheet lined with foil—it is important that the pieces of meat must not touch each other.

- ❄ Cook at your oven's lowest temperature for 24 hours or for 12 hours in a dehydrator.

- ❄ Test the meat by bending it gently: when it is ready and dried enough it will bend slightly before snapping.

- ❄ Let cool completely. Store in plastic bags.

- ❄ To ensure that any bacteria present are destroyed, the United States Department of Agriculture officially advises that jerky meat should be heated to 300 to 325 F (160 C) before hydration.

Blowing in the wind

Different regions of the globe boast their unique fish-drying traditions. India, for example, has its famous Bombay duck, while in China shark's fin and shrimp are dried (as is snake and duck), and in the Middle East octopus is strung up to dry. Lake Iseo in Lombardy, northern Italy, is home to the largest lake island in Europe, known as Montisola. Fishermen here are masters of their craft. They fish from small boats, then land their catch and string it up on road-side trellises, where they blow in the wind to dry.

Japanese cuisine uses many dried and semi-dried fish. *Katsuobushi*, a 1,500-year-old recipe, is the flavoring used for the famous dashi broth. This flaked, dried, fermented and smoked skipjack tuna is considered to have amazing powers, including lowering blood pressure by suppressing blood vessel contraction. *Naboshi* are dried sardines, which are used for *tazukuri*—a traditional dish of sweet and sour sardines served at New Year. *Mirinboshi* is seafood dried after being soaked in mirin (sweet rice wine), while *maruboshi* is fish dried after soaking in salt water. *Himono* is dried seafood and *Ichiya-boshi* is air-dried fish.

The Vikings favored drying since settlement began and preserving was a priority to prepare for the long, cold, dark winters. The cold, dry air was perfect for drying fish and on long voyages they hung up the fish they caught on rigging to dry in freezing winds until it resembled wood. In some parts of Scandinavia this is still the practice. The word "stockfish" or dried fish is derived from a Dutch, or possibly German, word meaning "a piece of wood." Stockfish has been traded around the world since the ninth century.

Norway has survived for centuries on fishing and exporting stockfish and salt fish. Because there was very little farmland and a poor climate for growing food, the country relied on the revenue from the export to import everything else. The island of Sørøya lies off the coast of northern Norway on the edge of the Arctic in the midst of the world's richest fishing grounds. When the days start to draw out between January and April, the cod returns here to spawn and this is when the best fish are caught and the best traditional *tørrfisk* or stockfish is made. The fish are caught with a hook and line from small boats and delivered for processing in less than two hours after catching, all helping to produce a superior artisan product. The cleaned fish are sorted into similar sizes, paired skin on, and tied together through the tail with a cotton string. They are then hung, carefully spaced apart for the air to circulate, from wooden racks or *hjeller* in the cold, dry, winter air. This process can take anywhere from two to three months, depending on fish size and climatic conditions.

Ninety percent of the stockfish produced in Norway is in fact exported to Italy—most to Venice then Liguria, Naples,

left **Dried stockfish**

Ancona, and Palermo where it still plays an important role in the traditional cooking. It was first introduced to Venice in 1423 by a rich Venetian nobleman who discovered it when he was shipwrecked on the island of Lofoten. He was impressed by this magnificent fish that could be preserved without the use of expensive salt and when he eventually went home he took stockfish back with him. The fish caught on because unlike fresh fish that went off quickly it could be kept indefinitely loosing none of its taste or nutritional value. A flourishing trade was eventually established by Dutch, Norwegian and Genoan merchants with these Italian ports.

Within Norway, however, stockfish is still associated with poverty and the desparate times when there was nothing else to eat, and is mainly regarded as an export product, so there are very few typical Norwegian recipes. It is usually eaten as a dry snack or made into *lutefisk*, stockfish that has been soaked in a lye solution for several days to rehydrate it.

The lye-soaked stockfish is salted and baked, and then served with butter, pea stew, crispy bacon and mustard; the finished fish, sometimes called lyefish, is jelly-like. It is believed that *lutefisk* was brought by early Norwegian settlers on their ships to North America, and that was all they had to eat. Today *lutefisk*, with its links back to those early days of hardship and courage, is celebrated in ethnic and religious celebrations, and served by Norwegian-Americans at Thanksgiving and Christmas.

Truffle of the sea

Bottarga, the amber-colored cured roe of the mullet or tuna, is largely a specialty of Sardinia, although it is also produced in Sicily, Spain and the South of France. The roes are salted and air dried, creating an amazingly intense flavor with a bitter, almost almond aftertaste. Although it was much appreciated in ancient times by Carthaginians, Egyptians and Romans, it was very much the preserve of the seafarer until fairly recently. Today this "truffle of the sea" is a prized gourmet product, exported from Sardinia all over the world to France, Germany, Japan, Spain and the USA It is served sliced thinly or dried and ground to a fine powder to enhance pasta dishes.

The tuna mattanza (literally slaughter) has taken place for hundreds of years in May in Sardinia around the island of Carloforte, where the fish come in thousands to spawn in the shallow waters. Up until the 1970s, before the introduction of modern industrialized fishing vessels, the tuna mattanza was huge and *bottarga di tonno* was made by fishermen in their homes, the roe being the fishermen's perk. Back then this was no gourmet specialty, but something to keep the fishing folk going through the winter when there was no other food.

Tuna fish bottarga is more problematic to make than any other because the skin is thick, making it difficult for the salt to penetrate the roe and for the leaching of the water from the roe. The roes are laid out on a bed of salt, buried in salt and a 4½-pound (2-kg) weight placed on top. After one or two days the liquid from the roe turns the salt yellow. This is scraped off, new salt is added, and the weight's replaced. The roe is massaged every day by hand with firm but delicate strokes, starting at the thin end and working toward the fat end. Today this process is carried out on stainless steel benches, but in the past soft wood tables were used, which absorbed the water. At this point the once-shapely pink roes have shrunk down to something that resembles a plank of wood, varying in weight from 2 to 11 pounds (1 to 5 kg). They are washed, dried and hung up, traditionally in the sun but nowadays laid out on a rack and turned in a temperature-controlled room for 15 to 20 days. The bottarga is then vacuum packed and stored in wooden boxes with straw packing.

When the tuna fish season draws to a close, the mullet season starts and continues until September. *Bottarga di muggine*, bottarga made with mullet roe, is considered to be the finer of the two and is sometimes referred to as Sardinian or Cabras caviar. The roes come in pairs still attached to the umbilicus and have a fine skin that absorbs the salt quickly: between one and three hours depending on the size. They are rinsed and dried and then hung to dry for anywhere from a week to a month. The longer they hang, the darker the color, the harder the roe, and the stronger the taste, but it remains delicate for all that.

Spanish *mojama* or *mosima* is tuna loin that has been salted for 48 hours, submerged in running water for 12 hours, and then hung in the wind to dry. Phoenician traders are thought to have taught the craft to Iberian tribes and also showed them how to flood low-lying fields with seawater, which then evaporated in the sun to leave salt deposits. *Mosciame*, as it is called in Italian, is made in Sant'Antioco to the southwest of Sardinia. This highly prized sun-dried tuna fish loin is a delicacy if you are lucky enough to get hold of it!

BOTTARGA AROUND THE WORLD

Bottarga in Italy, *bortarga* in Spain, *boutargue* or *poutargue* in France, *karasumi* in Japan, and *batrakh* in the Lebanon, where it possibly all started thousands of years ago; bottarga is the amber-colored air-dried roe of the tuna, swordfish or mullet. It is a highly sought-after ingredient comparable to caviar and truffle. Tuna roe bottarga has a powerful, distinctive flavor, while mullet roe bottarga is delicate and swordfish bottarga is strong yet relatively delicate. It can be used grated like Parmesan and sprinkled on pasta and rice dishes; shaved like truffle and served on risotto, spaghetti, boiled potatoes, fried and scrambled eggs, boiled fish,

salads, vegetables, and meat and fish dishes; or presented as a starter cut into paper-thin slices served with bread and butter or olive oil and bread and some sliced celery, cucumber or tomato. In the Lebanon it is served with thinly sliced garlic, while in Japan it is sliced and grilled so that it is crisp outside and soft inside and served with sake. As with truffle, the simpler the dish bottarga is served on, the better for enjoying the taste.

It is thought that the Phoenicians first developed the technique of making bottarga and introduced it to the countries with which they traded around the Mediterranean. Today it is still produced in

Provence in France, in Spain, and Orbetello in Italy, as well as Sardinia and Sicily. It is also produced as a Slow Food Presidium by Imraguen women in Mauritania on the western coast of North Africa.

In Japan, mullet roe bottarga, or *karasumi*, together with the sea urchin and the salted entrails of the sea cucumber are heralded as the three greatest culinary delicacies of the country. *Karasumi*, however, is an import, originally finding its way to Japan from Sardegna along the Silk Road via China around 400 years ago. It has been an element of high Japanese cooking ever since.

SANT'ANTIOCO ANTIPASTO

SERVES 6

6 slices of bottarga mullet

6 slices of bottarga tuna

6 slices of bottarga tuna heart

6 slices of tuna salami

6 slices of mosciame (cured tuna loin)

6 slices of smoked swordfish

1 cucumber, cut into 24 bias-cut slices

2 large firm tomatoes, cut into 12 slices

Freshly ground black pepper as described

Extra virgin olive oil, for drizzling

This bottarga feast is delicious served with carasau, *the traditional thin, crispy flat bread of Sardegna, and* Fili di Ferro, *the local grappa.*

Thinly slice the bottargas, tuna heart, tuna salami, mosciame, and smoked swordfish. Arrange on a platter with sliced tomatoes and cucumber.

Drizzle lightly with extra virgin olive oil and season with freshly ground black pepper. Serve with *carasau* or bread and butter.

ASPARAGUS, EGG AND BOTTARGA BUTTER

SERVES 4

4 tablespoons butter, softened

½ to 1 tablespoon dried grated bottarga or to taste, plus extra to garnish

1 bunch of fresh asparagus spears, trimmed

2 tablespoons malt vinegar

4 free-range eggs

1 tablespoon bottarga shards (optional)

Sea salt as desired

Bottarga butter is a very simple and effective way of using dried grated bottarga (the most easily available) and maximizing the flavor. Simply soften the butter, stir in the grated bottarga, and pot in ramekins or roll into sausages, chill and slice. The rounds of flavored butter can be put on broiled meat and fish or boiled vegetables, rice and pasta. It can also be spread on crostini, toast, canapés and celery.

Put the softened butter in a small bowl, add the dried grated bottarga, and mix well. Let stand at room temperature for the bottarga flavor to permeate the butter.

Cook the asparagus spears in a saucepan of salted water for 5 to 7 minutes; pierce the stalks with the tines of a fork to test for doneness. Drain when ready.

Half fill a large pan with water and bring to a boil, reduce the heat to a simmer, and add the malt vinegar. Crack the eggs into a cup, one at a time, carefully tip into the simmering water, and cook until set, say 2 to 3 minutes. Using a slotted spoon, transfer to paper towels to drain.

Drain the asparagus and transfer to a shallow dish. Add half the bottarga butter and toss the asparagus in the butter. Transfer to serving plates, top each with a poached egg, a knob of bottarga butter, bottarga shards, if using, and garnish with grated dried bottarga. Serve at once with a glass of chilled Manzanilla sherry.

❧ **HOMEMADE COD'S ROE BOTTARGA**

❧ I asked expert Antioco di Fois if I could make bottarga with cod's roe. As the roe is even more delicate than mullet roe, he suggested trying the method for the mullet roes (see page 123), but to salt the cod's roe for a maximum of an hour, trying just 30 minutes on one side to begin with.

MAKES 20 TO 30

¾ cup (200 g) crème fraîche or sour cream

Juice and finely grated zest of ½ lemon

4 tablespoons dried grated bottarga, plus extra to serve, or 2 tablespoons bottarga shards

1 pack of blinis or other ready-made canapé bases

3 tablespoons small bottarga shards or tomato concassé (optional)

Stefano Cannas, chef patron of the fish restaurant Golfo di Cannas, in Sant'Antioco, welcomes his clients with a taste of Sardegnan gold. A bar of bottarga is put on each table and diners help themselves. A generous touch of genius that has made his name.

Preheat the oven to 400 F (200 C).

Put the crème fraîche in a bowl and add the lemon juice and zest and the grated bottarga or bottarga shavings.

Put the blinis on a baking sheet and put in the oven for 5 to 10 minutes until completely warmed through.

Spoon the crème fraîche generously onto the blinis and top each with a bottarga shaving or a tomato jewel or two, if using. Serve on a hot plate dusted lightly with dried grated bottarga.

CHINESE STIR-FRIED DRIED SHRIMPS

SERVES 4 AS A STARTER

1 eggplant weighing about 14 ounces (400 g)

3 to 6 tablespoons grapeseed oil

6 garlic cloves, finely chopped

½ cup (100 g) dried shrimp soaked in a few tablespoons of cold water to just cover for 30 minutes

1 tablespoon tamari soy sauce

1 tablespoon rice wine or dry sherry

1 tablespoon sugar (any kind)

Good pinch of Chinese five spice powder

Small bunch of scallions cut diagonally into 1¼-inch (3-cm) pieces

Sea salt and freshly ground black pepper as desired

Most Chinese stores and supermarkets sell dried shrimp but you could use fresh shrimp too. Make sure they are the tiny brown variety, which are full of flavor. Serve this as a starter before the steamed and smoked guinea fowl (see page 140).

Cut the eggplant into pieces 2 inches by ½ inch by ½ inch (5 cm by 1.5 cm by 1.5 cm).

Put a wok on high heat for 1 minute, add 3 tablespoons of oil, and swirl it around the pan. Add the eggplants and garlic, reduce the heat a little and stir-fry for 10 minutes or until golden. It may be necessary to add extra oil. Add the other ingredients including the shrimp soaking water and cook until the liquid has been absorbed. Season to taste with salt and pepper.

Switch off the heat and add the prepared scallions, stir once, and divide between four Chinese bowls to serve.

CORFIOT STOCKFISH STEW

SERVES 4

1 large onion, finely sliced

4 leeks, finely sliced

6 garlic cloves, finely sliced

½ teaspoon cayenne

Few oregano sprigs

1 tablespoon tomato paste diluted in 2 tablespoons hot water

3 large tomatoes, peeled, seeded and chopped

1½ pounds (700 g) stockfish (soaked weight–see recipe introduction), or fresh cod, whiting, monkfish or other thick-fleshed white fish, cut into 4 to 6 pieces

Sea salt and freshly ground black pepper as desired

Finely chopped flat-leaf parsely, to garnish

Extra virgin olive oil, for sautéing

Stockfish is air dried in the biting-cold Scandinavian wind until it becomes as hard as wood; no salt is used in its preparation. It needs seven days' soaking and at least one change of water each day before it is fit for purpose. During this time the fish swells up. It can be cut with a saw into individual portions, which reduces the soaking time considerably. Unlike salt fish, it is dried with the skin on.

While the fish is soaking it is quite smelly, but don't let this put you off. I also suggest soaking it overnight in milk before you finally cook it. Once cooked the smell disappears, leaving a deliciously rich meaty fish.

In the 19th century, stockfish was traded by the British to Corfu in boxes marked "stockfish," and since those times Corfiots have called it by its English name. When wandering the tiny everyday streets of Kerkyra (Corfu Town) you can't fail to come across boxes of stockfish and salt fish as they both feature heavily in the island cooking, reflecting the island's earlier domination by the Venetian Republic.

Put a large sauté pan over medium heat, and when hot, cover the base with oil. Add the sliced onion, leeks and garlic and cook for about 10 minutes until soft.

Add the cayenne, oregano, diluted tomato paste, and prepared tomatoes and simmer for 5 minutes. Add the fish portions and salt and pepper to taste and cook for another 30 minutes. If using fresh cod, cook for another 10 minutes or until the fish is cooked through. Check for seasoning again before serving.

Transfer the fish pieces to a warmed plate. Discard the skin and bone, lightly flake the flesh with a fork, mix into the vegetables, and garnish with parsley before serving.

NORWEGIAN STOCKFISH CAKES AND PEAS

SERVES 4

11 ounces (300 g) stockfish (soaked weight—see page 129), coley, haddock or lightly salted cod (see page 50) or firm-fleshed white fish

3 cups (700 ml) milk

⅓ cup (150 g) boiled potatoes, roughly mashed

¼ cup (50 g) lean home-cured bacon, rind removed, (see page 109), finely chopped

1 onion, finely chopped

1 tablespoon butter or bacon fat

2 tablespoons all-purpose flour, plus extra for flouring

¼ teaspoon freshly ground black pepper

¼ teaspoon mustard

½ beaten free-range egg

Sea salt as desired

Bacon fat or oil, for frying the cakes

MUSHY PEAS

2 cups (300 g) dried peas

½ teaspoon baking soda

1 teaspoon sea salt, plus extra as desired

1 tablespoon malt vinegar

1 tablespoon finely chopped mint

Freshly ground black pepper as desired

Most stockfish recipes come from Italy and Spain where stockfish was once consumed in large quantities. The Norwegians are less enthusiastic about it and traditionally eat it dry as a snack with aquavit and beer. I have reworked this Norwegian fishcake recipe using stockfish and added the traditional accompaniments for lutefisk *(see page 123): bacon and green pea stew—or mushy peas as we call them.*

Soak the fish for 6 or 7 days and then drain well. Remove the skin and bone the fish carefully. Soak overnight in half of the milk. Soak the dried peas for the mushy peas overnight in enough cold water to cover with the baking soda added.

Drain the soaked peas and rinse. Put in a saucepan, cover with cold water, and add the salt. Bring to a boil, skim the surface, and then simmer gently until the peas turn to a mush, by which time most of the water will have evaporated: say 20 to 30 minutes. Drain if necessary. Add the vinegar and mint and salt and pepper to taste. Stir well and keep warm.

Discard the soaking milk from the fish and transfer the fish to a saucepan, cover in the remaining milk, and simmer gently for 5 minutes. Drain well and fork the fish and mix with the mashed potatoes.

Fry the finely chopped bacon and onion in the butter or bacon fat until crispy.

Add the bacon, onion and cooking fat, flour, black pepper, mustard, egg and salt to taste to the potato mixture and mix well. Shape into cakes and dip in flour. (The fishcakes can be chilled at this stage until required, but it may be necessary to flour them again lightly before frying.) Fry in bacon fat or oil until well browned on both sides. Serve at once with the mushy peas.

A whole smoked eel

4SMOKED

AN ADDICTIVE HABIT

Smoking is one element of a three-fold cure for fresh foods. It starts with dry salting or brining, goes on to drying, and ends with smoking—all three processes help to preserve the produce. In the past this combined process was called "kippering," hence the word "kipper" for a smoked herring.

Traditionally, meat and fish were cured to see the family through the winter and then hung up high in the chimney above the smoldering wood fire to smoke overnight, after which they were cut down and hung from the rafters until needed. During smoking, tarry deposits from the smoke would fall on the flesh and act as an antiseptic. This, combined with the salt already absorbed, inhibited the development of bacteria that would otherwise have caused the food to decay. The demise of the open hearth in favor of more convenient stoves and cooking ranges brought home smoking to an end until home smoke boxes started appearing on the market. Modern tastes as well as needs have changed. We use less salt and more subtle smoking techniques because the necessity to preserve food in this way no longer exists. In the Western world we smoke food only for flavor and find lightly salted and smoked produce more palatable, although in some remote regions of the world smoking is still an essential preserving process. This means that although today's smoked fish and meat lasts longer than fresh fish and meat, it no longer has an indefinite shelf life and should be stored in the freezer if you want to keep it long term.

Home hot smoking can be improvised in a steamer or wok (see page 138).

SMOKING TRADITIONS

The native people of the Caribbean, the Arawaks and Caribs, dried and smoked meat on green wood lattices over fires of bones and hides. The Caribs called this *boucan*, and the Spanish *barbacoa*, which eventually evolved into the word "barbecue" or "barbeque." Red herrings, originally prepared in the 14th century around Yarmouth in East Anglia in eastern England, were cured whole, hard salted, dried and long smoked, which turned them red, hence the name. The cure was so intense that red herrings could be transported all over Europe without fear of spoiling and barrel loads were shipped to Italy, Greece, France and Holland. It is not unusual to see boxes of imported smoked herring in these countries even today alongside the local catch in the fish market. Although this kind of cure provided sustenance where it was most needed, it was not to the taste of the more sophisticated palate. The bloater (smoked mackerel or herring) offered a milder smoke taste, but did not travel well and consequently could only be consumed locally.

THE SMOKED SALMON STORY

Of all the smoked products, salmon is king and smoked Scottish salmon is the king of kings. However, it was Jewish immigrants from eastern Europe who introduced the trade to the U.K. at the beginning of the 20th century, smoking imported Baltic salmon preserved in barrels of salt water. The many rivers of Scotland and Ireland and the Wye, Usk and Severn in England and Wales were renowned as salmon rivers and salmon fishing was the sport of the aristocracy at the time. This, coupled with the fact that salmon was a seasonal delicacy, brought kudos to its consumption.

The early eastern European makers of smoked salmon in London soon realized that there was no need to import fish from the Baltic, as there was an abundant supply of wonderful fresh Scottish salmon being brought to London. As the popularity of smoked salmon spread, canny Scot smokers decided to grab some of the action. Until the 1970s when techniques changed and salmon farming took over, Scottish smoked salmon reigned supreme the world over. The Scot curers put more emphasis on the smoke, whereas the London cure of those founding Baltic smokers was and is more delicate, with the taste of fish over smoke.

The majority of farmed salmon live in confined spaces and have fatty flesh, very different from the flesh of the wild fish that swim free in the sea. Some farmed salmon is inexpensive and is therefore no longer treated with due consideration. Rather than being salted and then smoked in the fullness of time, it is injected with brine and sprayed with smoke flavoring. It is a very different product from the one the early 20th-century well-heeled enjoyed and really has no right to be called smoked salmon. There are of course still smokehouses producing fabulous handmade smoked salmon from wild and organic farmed salmon. Naturally it is more expensive, but you get what you pay for.

Improvised hot smoking in the kitchen

You can hot smoke at home without going to the trouble or expense of buying a special kit. Simply use a heavy-based lidded wok or steamer with a cooking rack inside, or use the steamer basket. You can even use a covered heavy-based roasting pan with a trivet. If you don't want to ruin said pots and pans forever, line the base and sides with several layers of foil.

You can use rice, tea leaves, sugar or even sawdust to smoke and aromatize it with your own choice of herbs and spices. Set your improvised smoker over high heat for 10 minutes, which is long enough to ignite your fuel. I have found plain sugar the best fuel for indoor smoking, as it does not leave the kitchen or me with the overpowering aroma of smoke. Unless you have a professional venting system in your kitchen, use a gas grill outdoors to ignite your fuel, then you can puff away.

Hot smoking is basically cooking with the added element of smoke and therefore you can more or less follow the cooking times you would use for other quick-cooking processes. Scallops, oysters, mussels and shrimp take a few minutes, thin fillets of fish not much longer, duck and chicken breasts 20 to 30 minutes, and big pieces of meat much longer. But there is no substitute for experimenting to achieve the right results. As a general guideline, when the meat or fish turns opaque, it is ready.

The best results for hot smoking are achieved by curing in salt and sugar marinades overnight before smoking. It is easy to make your own delicious home-smoked dishes this way. Try the recipes on pages 140 to 146, also try experimenting with thick fillets of salmon, other fish, chicken and game bird breasts.

❧ SMOKEHOUSE RULES

- ❧ Only choose best-quality, fresh produce.
- ❧ Wait for rigor mortis to pass if freshly killed.
- ❧ In the case of wild fish, freeze for 48 hours before starting the curing process, to kill any parasites that may be present.
- ❧ Thoroughly clean, gut and open out fish, making sure to remove blood channels, or fillet, trim or cut meat and other produce.
- ❧ Weigh and record weight.
- ❧ Make a bed of coarse sea salt in the bottom of a noncorrosive container.
- ❧ Layer the product on top, in the case of fish layer flesh to flesh, skin to skin, and sprinkle each layer with salt as you go.
- ❧ In the case of fish, moderate the amount of salt in proportion to its thickness: where the fish is thinner it will need less salt.
- ❧ Put a weight on top; I use several tetra packs of long-life juice for

big pieces of meat and fish and a sardine can for small fish.

- ❧ Leave the product for 8 to 24 hours, depending on its weight, amount of salt used, degree of weighting and so on; aim for a 15 percent weight loss at the end of salting.
- ❧ Wipe the excess salt off and soak the product in cold water for 5 minutes.
- ❧ Hang up or arrange on racks at room temperature for 24 hours to dry (trout and eels are hung up to smoke still wet) at about 70 F (21 C). Quail, partridge and small game birds need only 3 hours drying; small items such as scallops and shrimp will need just an hour. Another 10 percent weight loss should occur during smoking.
- ❧ Use hardwoods; soft woods are unsuitable. Choose oak, beech, ash, sycamore, hawthorne, blackthorne, plum, apple, pear or juniper in chips or sawdust. Experiment with using spices,

herbs, sugar and teas in a domestic situation.

- ❧ Smoke according to the product and try to keep the smoking light. Don't be disappointed if you fail to achieve the right result at first—practice makes perfect and imperfect results make good croquettes and fish cakes!
- ❧ Cold smoke at 70 to 80 F (20 to 25 C) for long periods. Create a good head of smoke before putting the product in the smoker and keep it constant throughout. Don't open the door unnecessarily. Put a bowl of water on the smoker floor to increase moisture. Hot smoke at 140 to 150 F (60 to 65 C) for short periods.
- ❧ Hot-smoked food is best served immediately, cold-smoked rested overnight; freeze anything you don't eat in a few days.
- ❧ Before you embark on home smoking, read how the experts do it in this chapter.

❖ FISH AND MEAT SUITABLE FOR HOT SMOKING

- ❖ Mackerel
- ❖ Trout and salmon
- ❖ Eels—can also be cold smoked; a great delicacy, but non-sustainable
- ❖ Arbroath Smokies—haddock with heads removed, gutted, tied in pairs by the tail and smoked (originally over peat)
- ❖ Shellfish such as oysters, mussels, scallops and shrimp—shells on or off
- ❖ Octopus
- ❖ Buckling—un-gutted herring, originally from Suffolk, eastern England
- ❖ Sprats—un-gutted
- ❖ Chicken, duck, goose and turkey
- ❖ Pheasant, quail, grouse, pigeon and mallard
- ❖ Venison, lamb and beef
- ❖ Ham

1
2 3

HOT-SMOKING TECHNIQUES. **1. Rice, tea leaves and sugar in a wok ready to be ignited for smoking. 2. Apple lops (freshly cut twigs from an apple tree) and leaves smoking on a barbecue. 3. Apple wood smoked duck breasts.**

CHINESE SMOKED GUINEA FOWL WITH NOODLES

SERVES 4

1 guinea fowl or chicken, weighing 3¼ to 4½ pounds (1.5 to 2 kg)

5 teaspoons coarse sea salt

1 egg-size piece of fresh ginger root, peeled and halved

4 tablespoons dark brown sugar

2 tablespoons sesame seeds, toasted in a dry pan

Sesame oil, for brushing

NOODLES

4 portions of Chinese noodles

1 tablespoon tamari

2 tablespoons sesame oil

DIPPING SAUCE

1 tablespoon tamari

2½ tablespoons white wine vinegar

2½ tablespoons superfine sugar

1½ tablespoons sesame oil

½ tablespoon Tabasco sauce

½ tablespoon salt

TO SERVE

Spicy Cucumber Salad (see page 145)

Plum Chutney (see page 233)

EQUIPMENT

Steamer or wok

This is a traditional Chinese recipe for steaming and smoking chicken, which lends itself well to game birds. I used guinea fowl, but try pheasant, quail and partridge this way. The flesh is soft and delicate, run through with the subtle flavors of ginger root, and sesame.

Wipe the bird inside and out and rub with the salt. Put in a noncorrosive dish, cover loosely with parchment paper with a weight on top, and let stand in a cool place overnight.

Pour off any excess water that may have formed. Pour enough boiling water into the steamer or wok to come within 2 inches (3 cm) of the steamer basket, or a cooking rack if using a wok. Put one piece of ginger in the water and the other piece inside the bird. Put the bird in the steamer basket or on the rack so that the steam can circulate around the bird. Bring the water to a rolling boil, put the lid on, and simmer continuously for 45 minutes. Keep a kettle handy and top up the water level as necessary.

Put all the ingredients for the dipping sauce in a bowl and whisk together. Divide into four dipping bowls.

Once the bird has steamed, test for doneness by waggling a drumstick. If the leg moves freely, the bird is ready. Put the bird on one side and pour away the water. Dry the steamer or wok and line the base and lower sides with at least three layers of foil. Sprinkle the foil with the sugar. Put the bird in the steamer basket or on the cooking rack over the sugar. Line the lid with more foil, bringing it up over the lid to seal the pan tightly to stop the smoke from escaping (optional).

Set the pan over medium heat for 10 minutes, by which time the sugar should have ignited. Smoke the bird. Switch off the heat and leave for 5 minutes before opening.

While the bird is smoking, cook the noodles according to the package instructions, drain, and dress with the tamari and sesame oil. Spread out on a serving dish, cover, and keep warm.

Working quickly, transfer the smoked bird to a chopping board. Pour off any juices that might have accumulated inside the bird and reserve. Brush the bird with sesame oil, then carve as follows; a short, sharp-bladed knife is useful for this. Cut off the wings and legs. Cut the body in half lengthwise through the breast and backbone. Lay the flat halves on a board, skin side up, and use a cleaver to cut through the bones into 1-inch (2-cm) wide pieces. This is easier said than done unless you are an expert with a Chinese cleaver. Alternatively, cut through the bird with a sharp knife and leave the breastbones on the board. Arrange on the bed of noodles as if the bird were still whole. Cut the wings and legs into pieces and arrange these on the noodles too. Pour the reserved juices over the meat and sprinkle liberally with the toasted sesame seeds.

Serve warm or at room temperature with Spicy Cucumber Salad, the dipping sauce, and Plum Chutney.

SMOKING THE GUINEA FOWL. 1. Water boiling in a steamer. 2. The guinea fowl in the steamer basket.
3. Igniting the sugar ready for smoking. 4. The smoked guinea fowl.

Chinese smoked guinea fowl with noodles

CINNAMON AND ORANGE SMOKED DUCK

SERVES 4 TO 8

½ cinnamon stick

2 star anise

Zest of 2 oranges, pared with a potato peeler and dried in a low oven for 24 hours

1 tablespoon coarse sea salt

1 tablespoon demerara sugar

2 duck breasts

EQUIPMENT

Steamer

Alan Murchison (see below) recommends eating the smoked duck within 36 hours of smoking; after that time it loses its fresh taste.

Put the cinnamon stick, star anise, and dried orange zest in a blender and reduce to a fine powder. Put in a noncorrosive bowl, add the salt and sugar, and mix well.

Rub a small amount of the salt, sugar and spice mixture into the duck breast skin, cover, and let marinate in a cool place for 3 hours.

After this time, wipe off any excess marinade. Put the duck, skin side down, in a nonstick skillet, set over medium heat, and cook until the duck fat is rendered and the skin turns golden. Check on the skin from time to time to make sure it does not burn. If the skin is getting too dark reduce the heat. This may take 15 to 20 minutes. Pour off the excess fat as it melts. Keep the fat for making confits and rillettes (see pages 185 to 197).

Line the base of a steamer with six layers of foil, making sure that the foil goes 2 inches (5 cm) up the sides of the pan. Sprinkle with the remaining salt, sugar and spice mixture.

Either light the sugar with a blowtorch or set the pan over high heat. When the sugar has caramelized and is smoking well, put the duck breasts in the pan or steamer basket over the smoke. Set the pan over low heat and cook for 20 minutes, turning the duck once.

Alan serves this in a stunning terrine with sultanas soaked in a port and red wine reduction and quince purée. I served mine sliced while still warm on toasted brioche with the sultanas and Membrillo (see page 232) diluted 50/50 with boiling water.

PLAYING WITH SMOKE

An elegant country house restaurant, L'Ortolan, is set in a charming garden just on the outskirts of Reading in Berkshire, southern England. The restaurant's energetic and experimental chef patron, Alan Murchison, changes his menu four times a year, and when I asked him how he comes to new dishes, he responded simply, "We play about with food." This echoes the philosophy of his book *Food for Thought*, which kicks off with a quote from Benjamin Franklin, "We do not stop playing because we grow old, we grow old because we stop playing."

L'Ortolan smokes scallops, salmon, cheese, pigeon and venison, and Murchison agreed to show me how he was smoking duck breast for the restaurant, igniting sugar in a pot on the stove using sugar as the fuel for the smoke, as they do in China (see page 140). He grinds the spices and then adds them to equal quantities of salt and sugar, which he uses first as a marinade and secondly to fuel the smoke.

Murchison totally loves the combination of aromatics and he kept saying "that smell," giving me the marinade to inhale. Once the smoke was going and the duck breasts in situ, he lifted the lid and with a great grin announced, "The smell is awesome!" And so it was.

He says you can smoke anything this way, and believe me you will: "Try smoking seared tuna loin with soy, confits of duck or scallops with wasabi and ginger." Playing is just what you want to do once you get the smoking habit.

SMOKING THE DUCK. 1. Sugar, salt, star anise, cinnamon and dried orange zest ready for grinding. 2. Rubbing the spiced cure into the duck breasts. 3. The hot-smoked duck breast ready to serve.

SMOKED

SMOKE BOX SIDE OF HOT-SMOKED SALMON

SERVES 6 TO 8 AS A MAIN COURSE AND MANY MORE AS AN APPETIZER

1 side of salmon, weighing 2¼ pounds (1 kg)

5 tablespoons sea salt

3 tablespoons unrefined cane sugar

Vegetable oil, for brushing

❧ **VARIATION** For a more exotic hot smoke, add one or two of your favorite herbs and spices to the cure, or try this more complex combination of spices:
2 teaspoons each of crushed black peppercorns, crushed white peppercorns, crushed coriander seeds, crushed mustard seeds, ground cinnamon, ground ginger, and 2 crushed bay leaves.

Hot-smoked salmon is cured salmon cooked at a low temperature and smoked at the same time. The more familiar smoked salmon is simply cured and smoked, not cooked.

Cut clean slashes 4 inches (10 cm) apart in the skin with the point of a small sharp knife under the thickest part of the fish, taking care not to damage the flesh.

Mix the salt and sugar in a small bowl and cover the base of a stainless steel, ceramic, glass or plastic container with a very thin layer of salt and sugar cure. Lay the fish, skin side down, on the cure and then sprinkle what is left over the flesh, moderating the density according to the thickness of the fish; the thickest part will need the most, while the thin tail end will require hardly any. If you are curing several sides of salmon or fish, lay flesh to flesh and then skin to skin and so on.

Cover the fish lightly with plastic wrap and put a weight on top (see page 138). Let stand overnight or for 24 hours for bigger fillets, less for smaller ones. After this time, rinse the fish and dry or wipe down the residual cure, put on an oiled rack in a cool place, and let dry so that the air can circulate around it.

Preheat a commercial-built home smoke box to 150 F (65 C) and then put the fish in the smoker for 2 hours. Keep an eye on it to ensure that the smoker is maintaining an even temperature. It may take longer or less time, depending on the quantity of fish you are smoking, the size and the thickness of the fillets, and also the weather outside. Lift out the salmon and carefully insert the point of a sharp knife into the thickest part of the fish to see if the fish has turned opaque inside. Remember that you want it to be just cooked, succulent and juicy, not dry. If the salmon is not ready, return the rack to the smoker and smoke for another 30 minutes, then check again. If you are smoking more than one salmon side, it may be advisable to smoke for longer and to rotate the racks so that all the fish get an even smoke.

For a golden result, paint with vegetable oil halfway through the smoking progress. When ready, rest for 20 minutes and eat hot or let rest and cool at room temperature, then wrap in foil and refrigerate until required.

THE HEREDITARY SMOKER

Lance Forman is the great-grandson of the founder, Aaron, of H. Forman and Son, makers of world famous cold-smoked Scottish salmon in east London since 1905.

"Hot smoking is relatively new at Foremans," says Lance. "The problem is getting enough smoke into the fish in a short time. A cold smoke takes 24 hours, a hot smoke has to be realized in two hours or it dries out." In their new state of the art factory, they grind oak logs, causing friction, burning and smoke. This gives complete control

and intense amounts of smoke in a very short time, creating soft and buttery hot-smoked salmon.

Work starts at 4:00 a.m. with the arrival of the salmon six days a week from the Shetland Islands or the west coast of Scotland. Wild fish are caught and delivered the same day and farmed fish are harvested and delivered within 48 hours. All wild fish have to be frozen to kill any parasites. Lance maintains freezing enhances the smoking process. Wild salmon is caught in the summer and then

frozen for smoking all year around.

The salmon are gutted, cleaned and filleted; three or four oval incisions are made in the skin to aid salt and smoke absorption. Next they are laid, skin side down, on stainless-steel racks and lightly salted with rock salt. After 24 hours the excess salt is rinsed off, the fish is soaked in fresh water, and then dried before smoking. Hot or cold smoked, wild or farmed, the product is exceptional. Lance's ideal is smoked wild Scottish salmon with a glass of champagne.

SMOKING THE SALMON. **1.** Slashing the salmon skin at the thickest part. **2.** Sprinkling the salt and sugar mix on the salmon flesh. **3.** The salmon after 24 hours, cure is ready for draining. **4.** The salmon in the hot smoke.

SERVES 4

1 pound (500 g) small zucchini, washed and dried

4 tablespoons extra virgin olive oil, plus extra for drizzling

1 tablespoon lemon juice

2 heaping tablespoons finely chopped mint leaves, plus extra sprigs to garnish

1 cup (150 g) hot-smoked salmon (see page 148), flaked

1 baguette

1 garlic clove, halved

Good-quality balsamic vinegar, for drizzling

2 tablespoons pine nuts, toasted

Sea salt and freshly ground black pepper as desired

A side of hot-smoked salmon is a great centerpiece for a party, especially when you have smoked it yourself. However, there is some really good smoked salmon made commercially (see pages 284 to 285). They are sold in handy packs and are great for making simple summer appetizers and salads such as this one.

Shave the zucchini lengthwise into ribbons using a mandolin or potato peeler. Put in a bowl and add the olive oil, lemon juice, salt and pepper. When ready to serve, add the chopped mint and the salmon and toss.

Cut the baguette into four or eight diagonal slices, depending on size. Toast the bread and then rub with the garlic, sprinkle with salt, and drizzle with olive oil. Divide between four plates to serve.

Pile the zucchini and salmon salad on the toast, drizzle lightly with balsamic vinegar, sprinkle with the toasted pine nuts, and top with a mint sprig. Serve at once.

Introducing the cold-smoking craft

Cold smoking, as in classic smoked salmon, is the most difficult curing craft to perfect and you may find reading how the experts do it helpful (see below and page 158). Unlike hot smoking, cold smoking is not possible using a wok or steamer or any other improvised home smoker where heat and smoke are one, but requires a more complex gadget.

One option is to go the DIY route and rig up something ingenious outdoors. This can be an old refrigerator, dustbin, oil drum or filing cabinet—take your pick! The important principle is that you must distance the smoke from the heat source, so you need a length of vacuum cleaner, washing machine or tumble dryer hose to channel the smoke from a receptacle such as a biscuit tin or oil can containing smoldering sawdust (see page 138 for recommended types of sawdust to use). If this sounds like a fun way to spend your Saturday afternoons, read Keith Erlandson's book *Home Smoking and Curing*, which has been around since 1977—it's incomparable. He suggests all sorts of clever gizmos and gives helpful drawings too.

Should you live in a wonderful old house with an inglenook fireplace and keep a fire smoldering 24/7, you could try stringing up a salmon or a side of bacon in the chimney; you might find an old hook for the purpose still there. But be warned: this will produce a level of smokiness we are no longer used to. You could even try hanging it up overnight over the embers of a dying campfire and have a bit of fun in the process.

Alternatively, you could do as I do and use a commercial-built smoke box with a thermostat. The key point to remember is to keep the heat low and constant. Get it to the right temperature, 70 to 80 F (20 to 25 C), then hold it there, so don't think you can simply put your fish in and abandon it. To start with, weigh what you are smoking at hourly intervals. Lance Forman (see page 148) advises a 15 percent weight loss during salting and 10 percent during smoking for the perfect cold-smoked salmon. In time you will only have to look at your smoked result to judge when it is right.

The crown of the smoker's craft is of course smoked salmon (see below), but don't waste money experimenting with it. Start with smaller fish that cold smoke well (see box below). Trout is the closest to salmon, so begin with that and build up to salmon. I can't give hard and fast cooking times and temperatures; smoking does not work in that way. But Rinaldo Dalsasso's recipe for Lake Garda Cold-smoked Rainbow Trout (see page 154) will kickstart your cold-smoking apprenticeship. For a plainer smoke, omit the herbs and orange zest and simply use salt and sugar. Create your own mixes of herbs and spices to make new flavors.

❀ FOODS SUITABLE FOR COLD SMOKING

- ❀ Kippers—herring
- ❀ Red herrings (see page 135)
- ❀ Salmon and trout
- ❀ Swordfish and tuna
- ❀ Herring—bloater and kippers are split back to belly and opened up
- ❀ Whiting and pollock
- ❀ Venison and wild boar
- ❀ Beef, lamb and mutton
- ❀ Ham, bacon, sausages and salami
- ❀ Biltong—ostrich, antelope and so on
- ❀ Mild soft and hard cheeses from Parmesan to Cheddar, but no blues
- ❀ Nuts, grain, eggs, milk, salt, sugar and fruits

THE INTUITIVE SMOKER

Michael Leviseur, master of the award-winning Organic Smokehouse in Shropshire, has learned his craft by trial and error. He cured his salmon in plastic boxes, the base of which is covered with a thin layer of sea salt, and the fish is layered with more salt, flesh to flesh, skin to skin. The box is closed and left for 10 to 12 hours. The fish is then washed, strung, hooked and hung for 24 hours and smoked for 18 to 20 hours depending on the weather.

When the weather is damp the smoking takes a little longer. Michael knows instinctively when the product is ready. He uses the centuries old draft-smoking method with air-dried, naturally fallen oak. The process is slow and gentle giving greater depth of flavor.

Michael's advice for the home smoker: "Experiment with trout. It's all about the quality and freshness of the fish to start with. The feel, the smell and the firming up of the flesh as the fish is cured and smoked." Michael works on a total of 30 percent reduction between salting, drying and smoking in weight loss.

COLD-SMOKING RAINBOW TROUT. 1. Salt, sugar, herbs and orange zest are added to the trout fillets. 2. After 24 hours water has leached from the trout. 3. The trout fillets and shrimp and scallop skewers (see page 145) cold smoking.

SMOKED

LAKE GARDA COLD-SMOKED RAINBOW TROUT

SERVES 12 AS AN APPETIZER

3 tablespoons coarse sea salt

3 tablespoons golden granulated sugar

Few fennel fronds and thyme, sage and rosemary sprigs

Zest of 1 orange, pared in julienne

2¼ pounds (1 kg) rainbow trout fillets

The Trentino region of northern Italy is home to the northern reaches of Lake Garda and has many rich waterways producing significant numbers of trout, which have been farmed for centuries along with tench and Arctic char. The quality of the lake water, fed by mountain streams, makes for exceptional fish farming and the resultant harvest. Michelin-starred chef Rinaldo Dalsasso maintains the quality of the salmon is quasi wild. Try Rinaldo's fennel, herb and orange rub prior to cold smoking trout or salmon rather than using a plain salt and sugar rub.

Combine the salt, sugar and herbs. Sprinkle the base of a noncorrosive container with the salt mixture. Lay the fish on top, skin side down, and sprinkle with the remaining salt mixture, taking care to moderate the amount of salt in proportion to the thickness of the fish. Top with the orange zest, place a light weight on top, and let stand in a cool place for 24 hours.

Rinse off the salt mixture, pat dry, put on an oiled rack, and cold smoke lightly and slowly (see page 152). If you do not have a smoker suited to cold smoking, you can give the fish a quick hot smoke (see page 138).

I cold smoked my fish, weighing 6 ounces (180 g) each, in my purpose-designed smoke box at 80 F (25 C) for 2½ hours (it was a cold, still evening), by which time they had lost the desired 10 percent weight, but more importantly they looked just right. If the smoker had been full, it may have taken twice the time to smoke. It may take you longer or less time; the quantity of fish you are smoking and the size and thickness of the fillets are all influencing factors, as is the weather outside.

SERVES 4

7 ounces (200 g) cold-smoked rainbow trout or salmon, cut into ¼-inch (5-mm) thick slices

2 cups (120 g) salad leaves

Handful of arugula leaves

Handful of small strawberries and/or raspberries

3 tablespoons extra virgin olive oil

Few drops of good-quality balsamic vinegar

Sea salt and freshly ground black pepper as desired

This is how Trentino chef Rinaldo Dalsasso serves his own home-cured smoked trout. If you don't want to smoke your own, buy a side of cold-smoked trout or salmon and slice it yourself (see pages 284 to 285 for recommended producers).

Divide the smoked trout or salmon between four serving plates.

Combine the salad leaves and berries in a salad bowl. Add the olive oil and balsamic vinegar, season with salt and black pepper, and toss lightly. Arrange alongside the smoked trout or salmon and serve at once.

SWEDISH COLD-SMOKED LOIN OF VENISON

SERVES 8 AS AN APPETIZER

1 ¼ pounds (600 g) top loin of venison

4 tablespoons sea salt

3 tablespoons black peppercorns

3 tablespoons pink peppercorns

2 garlic cloves, chopped

Few tarragon and thyme sprigs

2 tablespoons dark rum

This recipe can be adapted to smoke lamb, fillet of beef and any game meat. Hand-sliced the venison is delicious; machine-sliced paper thin it is sublime.

Trim the skin, fat and membrane from the loin. Put the salt and spices in a mortar and crush with a pestle, then pound with the garlic, herbs and rum to make a paste.

Rub the paste into the meat. Put in a plastic bag and refrigerate for 3 days, turning the meat from time to time.

After this time, remove the excess spices and cold smoke at 80 F (25 C) for 12 hours (see page 152). Slice thinly and serve with a slice of pomegranate or pickled fruit.

MY FAVORITE SMOKED DISHES

I love breakfast, it really is my favorite meal of the day, and smoked fish such as salmon, haddock and kippers provide a wealth of variety. I know the smell of cooking fish in the morning is not for everyone... My father was a fan, too, and I used to hate it.

So if you are not a breakfast enthusiast, they also make wonderful lunches and suppers especially when made into things like kedgeree, cullen skink, pastes and patés. Serve the following recipes with good bread, butter and something cooling like eggs and salads to complete your meal whenever you choose to serve it.

KEDGEREE

SERVES 4

1 tablespoon butter

1 onion, finely chopped

Good pinch of saffron strands

Good pinch each of crushed cardamom seeds, cumin seeds and coriander seeds

½ teaspoon sea salt

11 ounces (300 g) basmati rice

14 ounces (400 g) smoked haddock fillets

Bunch of parsley, chopped

4 hard-cook eggs, quartered

Kedgeree is most commonly known as originating in British colonial India. Scottish food writer Christopher Trotter in his book The Scottish Kitchen, *however, traced its origins in Scotland to 1790. Scottish soldiers then took it with them to India.*

Put a saucepan on high heat for 1 minute. Reduce the heat, add the butter, and when melted add the chopped onion. When it starts to soften, add the spices and salt and stir well. Now add the rice and stir for a few minutes.

Add 3 cups (700ml) water, bring to a simmer, and cook for another 15 minutes. Put the haddock on top of the rice, cover the pan with a lid, and cook for another 5 minutes.

Put the fish in a dish and flake with a fork, discarding the skin and any bones. Drain off any water from the rice and discard. Add the rice, half the chopped parsley, and the hard-cook eggs to the haddock and stir well. Garnish with the remaining parsley.

SMOKED

CULLEN SKINK

SMOKED HADDOCK CHOWDER WITH PARSLEY AND CHIVES

SERVES 6

3½ cups (800 ml) whole milk, plus extra if needed

1 small onion or shallot, studded with 6 cloves

Generous pinch of saffron strands

1 pound (500 g) natural smoked haddock fillets, or any other lightly smoked white fish

2 tablespoons butter or olive oil

1 large onion, finely chopped

¾ cup (250 g) potatoes, peeled and cut into small cubes

Freshly ground black pepper as desired

Chopped parsley and snipped chives, to serve (optional)

Cullen Skink is a well-known traditional recipe from Scotland that was introduced to me by Tones, an entusiastic cook in our family living in Nairn. The soup is rich and creamy, the haddock flesh smooth and smoky. Neil Robson (see below) explains: "Haddock is open-flaked and so takes in more smoke than other fish and because of this needs careful watching." He smokes haddock as well as kippers and salmon in his Northumberland smokehouse. The haddock is gloriously sweet and smoky even if it isn't Scottish. It is made from fresh, locally caught haddock, soaked in a light brine for 10 to 12 minutes, and smoked flat for six hours.

Put the milk in a large saucepan with the clove-studded onion and the saffron strands. Bring the milk to simmering point, switch off the heat, and let stand for 1 hour or as time allows for the flavors to infuse. After this time, bring the milk to simmering point again, add the haddock, and gently poach for 3 minutes. Using a slotted spoon, transfer the fish to a plate and carefully flake with a fork, discarding the skin and any bones. Cover and reserve. Strain the milk and reserve.

Melt the butter or heat the oil in a saucepan over low heat, add the chopped onion, and cook until soft. Add the cubed potato and cook for 2 minutes. Add the strained milk and simmer gently until the potato is tender, say 20 minutes. Reserve half the potato cubes for later use and then transfer the remaining vegetables and milk to a blender and blend until creamy. Add black pepper to taste.

When ready to serve, gently reheat the soup, taking care not to let it boil. If the soup is very thick it may be necessary to dilute it with extra milk. Divide the reserved haddock and potato cubes between six warmed dishes and pour the soup on top. Sprinkle with chopped parsley and snipped chives, if liked, and serve at once.

THE SAVVY SMOKER

On arrival in Robson's yard I was greeted not by the smell of herring, as I had anticipated, but by the sweet smell of the wood smoke swirling and drifting skyward from the smokehouse shutters. Inside the smokehouses the stone walls, brick floors and timbers are as black as night, thick with 150 years of tar. Shafts of light from above pierce the dark, catching a glimpse of gleaming kippers.

Herring are cut open from back to belly to make kippers, giving them their distinctive oval shape. They are washed and brined for 20 minutes and pinned open on rods of tenterhooks and left to drip.

Nine piles of wood shavings and sawdust are laid out on the floor, lit, and the doors closed. Not too much heat, 70 F (20 C), otherwise the kippers would cook and fall off the hooks. The fire is kept slow

for three and a half to four hours. Once the fish stiffen up, the heat is raised to 85 F (30 C). Adjustments have to be made according to temperature, wind strength and direction, and humidity. There are no controls; smoking at Robson's is controlled by know-how; more or less sawdust and the opening and closing of shutters. There are two more firings and after 14 to 16 hours of smoke they are ready.

EGGS BERNADETTE

SERVES 1

1 small thick piece of smoked haddock fillet, weighing 3½ ounces (100 g), or any other lightly smoked white fish

2 tablespoons malt vinegar

1 very fresh egg

1 tablespoon mayonnaise

1 firm tomato, seeded and diced into concassé (tomato jewels)

This is my personal take on Eggs Benedict, which I often eat for breakfast. A perfect start to a perfect day!

Bring 2½ inches (6 cm) of water to a boil in a saucepan, then reduce the heat to a simmer. Add the smoked haddock and poach gently for 4 minutes. Drain.

At the same time, bring 2½ inches (6 cm) of water to a boil in a separate saucepan. When it comes to a boil, add the malt vinegar, crack an egg into a cup, and gently tip it into the center of the boiling water. Reduce the heat and simmer for 2 minutes or until the white has set. Using a slotted spoon, transfer the poached egg to a sheet of folded paper towel to drain.

Transfer the smoked haddock to the center of a warmed plate, top with the mayonnaise, and perch the poached egg on top. Scatter the tomato jewels over the top and around the egg. Serve with soft wholemeal bread and butter.

KIPPER PASTE

SERVES 4 TO 6

2 kippers or a pack of
4 kipper fillets

1 bay leaf

Juice of ½ lemon

6 tablespoons butter,
softened

3 hard-cooked egg yolks

Freshly ground black pepper
as desired

In Scotland in days gone by a salmon that had spawned and was therefore in poor condition for eating was called a kipper. These spent salmon were split and smoked, or "kippered," and this is where the expression "feeling kippered," meaning "worn out," comes from. Later in 1843 an innovative fish merchant called John Woodger, just over the Scottish border in Northumberland, England, started smoking herring and called them kippers. Woodger packed his kippers in boxes and sent them by rail. They soon caught on and before long they became a mainstay of the British breakfast table.

Lower the kipper gently into a saucepan of simmering water. Add the bay leaf and bring to simmering point. Switch off the heat and let stand for 5 minutes. Drain off the water and put the kipper on paper towels to drain. Transfer to a plate and remove the fish from the bones, taking great care as the bones are very fine.

For a smooth paste, put the kipper in a blender, add the lemon juice, butter, egg yolks and black pepper, and blend until smooth. For a coarser texture, mash the ingredients together with a fork. Spoon into a dish and serve with brown toast.

❧ **VARIATION** For smoked mackerel paste, use mayonnaise instead of softened butter and add 1 tablespoon creamed horseradish.

HOW BEST TO COOK A KIPPER

The picturesque fishing village of Craster is world famous for kippers. Neil and his father Alan Robson are third and fourth generation kipper makers and there is nothing they don't know about kippering. Their advice: preheat the broiler and line a pan with foil. Turn the kipper cut side up, add a knob of butter, and set under the hot broiler. When the fish bones curl up your kipper is ready. Serve with a wedge of lemon and enjoy the rich, dark, intensely smoky flavor, and close your eyes and listen to the sea pounding on the rocks along the coastline.

SMOKED EEL WITH GARLIC BEURRE BLANC

SMOKED

SERVES 4

2 cups (160 g) mixed leaves, ideally lettuce, rocket and a little curly endive

7 ounces (200 g) smoked eel

4½ ounces (125 g) pancetta

4 tablespoons butter

BEURRE BLANC

1 shallot

4 garlic cloves

Pinch of sea salt

Pinch of freshly ground white pepper

½ glass dry white wine

1 tablespoon heavy cream

⅔ cup (150 g) unsalted butter, cut into small cubes

VINAIGRETTE

½ teaspoon sea salt

½ teaspoon cracked black pepper

½ teaspoon Dijon mustard

2 teaspoons white wine vinegar

2 tablespoons olive oil

Smoked eel is among the world's greatest delicacies and hugely underrated in many countries. Whether served on blinis with caviar and horseradish, in a potato salad, on warm crostini with radicchio, pancetta and sour cream, or in this delicious recipe by Rowley Leigh (see page 52), it should not be missed.

Wash and dry the salad leaves. Cut the smoked eel into 8-inch (20-cm) long slices, lay out on a tray, and keep chilled. Dice the pancetta into very small pieces. Put it in a small saucepan, cover with cold water, and bring to a boil, then drain and refresh in cold water.

Fry the blanched pancetta in the butter, turning regularly until perfectly crisp on all sides, then drain well and reserve.

Make the vinaigrette by mixing the salt, pepper, mustard, and white wine vinegar very well together before whisking in the olive oil.

For the beurre blanc, chop the shallot and garlic quite finely and put in a small saucepan together with the salt, white pepper and white wine. Stew on a very gentle heat for 10 minutes, reducing the liquid to a syrupy tablespoonful. Add the cream and bring quickly to a boil before adding the cubed butter, whisking very well as you do so. The butter will combine with the reduction into a smooth, pale sauce. Strain the result through a fine sieve into a warm (not hot) bowl.

To assemble the salad, dress the leaves lightly with the vinaigrette and arrange in the middle of the serving plates. Drape three slices of eel per person over the salad and sprinkle with the pancetta. Place the salads under a hot broiler for 30 seconds or until the leaves are just starting to wilt. Remove immediately from the broiler, anoint the salads with 1 to 2 tablespoons of the beurre blanc, and serve immediately.

SMOKED EEL: THE ETHICAL OPTION

There is a long tradition of fishing for elver, or glass eel, on the River Severn. Transparent baby eels arrive in the Severn between February and May from the Sargasso Sea on a journey that takes two years or more. After a year they become grown eels and remain in the river waters for around 12 years until ready to make the long journey back to the Sargasso Sea to spawn.

Richard Cook's Severn and Wye Smokery is a stone's throw from the banks of the River Severn. He smokes salmon and other specialties but his flagship product is smoked eel. Richard's eels, however, do not grow up in the Severn but make yet another journey.

He collects the elvers from the river and ships them to Lock Neagh in Northern Ireland, the world's largest fish farm, where they are left to grow and then sent back to the Severn to be smoked. He explained, "There has been a huge drop in eel numbers in all U.K. waters since defenses have been built up to protect the land from flooding and the elvers can't reach their natural habitats to grow into eels." There is a strong lobby against this trade, but Richard is emphatic that there is no exploitation of the eel and works very closely with Peter Wood who is the eel welfare vet.

The farmed mature silver eel has superb fat and is perfect for hot smoking. It is gutted, brined, and hung to air-dry quickly to take the moisture out. It is then put in the smoking kiln. Richard says that it is essential to try to shrink the skin immediately. The belly is opened during smoking.

Everything is smoked with locally and ethically sourced oak. The wood is chipped and wet for cold smoking, larger for hot smoking. They have gone back to a traditional, powerful smoked product. When I asked him what makes a good smoked product, his answer was simple: "The quality must be good, the raw material is king."

CANAPÉS WITH COLD-SMOKED FISH AND MEAT

Everybody loves canapés; just a taste of something delicious with a drink before dinner. They don't have to be complicated or take a long time to make but they do need to have impact. Smoked trout, salmon, mackerel and kipper make great canapés, as do smoked meats and smoked seafood. The beauty of smoking your own is that you are quite likely to have bits in the refrigerator that need using. It's even worth smoking your own just to make canapés. Make sure you slice meats paper thin.

Canapés should be freshly made because the bases will go soft if not eaten straight away.

SMOKED SALMON AND VENISON CANAPÉS

MAKES 24

½ cup (100 g) cream cheese

1 tablespoon creamed horseradish

Coarsely ground black pepper as desired

1 lemon, halved

1 pack of ready-made blinis or 24 toasts or brioche rings (see below)

3½ ounces (100 g) cold-smoked meat and fish, thinly sliced and cut into canapé-size squares

Wrap the cream cheese in salmon and venison strips to stop the canapés going soft.

Mix the cream cheese with the horseradish, a good pinch of black pepper, and a few drops of lemon juice. Spread each blini with a small dollop of cream cheese, top with a rag of smoked meat, or fish and add a squeeze of lemon and a pinch of black pepper.

❧ VARIATIONS

❧ To make the cherry tomato and black pudding canapés in the photo, cut the top off 24 cherry tomatoes and remove the seeds. Turn the tomatoes upside down and drain on paper towels. Cut 12 tomato lids in half and put these to drain with the tomatoes and discard the others. When ready to serve, use 3½ ounces (100 g) black pudding to fill the tomato shells, balance half a lid on top, and decorate with a small parsley leaf. Makes 24.

❧ To make the smoked trout and strawberry rolls in the photo, cut six large strawberries into quarters. Pepper the strawberries. Use 2½ ounces (75 g) smoked trout cut into thin strips to wrap around the strawberries and drizzle with a few drops of lemon juice. Makes 24.

SMOKED SHRIMP AND SCALLOP CANAPÉS

MAKES 24

24 homemade canapé bases (see below)

3½ ounces (100 g) black pudding (see page 96)

12 smoked shrimp (see page 145)

12 smoked queen scallops (see page 145)

1 lemon, halved

Freshly ground black pepper or crushed red pepper flakes as desired

Put canapés in the oven for five minutes if you've made them in advance to crisp up the bases. Alternate between black pudding and cream cheese to ring the changes.

Spread the canapé bases with a generous dollop of black pudding and top with a smoked shrimp or queen scallop set at a cheeky angle. Arrange on an ovenproof serving plate and put in a preheated oven at 400 F (200 C) for 5 minutes to warm through. When ready to serve add a few drops of lemon juice and a grinding of black pepper or crushed red pepper flakes.

❧ HOMEMADE CANAPÉ BASES

Canapé bases can be bought ready-made from the supermarket—either toasted squares of bread, blinis, mini oatcakes, or tiny pastries. However, you can make your own quite easily:

❧ Simply cut sliced bread into 1-inch (2.5-cm) squares.

❧ Paint lightly with sunflower oil.

❧ Bake in a preheated oven at 400 F (200 C) until golden. Let cool.

❧ Alternatively, cut brioche rolls into ½-inch (1-cm) thick rounds and proceed as above.

❧ Store in a tin until required.

Potted rillons of pork (see page 185) and confit of rabbit (see page 193)

5 POTTED

NATURAL PRESERVATION

The action of cooking food extends its life, and protecting it from the air around it prolongs its life even further. Before the invention of the modern vacuum pack, animal fats, pastry crusts and stoneware pots were used to perform the same function—that is, to stop bacteria in the air reaching the foods contained within and contaminating them.

Today, most of us believe that if something is preserved commercially we can depend on it, and have lost sight of the fact that many natural substances that kill or guard against bacteria have been used for centuries to preserve food. We trust a vacuum pack because it has a use-by date stamped on it, yet we would find it difficult to put such faith in a layer of pastry, lard or butter, which in fact does exactly the same thing.

We may feel secure in the knowledge that a product has a use-by date, but should the packaging be damaged and the food contaminated by air before these dates have expired, we would soon recognize by its smell and appearance that it should be discarded. Our noses tell us when food goes off, and it is our noses that we must learn to trust when preserving food at home.

A POTTED HISTORY

Preserving food by sealing it in some kind of animal fat in an airtight environment dates back to prehistory. It is known that in Greenland in former times, all kinds of primary produce were preserved in seal blubber in a skin bag, probably made from the seal's stomach, to store it through the winter, and great care was taken to make the bag thoroughly airtight.

Native Americans made a meat preserve known as "pemmican," derived from the Cree term *pimikan*, which literally means "manufactured grease." Air-dried meat was pounded with berries to improve the flavor and the marrow from the animal bones melted down, poured over the meat, and left to cool to a stiff paste. This was then packed into rawhide sacs and another layer of fat spread on top to create a barrier to keep out the bacteria and lengthen the storage time. This nutritious concoction also fueled fur traders and explorers on their long winter journeys.

Before the advent of refrigeration, cooked meats and fish were packed into pots and sealed under a layer of melted clarified butter, lard, duck or goose fat to prolong their shelf life, or encased in a pastry crust. It is interesting to note that many recipes written in the 17th and 18th centuries give the choice of using either a pie crust or a pot for this purpose. The pastry crust was invented during the Middle Ages in England, not to be eaten but solely as a protective airtight casing for food. The Cornish pasty, for example, was originally made with rock-hard pastry to protect and transport the miner's meal underground; the crust was not intended for consumption. By the 17th century, the pie crust was being replaced by fat and stoneware pots. As the quality of stoneware improved, the pots became stronger and more fit for purpose, and unlike the pastry case they could be reused. Game birds well rubbed with allspice, mace, pepper and salt were cooked breast down in butter in a lidded casserole until the meat was quite tender. They were then left to cool, closely packed in stoneware jars and covered with clarified butter. Until recently in Sardinia where blackbirds were fair game, they were cooked and packed into jars and preserved under a layer of pork fat flavored with myrtle to preserve them.

In the Veneto region of Italy, in the provinces of Treviso, Padua and Vicenza, they make something called *oca in onto*, or potted goose, an *onto* being a terracotta pot. As traditional dishes go in the area—and there are many—it is held somewhat in awe. In days gone by, the goose was the *maiale dei poveri*, or poor man's pig, and smallholders made salamis, hams and all the delicacies normally associated with pork from goose instead. Potted goose was prepared and secreted away during the winter to be brought out in the spring to celebrate high days and holidays such as Easter and the great Venetian feast of St. Mark.

❧ THE PRINCIPLES OF POTTING

- ❧ Cook fish, meat, and poultry well.
- ❧ Pound to a smooth paste, break up with a fork, or, in the case of shrimp, leave whole.
- ❧ Put into ovenproof pots with clarified butter.
- ❧ Set in the oven in a water bath—a shallow ovenproof dish filled with boiling water to come halfway up the sides of the pots— to cook.
- ❧ Let cool.
- ❧ Seal with a layer of clarified butter and refrigerate until needed.
- ❧ Bring back to ambient temperature before serving.

Oca in onto is also known as *oca in pignatto* or *confit alla veneta*, but unlike the French confit, the goose portions were generally simply salted for a few days, washed, dried, and sometimes even smoked in the chimney before being layered with melted goose fat and bay leaves. The pots would be topped up with a final layer of goose fat and then sealed and left for one or two years. In some cases, the goose was lightly roasted first with oil and rosemary in a pan with a lid. After a few hours' gentle cooking, the goose pieces would be immersed in fat. The goose joints were then potted whole or sometimes the meat was scraped off the bone first. It is interesting to note that Napoleon invaded Venice and the Adriatic coast, and this tradition of potting goose may well have been introduced by the occupying French.

POTTING RESURGENCE

Like most of the other curer's crafts, potting became very unfashionable during the second half of the 20th century as we embraced the convenience of modern food technology. However, mass-produced potted meats and fish remained popular. In England Shippam's and other branded tiny glass pots have been beloved by decades of children in their teatime sandwiches.

Potting is a culinary gem that has stayed out of favor for far too long, but is now being restored to its rightful place, alongside the French evergreens of pâtés, terrines and parfaits. Potting will lengthen the refrigerator life of all kinds of fresh meat, poultry, fish and game. It can also increase the shelf life of small amounts of leftover ingredients, transforming them into mouth-watering delicacies with the addition of spices, fresh herbs, cream and butter. Hot buttered toasts spread thick with potted meats and fish will rival their Mediterranean cousins, the much-vaunted crostini and canapés, and provide a new dimension to your cocktail, lunch and supper parties.

The prince of potted foods is perhaps the delicate and diminutive brown-fleshed potted shrimp (see page 175). But lobster tails and crabmeat come a close second, encapsulated in a smooth, cold, buttery casing; be sure to use only the very best butters.

POTTED PREFERENCES

All the recipes in this section can be interchanged to pot any kind of fresh or leftover fish, seafood, meat, poultry or game. You can vary the spices and herbs to make your own versions. Simply add your chosen flavorings to the cooked meat or fish of your choice, then pound or process in a blender to a smooth paste with some melted butter or cream. Fill ramekins and transfer to a water bath—a shallow dish of boiling water—to heat through in the oven. Top up with clarified butter (see page 172), refrigerate, and serve when required with hot wholemeal toast, wafer-thin, crisp melba toast (see page 178), or crispbreads—the perfect accompaniment to potted meats and fish.

POTTED

❧ **CLARIFIED BUTTER**

❧ Put the required amount of butter in a small saucepan and set over a low heat to melt.

❧ When the butter has melted, take the pan off the heat and leave it to stand for a few minutes. The butter will separate.

❧ When clarifying organic butter, as in the photograph, a creamy scum may form on the surface; this should be skimmed and discarded.

❧ Carefully pour off the clarified butter that has risen to the top of the pan. Discard the cloudy substance in the bottom of the pan.

POTTED SHRIMP. 1. Ingredients. 2. Pouring over clarified butter.
3. Topping up with the clarified butter. 4. Ready for the refrigerator.

SERVES 4

1 cup (225 g) unsalted butter

Pinch each of ground white pepper, cayenne, ground mace and ground nutmeg

1 cup (300 g) cooked peeled brown shrimp

EQUIPMENT

4 buttered ramekins

Potted shrimp is the king of potted dishes: simple to make, delicious to eat. Make sure you buy those tiny, meaty brown shrimp... no other will do!

Preheat the oven to 325 F (160 C).

Put the butter in a small saucepan and set over low heat to melt. When the butter has melted, take the pan off the heat and let stand for a few minutes. Carefully pour off the clarified butter that has risen to the top of the pan and discard the cloudy substance left in the bottom of the pan.

Reserve a quarter of the clarified butter for later use. Return the remainder to the pan. Add the spices and shrimp, stir well, and cook over low heat for 2 minutes. Let cool. Pack the cooled shrimp into ramekin dishes and top with the clarified butter.

Transfer to a shallow ovenproof dish, add boiling water so that it comes halfway up the ramekins, and cook in the preheated oven for 15 minutes. Let cool.

Top up each ramekin with a thin layer of the remaining clarified butter, making sure that the shrimp are completely submerged. Put in the refrigerator to set.

Take the potted shrimp out of the refrigerator 20 minutes before serving to bring back to room temperature. When ready to serve, run a palette knife around the sides of the ramekins and turn the potted shrimp out onto serving plates. Serve with Melba Toast (see page 178).

above **Flaking the cooked salmon and capers**
opposite **Potted salmon and pumpernickel canapés**

POTTED SALMON

SERVES 4

14 ounces (400 g) skin-on salmon fillet

1 tablespoon salted capers, rinsed repeatedly in cold water and squeezed dry

2 teaspoons fresh fennel seeds or 2 tablespoons fennel fronds, finely chopped, plus extra fronds to serve

Good pinch of ground white pepper

1⅓ cups (300 g) clarified unsalted butter (see page 172), cooled

½ cucumber, cut in half lengthwise and diagonally sliced, lightly salted, and drizzled with rice vinegar

Sea salt, as desired

Olive oil, for frying

EQUIPMENT

4 buttered ramekins

Serve as a starter or as a light lunch with salad and hot wholemeal toast or home-made melba toast (see below). Alternatively, serve as canapés on pumpernickel bread (see page 177).

Preheat the oven to 300 F (150 C).

Set a large nonstick skillet over high heat, and when hot, cover the base with a film of olive oil. Add the salmon quickly to the hot skillet, skin side down, and reduce the heat to medium. Cook for a couple of minutes, then turn and cook it for a minute or two on the other side. Add the capers, cover the pan, and cook until the salmon has just cooked through. This should take only a couple of minutes, but will depend on the thickness of the fillet. Introduce the tip of a knife into the thickest part of the salmon to check for doneness.

Transfer the salmon to a plate and pull away and discard the skin. Add a tablespoon of water to the skillet and scrape up the juices and capers, then add them to the salmon. Add the fennel, white pepper, and a little salt. Flake the fish or mash to a rough paste with a fork, checking for bones as you do so.

Spoon the salmon paste into the buttered ramekins, press down flat, and cover with two-thirds of the clarified butter. Transfer to a shallow ovenproof dish, add boiling water so that it comes halfway up the sides of the ramekins, and cook in the preheated oven for 10 minutes. Let cool.

Pour the remaining clarified butter over the salmon until it is completely submerged. Put in the refrigerator to set.

Take the potted salmon out of the refrigerator 20 minutes before serving to bring back to ambient temperature. Serve either straight from the pots or turn out onto a plate so that the butter layer is underneath. Top each with a fennel frond and serve with a few slices of the cucumber.

❧ **TO MAKE PERFECT MELBA TOAST**

❧ Cut the crusts off 12 slices of medium-sliced white bread and put under a hot broiler to brown on both sides.

❧ Remove the toast and carefully cut horizontally through each slice, giving 24 paper-thin slices.

❧ Reduce the broiler to medium and return the toast to the broiler, untoasted side up. It will curl up in the heat. Let cool.

POTTED CRABMEAT

SERVES 6

1⅓ cups (300 g) unsalted butter

Few thyme sprigs, plus extra to serve

Pinch of crushed red pepper flakes

1 cup (400 g) brown crabmeat

Juice of 1 lemon

6 fresh thyme sprigs, to garnish

Sea salt and freshly ground black pepper, as desired

EQUIPMENT

6 buttered ramekins or a single 8-ounce (250-ml) ovenproof pot with a lid

This is a brilliant way to use those pots of crabmeat that are 90 percent brown and 10 percent white meat; simply scrape off the white meat and set aside for a garnish.

Preheat the oven to 325 F (160 C). Put the butter in a small saucepan, add the thyme sprigs and chili flakes, and set over low heat to melt. When melted, take the pan off the heat and let stand for a few minutes. Carefully strain off the clarified butter that has risen to the top of the pan and discard the cloudy substance that has settled at the bottom with the thyme and chili. If any bits of thyme or chili escape into the clarified butter, strain it through a sieve. Let cool.

Put the brown crabmeat in a blender, add half the clarified butter, the lemon juice, and salt and pepper and blend until smooth. Taste and add extra seasoning if necessary. Divide the mixture between the ramekins or put in a single pot.

Transfer to a suitable ovenproof dish, add boiling water so that it comes halfway up the dishes or dish, and cook for 25 minutes in the preheated oven. Let cool.

Pour a film of clarified butter over the top to seal the crabmeat and top with a sprig of thyme. Put in the refrigerator to set.

Take the potted crabmeat out of the refrigerator 20 minutes before serving to bring back to room temperature. Run a palette knife around the edge of the ramekins and turn out, butter side down, or if using a single pot, simply spoon out onto fresh, crusty bread.

POTTED

POTTED DICED SHOULDER OF VENISON

MAKES 16 OUNCES (500 ML)

1 pound (500 g) shoulder of venison or wild boar, diced

1 blade of mace

1 heaping teaspoon juniper berries, crushed

½ cinnamon stick

½ teaspoon freshly ground black pepper

1 teaspoon sugar

¾ cup (200 ml) red wine

1 heaping teaspoon Forager's Jelly (see page 228) or redcurrant jelly

1¼ cups (100 g) fresh Portobello mushrooms, sliced

1 teaspoon sea salt

TO FINISH

⅔ cup (150 g) rendered pork fat (see page 193) or goose fat

1 tablespoon Forager's Jelly (see page 228) or redcurrant jelly

EQUIPMENT

Preserving jars, washed and sterilized (see page 204); size of your choice

Venison and wild boar, like other game meats, are relatively dry on account of their low fat content. Slow cooking these meats in pork fat and then sealing them under pork fat transforms the flesh, giving it a soft, fall-apart, melt-in-the-mouth texture.

To our 21st-century minds, cooking in pork fat can seem a little scary. But slow cooking the meat in part marinade and part fat reduces the cholesterol content of the dish. Potting the meat in its own juices rather than in the fat helps reduce the fat content further, though it does lessen the softening effect on the meat. However, I have found this an excellent way of potting game meat.

Serve the potted venison shredded in tiny pies as a starter (see page 183) or on crostini (see page 184) with Forager's Jelly (see page 228).

Put the venison, spices, and sugar in a shallow earthenware dish. Add the wine and heaping teaspoon of Forager's Jelly, put the sliced mushrooms on top, and sprinkle with the salt. Cover and leave at room temperature for 6 hours.

Drain off the marinade. Transfer the venison to a slow cooker or lidded casserole dish and add the pork fat. Cover the dish and cook overnight, in a low oven, 225 F (110 C) —or at your oven's lowest setting—or slow cooker.

In the morning, drain off the juices and the fat into a bowl and let cool and separate. Transfer the venison to the sterilized preserving jar and close. Pour off the fat, or lift off if it has solidified, from the venison juices and reserve. Transfer the venison juices to a small saucepan and add the level tablespoon of Forager's Jelly. Heat and stir until the jelly has dissolved, then open the jar containing the venison and pour the juices over the meat. Let cool. Top up the jar with a layer of the pork fat and seal. The juices will set to a jelly when cold. Keep in the refrigerator for a few days before using. It will keep for several weeks or longer.

To serve on crostini, spoon the potted venison on the baked crostini, top with a spoonful of Forager's Jelly and serve as finger food.

above Marinade ingredients
opposite left Diced shoulder of venison
opposite right Diced venison and sliced mushrooms in a red wine marinade

POTTED DICED SHOULDER OF VENISON. 1. Slow-cooked venison. 2.. Pouring venison juices over the potted meat. 3. Sealing the potted venison with pork fat. 4. Potted venison crostini with Forager's Jelly (see page 228).

MAKES 6

PASTRY

1⅓ cups (200 g) all-purpose flour, plus extra for rolling

½ tablespoon cornstarch

½ tablespoon powdered sugar, sifted

Pinch of sea salt

½ cup (120 g) butter, softened

2 small free-range egg yolks, plus 1 egg white, lightly beaten, for brushing

1 tablespoon dry vermouth or iced water

FILLING

2 to 3 cups (300 to 500 g) Potted Diced Shoulder of Venison (or wild boar) in it own juices/jelly (see page 180)

2 tablespoons finely chopped parsley

EQUIPMENT

(6) 4-inch (10-cm) tart pans

These little pies are heaven on earth: the pastry crumbles and melts in the mouth and the venison is rich and sticky. Pickled Walnuts (see page 243) or fruit jellies, such as Foragers Jelly (see page 228) make perfect foils. Serve as a starter or light lunch.

Put the flours, powdered sugar and salt in a bowl and add the softened butter, egg yolks, and vermouth or water. Quickly and lightly work the ingredients together into a smooth ball with your hands. Cover in plastic wrap and set in the refrigerator to rest for an hour.

Preheat the oven to 350 F (180 C).

Roll the pastry out thinly on a lightly floured surface and cut out six circles measuring about 5 inches (12 to 13 cm) in diameter to line the tart pans and six circles measuring 3½ inches (8.5 cm) in diameter for the lids.

Line the tart pans with the pastry and brush lightly with the egg white.

Shred the potted venison with two forks and fill the pans with the venison and its jelly. Brush the edges of the pastry lids with cold water, put them on top of the pies, and seal the edges down. Set the pies on a baking sheet and bake in the preheated oven for 20 to 25 minutes until golden.

Serve warm with Pickled Walnuts and/or Forager's Jelly.

POTTED LEFTOVER GAME, MEAT OR POULTRY

POTTED

SERVES 4 TO 6

1 pound (500 g) leftover
game, meat, ham, poultry or
fish

Scant ½ cup (100 ml) stock,
sauce or gravy

½ teaspoon cayenne, ground
allspice or ground mace

⅓ cup (100 g) clarified butter
(see page 172)

Sea salt and freshly ground
black pepper, as desired

EQUIPMENT

4 to 6 buttered ramekins or a
single ovenproof pot

*When using up leftover game and so forth, I find it useful to pot in small ramekins,
which can then be frozen and brought out, thawed and spread on hot toast or
crostini (see below) with Sweet Tomato Jam (see page 237) to serve with drinks.*

Preheat the oven to 325 F (160 C).

Put the meat in a blender with the stock, sauce, or gravy and then reduce to a smooth,
moist paste. Season with the spice and salt and pepper.

Press the mixture into the buttered ramekins or a single pot. Transfer to a shallow
ovenproof dish, add boiling water so that it comes halfway up the sides of the dishes
or dish, and cook in the preheated oven for 20 minutes. Let cool.

Cover with the clarified butter to seal and put in the refrigerator to set.

Take out of the refrigerator 20 minutes before serving to bring back to ambient
temperature. Serve with slices of hot toast or crostini with butter and Sweet
Tomato Jam.

❀ **TO MAKE PERFECT CROSTINI**

❀ Preheat the oven to 400 F (200 C).

❀ Cut a baguette diagonally into ½-inch
(1.5-cm) thick slices, brush with extra
virgin olive oil, and rub with the cut
sides of 2 to 3 garlic cloves cut in half
crosswise (optional).

❀ Arrange them on a baking sheet and
set in the preheated hot oven and cook
until golden on top, about 10 minutes.

❀ Turn the crostini and cook until golden
on the other side, about 5 minutes.

❀ Serve topped with rillettes, rillons,
confits, or potted meat and fish.

❀ Makes 30.

THE FRENCH FARMHOUSE KITCHEN

There is a whole range of exquisite, melt-in-the mouth potted meats that are quintessentially French and very much the preserve of the domestic kitchen. Meat, game and poultry are salted and various flavorings are added. They are cooked slowly and buried under pork, duck or goose fat, thus protecting the meat from airborne bacteria and preserving it, to create mouth-watering delicacies.

These specialties differ from their English counterparts in that they are cooked very slowly in their own fat or a mixture of pork fat and their own fat until the flesh falls off the bone or apart. The fat is then strained off, the meat either pounded, mashed or left whole and submerged under a layer of fat.

In today's climate of healthy eating, the consumption of so much rich fat does not come naturally, but

it's well worth transgressing once in a while. Goose fat is much vaunted, but duck and pork fat is equally delicious. Rillettes, confits and rillons, as these French specialties are known, are sensational, and their tender and flavorful flesh can be used in quiches and pies or served on their own with bread or salads. Confits and rillons can also be served reheated with potatoes fried in the excess fat.

RILLETTES AND RILLONS OF PORK

MAKES 16 OUNCES (500 ML)

1 pound (500 g) side pork meat, rind removed

2 teaspoons coarse sea salt

1 teaspoon fresh rosemary leaves

1 teaspoon fresh thyme leaves

1 teaspoon ground nutmeg

EQUIPMENT

Preserving jars, washed and sterilized (see page 204); size of your choice

Traditionally, rillettes are made with hunks of side pork cooked slowly, carefully shredded with two forks, and then potted in a deep layer of lard that will preserve them well. Alternatively, you could just leave the pork in pieces. Spread rillettes on hot crusty bread and serve with pickled cucumbers (see page 245), or use in a tart (see page 188). Rillons are the solid little cubes of meat before they are shredded and can be served hot or cold with a salad, or hot with potatoes fried in pork fat (see page 193).

Rillettes and rillons can also be made with goose, duck, rabbit, chicken and game. Duck and goose are potted with their own fat. Poultry and game will need the addition of pork or goose fat, and the meat is traditionally processed until smooth.

Cut the side pork into neat pieces about 1 inch x ½ inch (2.5 cm x 1 cm) and put in a slow cooker or casserole dish with a lid, add enough water to cover the base of the casserole dish, about ⅔ cup (150 ml), and the remaining ingredients. Cover the dish and cook overnight in a very low oven, 225 F (110 C)—or at your oven's lowest setting—or in a slow cooker.

Strain the pork pieces. For rillons, pack the pork pieces into the sterilized preserving jar and pour the pork juices over the top to seal, ensuring that the pork is completely submerged. Seal the jar. When cool the pork juices and fat will separate naturally.

Alternatively, to make rillettes, shred the pork carefully with two forks, mix with three-fourths of the pork juices, and then pack into jars. Seal the top with a layer of the remaining pork fat and seal the jar.

❧ **VARIATION** If making rillettes or rillons with rabbit, chicken or game, you will need to add ¾ cup (200 g) of rendered pork fat (see page 193) when cooking the meat.

RILLONS OF PORK. 1. Chopped side pork ready for the oven. 2. Freshly cooked rillons.

✿ THE RILLONS, RILLETTES AND CONFITS CODE

✿ Joint game and poultry or cut the meat into small pieces or chunks.

✿ Salt or marinate overnight or for 6 to 8 hours.

✿ Slow cook at between 225 F (110 C) and 250 F (120 C) for 6 to 8 hours or overnight.

✿ Drain off the fat and juices.

✿ For confits, poultry and game meat are best served on the bone.

✿ For rillettes, reduce rillons to a rough paste or shred using two forks and mix with melted fat or stock.

✿ Taste for seasoning.

✿ Pack into sterilized jars (see page 204).

✿ Cover with a layer of fat or half stock and half fat.

✿ Seal the jar and store it in the refrigerator or cold larder.

CONFITS OF RABBIT. 1. Rendering pork fat. 2. Making stock with the bones. 3. Rabbit joints in their marinade. 4. Adding rendered pork fat. 5. The slow-cooking rabbit. 6. Flaking the rabbit meat. 7. The finished potted rabbit.

7
6

A selection of washed and sterilized glass jars

6 *PICKLED

seasoned with salt, bay and spices and preserved in boiled vinegar. Cod, salmon, mackerel, smelts, red mullet, sardine, tuna and anchovy were all cured in this way. In Spain and Provence, this method of curing was known as *escabeche*, the produce being pickled in vinegar and then preserved under a layer of oil.

The abundance of oysters, mussels and cockles around the coast of Britain gave rise to the tradition of pickling them in vinegar. Cockles and mussels are still popular preserved this way today, though oysters less so (see page 212).

It was not only fish that was preserved this way; soused or pickled meats were also popular eaten with salad. Eighteenth-century English cook Eliza Smith featured the curing of sparrows, squab pigeons and larks in vinegar in her hugely successful *The Complete Housewife: Or Accomplished Gentlewoman's Companion*, also the basis of the first cookery book to be published in what was then the American Colonies in 1742. After cooking in water, white wine, sweet herbs, salt, pepper, cloves and mace until tender, readers were directed to preserve the birds in a strong cold pickle of "rhenish wine and white wine vinegar; put in an onion, a sprig of thyme and savory, some lemon peel, some cloves, mace and whole pepper; season it pretty high with salt… when the bones are dissolved they are fit to eat." The latter provided extra nutrition and protection from arthritis, something sadly lacking from our diets today.

Tongues, brawn, pig's ears and trotters were also cured in vinegar. On the low-lying "island" of Sant'Antioco, joined to Sardinia by an isthmus and a bridge, the climate is so humid that it is impossible to produce air-dried pork products, which is unusual for a Mediterranean country. Consequently, before the introduction of refrigeration, pork had to be pickled in vinegar to preserve it for the winter.

Just as the traditions of pickling spread around the Mediterranean in ancient times and then to northern shores in the Middle Ages with the Crusades, so with the colonization of the New World, and more recently emigration, these self-same traditions were introduced to North America. An invaluable recipe book, *The Williamsburg Art of Cookery*, was first published in 1753 and is a collection of early recipes from Virginia, some of which originated from books printed in England, others from those printed locally and many from little handwritten books that were the pride and joy of old Virginian families. There are recipes for pickling oysters, herring and mackerel and every fruit and vegetable found under the Virginian sun. Pickles, preserves and jellies were apparently such staple table delicacies in colonial Virginia that no inventory of a person of substance was without "preserving-kettles, stone and earthen jars, jelly glasses, pickle dishes and an abundance of utensils for making or serving them." Large supplies of earthenware and stoneware jars for the sole purpose of preserving were brought in from the British Potteries by sea to the Virginian rivers and harbors. The trade was so important to Britain that any colonial manufacturer, who might have diminished it, was carefully monitored.

BONING SMALL OILY FISH FOR PICKLING

It is necessary to bone most oily fish before pickling. Good fishmongers are happy to fillet mackerel and herring but they might be pushed if you asked them to fillet sardines, anchovies or sprats. In actual fact it is not difficult at all once you get the hang of it and it is a very useful skill to have, especially if you are a fisherman.

❧ Some fish will need scaling. Scrape off scales with a fish scaler or sharp knife.

❧ Cut, or cut and snap, the fish head off at an angle—roughly follow the gill line as a guide.

❧ Slide a sharp knife along the length of the tummy and cut the fish open from the base of the head to the tail.

❧ Scrape out all of the innards with the point of a sharp knife.

❧ Open the fish out and lay cut side down, skin side up on a board. Use your fingers to press it down flat.

❧ Run your thumb along the backbone from tail to head, gently but firmly, flattening the fish.

❧ Turn the fish over and you should find that the backbone has loosened itself and will pull away from the flesh easily.

❧ Trim the fish with a sharp knife to remove any ragged edges.

❧ For bigger fish run your fingers along the flesh and pull out any bones you can feel with tweezers.

HOME-PICKLED FISH PLEASURES

Pickled fish specialties that were originally created out of necessity have since become much-loved stars of the antipasto table. For centuries they were made both commercially and at home, but although there is still much artisan production, it is a culinary craft that has all but disappeared from the domestic scene. Yet such dishes can be recreated in the contemporary home, providing wonderful evocative flavors—and a barrel-load of beneficial omega-3 oil.

❧ RECYCLING AND STERILIZING JARS

❧ When making pickles for resale, health and safety laws dictate that they are not stored in recycled jars. However, if making pickles for domestic consumption, be they fruit, vegetable, fish or meat, there is absolutely no reason not to recycle jars—if you can successfully remove the labels. With some jars these can be easily removed by washing in hot, soapy water or in the dishwasher, whereas others need hard scouring or the use of a chemical solvent, depending on the type of glue used.

❧ Wash used jars and lids, then store them in a dust-free environment until required.

❧ When ready to use them, either put them through a dishwasher cycle or wash in warm, soapy water and let drain thoroughly. Transfer to a warm oven to dry and leave until required.

❧ When recycling lids, it is advisable to put a cellophane disc (jam pot cover) over the mouth of the jar before putting on the lid and screwing it down tightly. If using jars with rubber seals, make sure that the seals have not perished.

INLAGD SILL

SERVES 4

⅔ cup (150 ml) white wine vinegar

⅔ cup (150 g) granulated sugar

5 cloves

1 teaspoon crushed whole allspice

1 teaspoon yellow mustard seeds

14 ounces (400 g) herring fillets (if using fresh herring add ½ teaspoon sea salt)

1 small carrot, sliced

½ red onion, sliced

½ small leek, sliced

1 cup (30 g) dill, chopped

1 bay leaf

EQUIPMENT

(2) 8-ounce (250-ml) preserving jars, washed and sterilized (see page 204)

SWEDISH PICKLED HERRING

Anyone who counts a Swede among their friends will have feasted on pickled herring, herring torte, herring salad, herring and potato, herring and beet and many of their other traditional dishes. They will also know that the Swedish fish cure is particularly sweet. Thanks to the small Swedish food section beyond the checkout in Ikea stores, Swedish delicacies can now be found all over the world.

Put the preserving jars to warm in a preheated low oven at 225 F (110 C).

Put the white wine vinegar, sugar and 3 tablespoons (50 ml) of water in a saucepan and heat through gently until the sugar has dissolved. Add the spices and let cool.

Wipe the herring fillets clean and cut into smallish pieces. Put the prepared herring, vegetables and herbs into the sterilized preserving jars. Fill the jars with the cooled vinegar, seal and let stand for 2 to 3 days in the refrigerator.

Serve with boiled potatoes and horseradish or with hard bread.

❧ **NOTE** Your fishmonger will fillet the herring for you but you will still have to pull away small bones with tweezers or even cut a 'v' section out of the center of the fillet to remove a series of bones.

LEMON AND HORSERADISH HERRING

SERVES 4

⅔ cup (150 ml) white wine vinegar

5 cloves

1 teaspoon crushed whole allspice

1 teaspoon yellow mustard seeds

14 ounces (400 g) herring fillets (if using fresh herring add ½ teaspoon sea salt)

½ cup (100 g) fromage frais

½ cup (100 g) crème fraîche

1 tablespoon honey

1 tablespoon creamed horseradish

Juice and finely grated zest of 1 lemon

Freshly ground black pepper, as desired

EQUIPMENT

(2) 8-ounce (250-ml) preserving jars, washed and sterilized (see page 204)

Swedish herring, as already said, can be served in many ways—simply as in the previous recipe or with the addition of fromage frais and crème fraîche, which is left to marinate overnight. If you cannot find fromage frais and/or crème fraîche, use the same quantity of sour cream.

Put the preserving jars to warm in a preheated low oven at 225 F (110 C).

Put the white wine vinegar, 3 tablespoons (50 ml) of water and spices in a saucepan and heat through, then let cool.

Wipe the herring fillets clean and cut into smallish pieces. Put the prepared herring into the sterilized preserving jars. Fill the jars with the cooled vinegar, seal, and let stand for 2 to 3 days in the refrigerator.

Mix the fromage frais, crème fraîche, honey, horseradish, and lemon juice and zest together. Season to taste with pepper.

Drain the herring well and arrange in a shallow dish. Spoon the fromage frais mixture over the top and refrigerate overnight before serving. Serve with Swedish hard bread and butter.

Swedish pickled herring

SWEDISH SAVORY HERRING RINGS

SERVES 8 AS A STARTER

BASE

⅓ cup (75 g) butter

1 cup (200 g) pumpernickel crumbs (made in a blender)

CREAM

7 ounces (200 g) pickled matjes herring or canned smoked herring fillets, drained and skinned

1 red onion

1 cup (200 g) cream cheese

1 cup (200 g) crème fraîche

1 heaping tablespoon creamed horseradish

Finely grated zest of 1 lemon

2 tablespoons finely chopped dill

Sea salt and freshly ground black pepper as desired

TO GARNISH

Purple radish sprouts or finely chopped red onion

EQUIPMENT

8 tian rings (or round cookie cutters)

This fishy Swedish specialty is traditionally served on Midsummer's Eve, the longest day, which is a highpoint of the Swedish year and the cause of much celebration: eating, drinking, singing songs, building fires, and the making and wearing of floral crowns. The herring rings improve with keeping, so make the day before required. If you cannot find fromage frais and/or crème fraîche, use the same quantity of sour cream.

Melt the butter in a heatproof bowl in a microwave for 1 minute on high and stir in the pumpernickel crumbs.

Cut a piece of plastic wrap and stand a tian ring in the center. Put a level tablespoon of the pumpernickel mixture in the tian ring and press down to make an even layer. Roll the plastic wrap around the tian and twist it closed at the top. Transfer to a plate. Repeat seven times, then put in the refrigerator to set.

Chop the herring and the red onion very finely in a blender, but do not reduce to a purée. Put in a bowl with the cream cheese, crème fraîche, horseradish, lemon zest and dill and stir well. Add salt and pepper to taste.

Remove the plastic wrap from the top of the tian rings, then spoon the herring mixture onto the bases and level with a palette knife. Re-cover and leave in the refrigerator overnight.

Put a tian ring on each of the eight serving plates, slide off the rings, and serve garnished with radish sprouts or finely chopped red onion. Alternatively, serve with an arugula and radish sprout salad dressed with a little olive oil, balsamic vinegar, and salt and pepper.

THE SMORGASBORD

Unlike other countries, the Scandinavian nations have clung to their culinary traditions and continue to enjoy a raft of cured delicacies, particularly those made from the oily migratory fish that make their way to their shores and rivers in the summer months.

Herring is the star of all pickles served as part of the traditional smorgasbord (*Smörgås* meaning "open-faced sandwich" and *bord* meaning "table"), which started in the 18th century as a table of appetizers, washed down with aquavit (a Scandinavian flavored spirit); it is still the custom today to drink aquavit with pickled herring. From these humble beginnings it developed into a sumptuous spread that offered anywhere from 50 to 100 dishes.

Not surprisingly, today such an extravaganza is a thing of the past, except at Christmas time when it appears on restaurant menus. All the dishes are laid out on the table at once, but rather than piling them on a single plate buffet style, they offer the equivalent of a five- or six-course meal, beginning with the pickled herring dishes, served with boiled potatoes, crispbreads and cheese. These should be washed down with aquavit and chased with cold beer. Next comes the gravadlax (see page 156), eaten with a mustard and dill sauce, and smoked salmon with lemon. This is then followed by cold cuts of meat, salads and egg dishes. It is then finished with hot puddings and coffee.

FILLETES DE ATÚN EN ESCABECHE

PICKLED TUNA PIECES WITH CARROTS AND FENNEL

MAKES 24 OUNCES (750 ML)

(2) 11 ounce (300 g) tuna
steaks

Olive oil, for frying

¾ cup (70 g) red onion, thinly
sliced

½ cup (70 g) young carrot,
thinly sliced

¾ cup (70 g) fennel, thinly
sliced

2 bay leaves

6 large garlic cloves, crushed

1 red chili, deseeded and
chopped

1⅔ cups (400 ml) sherry
vinegar

Sea salt and freshly ground
black pepper as desired

EQUIPMENT

Preserving jars, washed and
sterilized (see page 204);
size of your choice

This is a simple pickled fish recipe from Spain. The beauty of using tuna is that the fish steaks can be pickled as cut by the fishmonger, whereas mackerel and herring need to be carefully filleted and boned first. Experiment with different vinegars, vegetables and spices. This pickle will keep indefinitely in the refrigerator; leave for five days before eating and keep for a maximum of three months to taste it at its best. Mackerel, herring, swordfish and salt cod can be prepared in the same way.

Put the preserving jar to warm in a preheated low oven at 225 F (110 C).

Heat a grill pan until searing hot and grill the fish lightly on both sides; just long enough for it to become stripy on the outside. Add salt and freshly ground black pepper and let cool.

Heat the oil in a medium-sized skillet. Add the onion and fry until it starts to soften, add the carrot and fennel, salt to taste, bay leaves, garlic and chili. Add the sherry or red wine vinegar and ⅔ cup (150 ml) of water and cook until the vegetables are tender. Let cool.

Put the fish in the sterilized jar and layer with the vegetables. Top up the jar with the pickling liquid and seal. Let marinate for 5 days. It will keep for 3 months.

❀ **VARIATION** For a milder, less vinegary preserve, after 24 hours strain off the vinegar, top up the jar with olive oil and reseal.

BOQUERONES

FRESH MARINATED ANCHOVIES

SERVES 4

14 ounces (400 g) freshly caught anchovies, small sardines or sprats

Juice of 4 lemons

2 garlic cloves, finely chopped

Scant 1 cup (100 ml) extra virgin olive oil

Handful of flat-leaf parsley, finely chopped

Few chili flakes

Sea salt crystals as desired

Walk around any fish market in the Mediterranean in summer and you will see heaps of freshly caught silvery, glistening anchovies.

Salted herring and anchovy were also mainstays in North America. "A Sallad of Anchovies" appears in The Williamsburg Art of Cookery *first published in 1742. The anchovies were washed in water or wine till the liquid became clear, then dried with a linen cloth. The tails and fins were taken off, the flesh flipped from the bones and laid on a plate, garnished with young onions, parsley, slices of lemon and beet, dressed with sweet oil and lemon juice.*

Small sardines and sprats can also be prepared in the following way.

Decapitate, clean and bone the fish (see page 203).

Rinse and pat dry, then lay out in a single layer, skin side down, in a noncorrosive dish. Squeeze half the lemon juice over, adding half of the finely chopped garlic. Cover and let marinate in the refrigerator overnight.

Pour off the marinade and add the remaining lemon juice. Cover and let marinate in the refrigerator for 2 hours.

Drain the fish again, then arrange on a serving dish and add the extra virgin olive oil, flat-leaf parsley, the remaining chopped garlic, chili flakes and a little salt rubbed through the fingers. Cover and let stand at room temperature for at least an hour or until required. Serve as part of a Spanish tapas with warm crusty bread.

PICKLED OYSTERS

MAKES 12

12 oysters, scrubbed and cleaned

White wine vinegar

White wine

1 small blade of mace

Zest of 1 lemon

1 teaspoon black peppercorns

EQUIPMENT

5-ounce (150-ml) preserving jar, washed and sterilized (see page 204)

Nothing compares to a raw oyster but if you are a pickle devotee, or you have access to a cheap and plentiful supply, this recipe is something you may find appealing. Start by experimenting with a dozen oysters and see how you like them. Serve with a few slender slices of cucumber and a few drops of tobasco sauce.

Put the preserving jar to warm in a preheated low oven at 225 F (110 C).

Remove the oysters from their shells, reserving the juices. Put the oysters and their juices in a pan and simmer for 10 minutes.

Transfer to the sterilized jar one by one, checking that there is no grit.

Measure the oyster liquid and to every 3 tablespoons liquid from the oysters, add scant ½ cup (100 ml) white wine vinegar and 3 tablespoons white wine, and boil up with the blade of mace, the lemon zest, and the teaspoon of black peppercorns. Remove from the heat and let cool.

Pour the pickle over the oysters to cover. Seal the jar, refrigerate and keep for 5 days before opening.

❧ **VARIATION** For a sweeter pickle you may like to add 1 tablespoon sugar to every scant ½ cup (100 ml) oyster liquid.

Fresh marinated anchovies

A WALK ON THE WILD SIDE

Antipasto mare

The beach at Vieste in Puglia, southeast Italy, is long and flat, and the perfect place for a morning walk any time of the year, but most of all on a sunny morning out of season when the continuous rows of recliners have been put away for the winter and the beach is left to revert to nature's way. In the months before and after high season, the calm of the Adriatic is churned up into a frenzy of waves as if to wash away any last vestige of the ending tourist season.

The reason for my visit to this area was the famed Puglian antipasto. Every restaurant in the region worth its salt offers amazing spreads of delicious things to eat to kick off a meal before embarking on the pasta, fish and meat courses. Huge platters with mozzarellas still warm from the buffalo; magnificent Caciocavallo cheeses made with milk from Podolica cows; *torte rustiche* (farmhouse pies) and calzoni filled with cheeses and vegetables; hams, salamis and other cured specialties; char-grilled, lightly floured, deep-fried and preserved vegetables and fish; octopus, squid, mussels and clams in varying sizes cooked in myriad ways—the elegantly dressed Puglian antipasto table heaves and groans with unimaginable culinary pleasures.

I made my way to the market to look for some local cured fish specialties, and fast-tracking heaps of glorious Mediterranean produce stacked in jars creating a colorful wall six feet (two meters) high, stopped me in my tracks. Big, bulbous and bright preserved bell peppers, eggplants, zucchini, olives, *lampasciuoli* (local onions), mushrooms and every other vegetable known to the Gargano peninsula were enshrined in beautiful Puglian olive oil. Next to these were stacks of jars of fishy concoctions. I bought a jar of rich pink-colored salted anchovies preserved in oil with chili, another jar of fresh marinated anchovies pickled in vinegar and finished in oil with parsley, chili and garlic, and a totally irresistible jar of *moscardini*—perfect, tiny pink octopus. The stallholder, Antonio, made most of the pickles himself, and with little encouragement, took the trouble to explain how he did so.

ALICI

SALTED ANCHOVIES

Alici and acciughe *are one and the same thing; I have never quite figured out if the origin of the two words is regional, but sometimes they are called* alici *and sometimes* acciughe. *Try preserving small sardines and sprats using the same method, as follows.*

Gut and bone the fresh anchovies (see page 203). If the anchovies are very tiny they can be left whole, simply remove the head. Put the fish to soak in water for 1 hour. Rinse, drain and dry carefully. Pack them into a noncorrosive container, skin side up, then cover in brine made with ¼ cup (100 g) fine sea salt for every 4 cups (1 liter) of vinegar and let stand at cool room temperature for 7 to 8 hours.

After this time, take them by the handful and wring them out. Lay them out on clean dish towels like little soldiers for half a day to dry, then transfer to washed, sterilized preserving jars (see page 204). Top up with olive oil, and add lots of finely chopped chili, a leaf or two of flat-leaf parsley, and a peeled garlic clove to each jar before sealing.

MOSCARDINI SOTT'OLIO

BABY OCTOPUS IN OIL

A moscardino *is a diminutive Disneyesque octopus, which, when cooked, is pale pink with tiny, upturned, frilly tentacles. It is delicious in seafood salads and sauces.*

Put the *moscardini* in a saucepan and cover with cold brine made with ¼ cup (100 g) sea salt for every 4 cups (1 liter) of water. Bring to simmering point very gently, then drain and transfer to a noncorrosive dish. Cover with white wine vinegar and let stand at cool room temperature for 7 to 8 hours.

Take out of the vinegar, spread out on clean dish towels, and let dry for 4 hours. Pack into washed, sterilized preserving jars (see page 204) and fill with the best Puglian olive oil available.

above **Williamsburg pickled mackerel cooked in an earthenware dish**
opposite **The mackerel transferred to a jar to store**

WILLIAMSBURG PICKLED MACKEREL

SERVES 4

4 mackerel, herring or large sardines, 5 to 7 ounces (150 to 200 g) each, filleted

1 teaspoon ground black peppercorns

½ teaspoon crushed white peppercorns

1 heaping teaspoon marjoram leaves, finely chopped, plus extra to serve

1 heaping teaspoon thyme leaves, finely chopped, plus extra to serve

1¼ cups (300 ml) white wine vinegar

¾ cup (200 ml) cold water

Olive oil, for drizzling and storing

Coarse sea salt as desired

EQUIPMENT

24-ounce (750-ml) tall preserving jar, washed and sterilized (see page 204) (optional)

This delicious recipe can also be adapted to pickle herring and sardines. It is based on a pickle recipe from The Williamsburg Art of Cookery *first published in 1742. The original recipe contained saltpeter, which would have preserved the fish long term. It was also for 14 fish. I have reduced the recipe down to more manageable proportions.*

Preheat the oven to 325 F (160 C).

Fillet the fish yourself or ask your fishmonger to fillet it for you. Run your fingers over the cut surfaces to check for pin bones and use tweezers to remove them. Trim any ragged edges from the fish fillets. Cut a "v" down the center of the length of the fish fillet to remove the central bones (see photo on page 220).

Wipe the fish fillets and arrange them in a single layer, skin side down, in an earthenware dish and sprinkle the ground pepper and chopped herbs on and around them. Cover with the white wine vinegar and water and cook in the preheated oven for 2 hours.

If using, put the preserving jar to warm in a preheated low oven at 225 F (110 C).

Drain off the vinegar. Drizzle with olive oil, scatter with freshly chopped marjoram and thyme leaves, and salt. Serve with salad and boiled potatoes.

If not being eaten straight away, pack the fish into the sterilized preserving jar, cover with oil, seal and label. The mackerel will keep for 1 month or longer.

MINTED MACKEREL

SERVES 4

4 small mackerel, herring or sardines, about 4 to 5 ounces (100 to 150g), filleted

¾ to 1½ cups (200 to 400 ml) white wine vinegar

Extra virgin olive oil, for drizzling and storing

2 tablespoons chopped mint

2 garlic cloves, finely chopped

Coarse sea salt as desired

EQUIPMENT

24-ounce (750-ml) tall preserving jar, washed and sterilized (see page 204)

This is a very delicate cure that leaves the fish soft and velvety and is delicious served straight away as a starter with a celeriac salad. If you want to preserve it, wind the fish fillets around the base of the jar and build upwards.

Put the preserving jar to warm in a preheated low oven at 225 F (110 C).

Steam the mackerel for a few minutes, or plunge into simmering water and bring back to a boil, then drain on paper towels. Arrange in a shallow noncorrosive dish, add enough white wine vinegar to cover, and leave at room temperature for 1 hour.

After this time, take the fish out of the vinegar marinade and put in a clean dish. Drizzle with the best-quality extra virgin olive oil, a tablespoon of the vinegar marinade, and scatter with the chopped mint, garlic, and salt to taste.

To store, cut the fish into 2-inch (5-cm) lengths, transfer to the sterilized preserving jar, top up with extra virgin olive oil and seal until required. The mackerel will keep for up to 1 month.

RED MULLET, POTATO AND ARUGULA SALAD

SERVES 4

4 red mullet, herring or large sardines, 5 to 7 ounces (150 to 200 g) each, scaled, gutted, filleted and heads and tails removed (you can ask your fishmonger to do this)

Scant ½ cup (100 ml) white wine vinegar

2 tablespoons water

½ teaspoon sea salt

Few flat-leaf parsley sprigs

1 teaspoon juniper berries, lightly crushed, or black peppercorns

8 scallions, thinly sliced (optional)

TO SERVE

2 tablespoons finely chopped flat-leaf parsley

Extra virgin olive oil

Sea salt crystals as desired

Lemon wedges (optional)

3 cups (500 g) small boiled new potatoes, halved

3 ounces (90 g) arugula

Franco Taruschio and I have been teaching recreational cooking together for the last ten years, and this is a dish we make as part of our basic fish skills class.

Fillet the fish yourself or ask your fishmonger to fillet it for you. Run your fingers over the cut surfaces to check for pin bones and use tweezers to remove them. Trim any ragged edges from the fish fillets. Cut a "v" down the center of the length of the fish fillet to remove the central bones (see photo on page 220).

Pick over the fish fillets to remove all the pin bones.

Heat the white wine vinegar with the water and salt in a small saucepan. Put the fish fillets in a noncorrosive dish in a single layer and scatter the parsley sprigs, juniper berries, and scallions, if using, over the top. Pour the boiling vinegar mixture over the fish fillets. Cover and let marinate at room temperature for 1 hour.

After this time, remove the fish from the marinade and arrange in a clean dish. Add some of the scallions, drained, if using, and scatter with the finely chopped parsley, a few drops of extra virgin olive oil, and a sprinkling of salt.

Arrange the potatoes and arugula on four serving plates and put the fish fillets on top. Drizzle with extra virgin olive oil and serve. Garnish with lemon wedges, if using.

**Assembling the rollmops
before pickling**

MAKES 8

4 herring, 5 to 7 ounces (150 to 200 g) each, scaled, filleted and heads and tails removed

1 onion, cut into rings and blanched in boiling water for 1 minute, or dill pickles

1½ cups (400 ml) white wine vinegar

⅔ cup (150 ml) water

1 bay leaf

1 teaspoon mustard seeds

1 teaspoon coriander seeds

2 tablespoons granulated sugar

½ teaspoon sea salt, plus extra for seasoning (do not add salt if using salted herring)

Freshly ground black pepper as desired

EQUIPMENT

16-ounce (500-ml) preserving jar, washed and sterilized (see page 204)

Most northern European countries have a strong fish-curing heritage thanks to the migratory herring. The quintessential rollmop is popular all over northern Europe and, due to the wave of early 20th-century emigration to North America, on this continent too. Filleted herring are rolled up, marinated in a pickle brine of white wine vinegar, bay leaf, mustard seeds, onion and salt ,and sweetened with a little sugar. Rollmops are also popular in Holland, but here the herrings are first salted, then soaked for 24 hours, changing the water every few hours, and finally filleted before being rolled up and preserved in a mixture of spiced water and vinegar.

In Germany it is common to see people eating Fischbrötchen, *a crusty roll filled with Bismarck herring. Herring salads are also popular with pickled cucumbers or gherkins (see page 245) and potatoes, beets or mayonnaise, as are rollmops, but all these German specialties are made with* salzheringe, *or salted herring, rather than fresh herring.*

Put the preserving jar to warm in a preheated low oven at 225 F (110 C).

Cut a "v" down the center of the length of the fish fillet to remove the central bones (see photo opposite). Lay the fish fillets, skin side down, in a shallow noncorrosive dish. Sprinkle with salt and pepper and place either a few slices of prepared onion along the fish or a dill pickle at the end. Roll up the fish and secure with a wooden toothpick.

Put the remaining ingredients in a saucepan and bring slowly to a boil, add the rollmops, and simmer for 2 minutes. Let cool slightly, pull out the toothpicks and discard, then transfer to the sterilized preserving jar. Top up with the marinade, making sure that it covers the fish completely, banging the jar lightly on a work surface to ensure there are no air bubbles trapped in the jar.

Seal the jar and store in the refrigerator for 1 week before opening. The rollmops will keep for up to 6 months.

The pickled rollmops

Rollmops with Pickled Gooseberries (see page 234)

SHIMI SABA

JAPANESE PICKLED MACKEREL

MAKES 8 OUNCES (250 ML)

1 large mackerel

1 heaping teaspoon coarse
sea salt per 5 ounces (150 g)
filleted mackerel

1 bottle of mirin

1 bottle of rice vinegar

½ teaspoon grated fresh
ginger root

EQUIPMENT

Preserving jars washed and
sterilized (see page 204);
size of your choice

Mackerel is venerated by the Japanese gourmet, although it is not eaten raw, sashimi style, but rather lightly cured in salt and vinegar first. This is called shimi saba. *Sea bream prepared in a similar way is known as* kodai sasazuke, *but you can also try using sea bass and herring.*

There is another Japanese tradition known as sake kasu: *salted white fish fillets are marinated in sake and sake lees for three days, then washed, dried and broiled until caramelized. This too is worth experimenting with; make a small quantity at a time until you get the right result. As with all pickled fish, a little goes a long way, as the flesh becomes solid and the flavor much more strident and therefore more satisfying.*

The Japanese mirin and rice vinegar pickle brine produces a texture that is much firmer and drier than it would be if the same fish was pickled in wine or malt vinegar.

Put the preserving jar to warm in a preheated low oven at 225 F (110 C).

Fillet the fish yourself or ask your fishmonger to fillet it for you. Run your fingers over the cut surfaces to check for pin bones and use tweezers to remove them. Trim any ragged edges from the fish fillets. Cut a "v" down the center of the length of the fish fillet to remove the central bones (see photo on page 220).

Lay the fillets out on a noncorrosive tray, skin side down, and sprinkle with salt, using less at the tail end of the fish where the flesh is thinner and more where the flesh is thicker. Cover and leave in the refrigerator overnight.

Rinse the fish fillets and pat dry, then leave them for a few minutes in the air to dry.

Cut the fillets slightly on the diagonal, creating rhomboids ½ to 1 inch (1 to 2 cm) long. Pack them into the sterilized preserving jar. Top up with equal quantities of mirin and rice vinegar and add the ginger root. Seal the jar and leave in the refrigerator for 1 week before opening. Serve with *Tsukemono*, Japanese Cured Vegetables (see page 242) and Pickled Ginger (see page 245).

opposite **Shimi saba with Pickled Ginger (see page 245) and Japanese Cured Vegetables (see page 242)**

Sarde in saòr venete

SARDE IN SAÒR VENETE

PICKLED SARDINES VENETIAN STYLE

SERVES 4

1 pound (500 g) sardines

All-purpose flour, seasoned with sea salt and freshly ground black pepper as desired, for dusting

2 small onions, finely sliced

¾ to 1¼ cups (200 to 300 ml) good white wine vinegar, plus extra for storing

1 tablespoon raisins, soaked in boiling water for 5 minutes and squeezed dry

1 tablespoon pine nuts

Sunflower oil, lard or olive oil, for frying

EQUIPMENT

16-ounce (500-ml) preserving jar, washed and sterilized (see page 204) (optional)

In the traditional form of this Venetian recipe, sardines were fried in lard and layered in white wine vinegar with some finely sliced onion and the addition of either lemon zest, pine nuts, or pre-soaked raisins. It was originally created by seafarers, who, having to stay away at sea for long periods of time, learned to prepare fish so that it would keep longer. The onion in the recipe would have been included to combat scurvy. Other kinds of fish and meat were also preserved in saòr.

It has been the custom in Venice since the 16th century to eat sarde in saòr *on the Festa del Redentore, the third Sunday in July. However, traditional Venetian eateries known as* bàcari, *specializing in antipasti or* cicheti *as they are called here, generally have them on the menu whenever sardines are plentiful. Around the Rialto markets, the* bàcari *are little more than holes in the wall in a desirable location, dispensing wine, aperitifs, and delicious little snacks. On these Sundays during lunchtime, bright young Venetian things, come hell or high water, spill out into the square quaffing their amber-colored aperols and crimson Camparis and devouring freshly made delicacies.*

Not far from the Guggenheim Museum is a tiny bar next door to the trattoria da Fiore in the Calle delle Botteghe, run by Australian-born Venetian David da Fiore. Here you can enjoy a feast of cicheti, *including* sarde in saòr venete *on white polenta, with a glass or two of Prosecco or wine.*

Pull off the heads of the sardines and the intestines should come away at the same time. Cut open along the belly and scrape out any remaining intestines, then bone (see page 203), rinse and pat dry.

Close the sardines and lightly dust in seasoned flour, shaking off the excess. Pour 2 inches (5 cm) of sunflower oil, lard or olive oil into a deep pan and set over high heat. Deep-fry the sardines swiftly in the hot oil until golden and transfer to paper towels to drain.

In a separate pan, fry the onions until transparent, taking care not to brown them. Add enough vinegar to cover and then leave until quite cold.

Layer the sardines, onions, raisins and pine nuts in a shallow dish, pour vinegar over the top, cover, and leave for at least 24 to 48 hours in the refrigerator before eating. If you wish, you can transfer to a sterilized preserving jar, top up with white wine vinegar, and keep for a month or two.

TURIN PICKLED TENCH

Giacomo Mosso is an artisan producer of carpione of tench in an area called Ceresole d'Alba 19 miles (30 km) outside Turin. The tench can survive in waters that are low in oxygen, but towards the end of the summer, when water levels are very low and the fish have to be caught, he preserves those that cannot be eaten straight away. This much-prized freshwater fish once played an important role in the gastronomy of the area. It was served either salted and fried for four minutes in bubbling hot oil or preserved in carpione in vinegar.

Put the preserving jar to warm in a preheated low oven at 225 F (110 C).

Lightly season the fish with salt. Heat 1 inch (2 cm) of sunflower oil in a large skillet and, when it starts to bubble, add the fish and fry for 4 minutes, turning only once and taking care not to damage the delicate fish skin. Transfer to paper towels to drain.

Fry the vegetables and garlic in the remaining oil until tender, then transfer to paper towels. Heat the wine vinegars and wine to simmering point and add the herbs.

Transfer the fish to the jar and layer with the cooked vegetables. Pour the hot vinegar and wine over the fish, making sure that the fish is completely covered. Seal and keep for 3 to 4 days in the refrigerator before opening. It will store for up to 2 months.

MAKES 16 OUNCES (500 ML)

1 pound (500 g) tench or trout, gutted and filleted

1 small onion, finely sliced

1 small carrot, finely sliced

1 garlic clove, finely chopped

3 tablespoons good white wine vinegar

3 tablespoons good red wine vinegar

¾ cup (200 ml) white wine or equal quantities white wine and water

Few sage leaves

1 bay leaf

Sea salt as desired

Sunflower oil, for frying

EQUIPMENT

Preserving jars, washed and sterilized (see page 204); size of your choice

❧ **VARIATION** If you can't get tench, use trout or any other freshwater fish instead.

THE LARDER: PICKLED FRUIT & VEGETABLES

I grew up in the countryside on the borders of Herefordshire and Gloucestershire, not far from where I now live. We had a huge vegetable garden where we grew everything from onions to asparagus and all manner of berries and fruit. We had a gardener who did the planting and tending but come summer we all had to get out into the garden to help pick the beans and peas and soft fruit.

There was no finer sight than my mother's pantry (that is what we called the larder) in autumn. The top shelf was dedicated to great big glass and earthenware jars filled with pickled onions and walnuts. The lower shelf was rammed with bottled fruit, plums, pears, damsons, greengages, gooseberries, rhubarb and black currants and the shelf below with tall jars of chutneys; bean, beet and apple were favorites. Then there were the jams, raspberry and strawberry, and the jellies: redcurrant, black currant and crab apple. Even to a small child all those shiny colorful jars gave a wonderful feeling of well-being.

With the advent of affluence, freezers and refrigeration, the larder and preserving belong to a bygone age but still "my heart with pleasure fills" to see a simple stack of sparkling pots of homemade fare in the kitchen cupboard. Judging by the resurgence of interest in preserving over the last few years, many other people feel this way too.

FORAGER'S JELLY

MAKES 8 TO 16 OUNCES (250 TO 500 ML)

15 cups (1.5 kg) elderberries, blackberries or hawthorn berries

1½ cups 400 ml water

Preserving sugar

Juice of 1 lemon

EQUIPMENT

Preserving jars with lids and caps, washed and sterilized (see page 204); size of your choice

Jelly making is a little more involved than making jam or chutney in that the cooked fruit needs to be left overnight in a suspended jelly bag to drip before boiling it with the sugar. But it is well worth the effort, especially when using berries gathered from the hedgerows. Bear in mind that the yield is lower than with jam.

If using hawthorn berries, be warned that they turn a peculiar green color when cooked, but the resulting juice, albeit it low in yield, is a glorious red.

Serve with Potted Diced Shoulder of Venison (see page 180) or any game meat.

Put the preserving jar/s to warm in a preheated low oven at 225 F (110 C).

Wash the fruit, drain well, and transfer to a large saucepan. Add the water and simmer for 10 to 15 minutes until the fruit is tender. Carefully transfer the fruit to a jelly bag and suspend over a bowl. Leave the juices to drip overnight.

After this time, measure the juice and transfer it to a stainless steel saucepan. Add 1¾ cups (400 g) preserving sugar to every 2½ cups (600 ml) juice (this quantity of fruit may yield less than 2½ cups (600 ml)). Add the lemon juice and set over low heat, stirring regularly until the sugar has dissolved.

Increase the heat and boil rapidly for about 5 to 10 minutes until setting point is reached. Pull the pan off the heat, take ½ teaspoon of the juice and set it on a cooled saucer in the refrigerator. Leave for 10 minutes. If the jelly has started to set, it is ready. If not, boil again for another 5 to 10 minutes, stirring and watching that it does not stick to the pan and burn. Test again. Be patient and if necessary boil up again for another 5 minutes. The setting time depends on how much water is in the fruit.

When ready, transfer to a wide-mouthed pitcher and pour into the warm sterilized jars, cover the surface of the jelly and seal with lids and caps while still hot. Let cool before labeling and store in the dark for a month before opening. The jelly will keep for 2 years or more.

1 2
3 4

A COLLECTION OF PICKLES. 1. Lindy's garden apple chutney. 2. Pickled mirabelles.
3. Membrillo. 4. Plum chutney. *opposite* Pickled mirabelles and Pickled tench (see page 227).

LINDY'S GARDEN APPLE CHUTNEY

MAKES 48 OUNCES (1 ½ LITERS)

2 ¼ pounds (1 kg) apples

1 pound (500 g) onions

⅔ cup (125 g) golden raisins

2 ¼ cups (500 g) demerara sugar

1 small egg-size piece of fresh ginger root, finely chopped

2 teaspoons crushed coriander seeds

½ teaspoon chili

1 tablespoon sea salt

4 cups (1 liter) malt vinegar

EQUIPMENT

Preserving jars with lids and caps, washed and sterilized (see page 204); size of your choice

We have a collection of apples trees in our garden. The largest and oldest is the garden's focal point with one of those circular garden seats running around its trunk. The tree offers ample shade for garden parties when the weather allows in summer, a canopy of frothy pink blossom in May, a frivolous crop of mistletoe for Christmas, and an abundant supply of picture book apples in autumn. The chutney is delicious with hard cheeses, omelets, boiled ham and English breakfast.

Chop the apples and onions finely. Put the apples, onions, golden raisins, sugar, chopped ginger root and dried spices, salt and half the vinegar in a stainless steel saucepan and bring slowly to simmering point. Cook for 1 to 2 hours over low heat. Stir regularly to prevent the mixture burning. Add extra vinegar as the chutney reduces.

Put the preserving jars to warm in a preheated low oven at 225 F (110 C).

Turn off the heat and leave the chutney to rest for 20 minutes before potting. Spoon the chutney into sterilized jars and seal with lids and caps. Let cool before labeling. Store in the dark for at least a month before opening. The chutney will keep for at least 1 year.

Like all chutney this improves with age.

MEMBRILLO

MAKES 16 TO 24 OUNCES (500 TO 750 ML)

2 ¼ pounds (1 kg) quinces

Zest of ½ lemon, cut with a potato peeler

Granulated sugar

Juice of ½ lemon

EQUIPMENT

Preserving jars with lids and caps, washed and sterilized (see page 204); size of your choice

QUINCE CHEESE

Delicious with cheese or as an after-dinner treat!

Scrub the quince, cut in half, and put in a pan with the lemon zest. Cover with water, bring gently to a boil, and simmer until really soft. This may take a couple of hours. Put the fruit in a jelly bag and drain off the water overnight and make jelly (see page 228).

Put the preserving jars to warm in a preheated low oven at 225 F (110 C).

Transfer the fruit pulp to a mouli legumes or blender and then sieve and reduce to a purée, discarding the skin and seeds. Weigh the fruit pulp and weigh an equal quantity of sugar. Put the fruit pulp and the weighed sugar in a stainless steel saucepan, add the lemon juice, and cook over gentle heat and stir until the sugar dissolves. Continue to cook over low heat until the pulp thickens and darkens to a soft shade of burgundy; this may take an hour or two. Take care to keep the heat low and to stir the mixture often.

When the quince cheese is really thick, spoon it into straight-sided, oiled, sterilized jars and seal with lids and caps. Let cool before labeling. Turn out and cut into slices when required. The membrillo will keep for at least 1 year.

❧ **NOTE** Quince cheese can be dissolved in an equal quantity of boiling water to make a delicious dressing for smoked duck.

PICKLED MIRABELLES

MAKES 24 OUNCES (750 ML)

2¼ pounds (1 kg) firm mirabelles (cherry plums), damsons, greengages or plums

2¼ cups (500 g) granulated sugar

⅔ cup (150 ml) white wine vinegar

7 cloves

1 star anise (optional)

EQUIPMENT

Preserving jars with lids and caps, washed and sterilized (see page 204); size of your choice

I had never heard of or seen a mirabelle plum, or wild cherry plum, until one day early in August when Rhaoul the forager phoned to ask me if I wanted any. He turned up on my doorstep in no time with a basket of lovely creamy yellow and soft red, cherry-sized plums that he had picked along the banks of the River Wye.

Two months later I found myself in Peck, a venerable culinary institution in the Via Spadari, Milan, and to my surprise there on the shelves among the peaches and the prickly pears was a basket of mirabelles.

Serve the pickled mirabelles with smoked duck breast or even ice cream.

Wash and dry the fruit in the sun, prick with a sharp fork, and put in a bowl.

Put the preserving jars to warm in a preheated low oven at 225 F (110 C).

Put the sugar, white wine vinegar, cloves and star anise, if using, in a large saucepan and heat gently, stirring from time to time until the sugar has dissolved. Pour the vinegar and sugar syrup over the fruit in the bowl and let stand at room temperature for 24 hours.

Using a slotted spoon, fill the warm sterilized jars with the fruit, taking care to drain off as much of the syrup as possible.

Return the pan containing the syrup to the stovetop, increase the heat, and bring to a boil. Continue boiling for about 10 minutes until the syrup has reduced by half.

Pour the syrup over the fruit to cover. (As the syrup is very hot and the jars may have cooled a little by this time, put a teaspoon or narrow metal object into each jar as you pour in the boiling liquid to conduct the heat away from the glass and prevent the jars from cracking.)

Seal with lids and caps while still warm and let cool before labeling. Store in the dark for 1 to 2 weeks before opening. The fruit will keep for at least 1 year.

PLUM CHUTNEY

MAKES 14 TO 16 OUNCES (400 TO 500 ML)

1 pound (500 g) plums, pitted and chopped

⅔ cup (100 g) onion, chopped

1 teaspoon whole pickling spice, tied up in muslin

½ cup (125 ml) malt vinegar

½ cup (100 g) granulated sugar

1 teaspoon sea salt

Pinch of dry mustard powder

EQUIPMENT

Preserving jars with lids and caps, washed and sterilized (see page 204); size of your choice

This lovely old country recipe can be made with any plums, greengages, damsons, apples, rhubarb or whatever fruit you have available. Plums and damsons make a marvelous purple-colored concoction.

Put the prepared fruit and onion in a stainless steel saucepan with the tied-up spices and half the vinegar and simmer over low heat for 30 minutes.

After this time, stir in the sugar, salt, mustard powder and remaining vinegar and simmer until the water in the fruit has evaporated and the chutney is creamy. This may take up to an hour, but remember to stir regularly, because if the mixture sticks to the bottom of the pan it will burn.

Put the preserving jars to warm in a preheated low oven at 225 F (110 C).

Let rest for about 20 minutes before potting. Spoon the chutney into the warm sterilized jars and seal with lids and caps. Let cool before labeling. Store in the dark for at least a month before opening. The chutney will keep for at least 1 year.

FRANCO AND ANN TARUSCHIO'S PICKLING GEMS

Franco and his wife Ann have been a force to be reckoned with on the culinary scene since they established the Walnut Tree Inn restaurant near Abergavenny, South Wales, in the 1960s. I have worked with Franco since he "retired" from his beloved restaurant; in reality, he continues to toil tirelessly, consulting, teaching, and being a hands-on grandfather.

Ann is Franco's éminence grise, researching and writing their recipes and books, and there is very little she does not know about food. These days, most of their cooking goes on at home in their contemporary, no-nonsense, airy kitchen.

Ann and Franco are dedicated pickle makers. In late summer and early autumn there is generally something bubbling away in the saucepan, be it the prosaic gooseberry or the exotic quince. Franco never turns up anywhere without bearing culinary gifts and homemade pickles provide perfect seasonal presents for friends and family.

The Taruschios are just as generous with their recipes. While I have been working on this book, I don't think a phone call has passed between us that did not produce yet another suggestion, followed by an email containing a recipe. The following are three of their pickling gems.

TARUSCHIO PICKLED GOOSEBERRIES

MAKES 14 TO 16 OUNCES (400 TO 500 ML)

4½ cups (450 g) gooseberries (slightly under-ripe are best)

1¼ cups (300 ml) white wine vinegar

⅓ cup (60 g) granulated sugar

Pinch of ground ginger

1-inch (2.5-cm) piece of cinnamon stick

6 cloves

EQUIPMENT

Preserving jars with lids and caps, washed and sterilized (see page 204) size of your choice

Gooseberries look beautiful pickled in jars, as the syrup goes a cloudy pink color. Serve with rollmops (see page 22), or mackerel and other oily fish.

Put the preserving jars to warm in a preheated low oven at 225 F (110 C). Top and tail the gooseberries.

Put the white wine vinegar, sugar and spices in a large stainless steel saucepan and heat gently, stirring regularly, until the sugar has dissolved.

Poach the gooseberries very briefly in the syrup. Remove the fruit with a slotted spoon and place in the warm sterilized jars. Pour the syrup when cold over the gooseberries. Seal with lids and caps. Label and store in the dark for at least a month before opening. The fruit will keep until the following season.

❧ **NOTE** When serving the gooseberries, sprinkle a little julienne of fresh ginger root on the top.

CHRAIN

MAKES 8 OUNCES (500 ML)

4 to 5 beets, cooked, peeled and cut into chunks

2 to 3½ cups (100 to 175 g) fresh horseradish, peeled and grated

1 tablespoon balsamic vinegar

2 teaspoons superfine sugar

Sea salt as desired

EQUIPMENT

Preserving jars with lids and caps, washed and sterilized (see page 204); size of your choice

ASHKENAZI COLD COOKED BEET AND HORSERADISH PURÉE

This is yet another Taruschio special. Serve with Corned Beef (see page 48), roast beef, smoked eel or whatever you enjoy with beets. Eaten off the spoon this chrain will blow your mind, or at least your sinuses, but when eaten with meat the flavor mellows to perfection.

Put the preserving jar to warm in a preheated low oven at 225 F (110 C).

Simply blend all the ingredients together in a blender until coarsely puréed. Transfer to the warmed sterilized jars and seal with lids and caps. The sauce will keep in the refrigerator in a washed, sterilized screw-top jar for a couple of weeks.

MAKES 96 OUNCES (3 LITERS)

9 pounds (4 kg) just-ripe damsons

2 cups (500 ml) red wine vinegar

8 cups (2 kg) preserving sugar

1 cinnamon stick

6 cloves

EQUIPMENT

Preserving jars with lids and caps, washed and sterilized (see page 20); size of your choice

This recipe from Franco and Ann Taruschio is a mainstay accompaniment to one of their signature dishes, Lady Llanover's Salt Duck (see page 25), which appears in their book Leaves from the Walnut Tree. *It is essential to pick the fruit at just the right time when it is all but mature; plump but still firm with just a hint of softness.*

Put the preserving jars to warm in a preheated low oven at 225 F (110 C).

Wash and dry the damsons, then prick with a silver fork.

Put the red wine vinegar and preserving sugar in a large stainless steel saucepan and heat gently, stirring regularly, until the sugar has dissolved.

Put the damsons in the syrup and bring the syrup back to a boil. At this point, remove the damsons quickly, using a slotted spoon, and lay them on flat trays to cool rapidly. Add the spices to the syrup and boil for another 5 to 10 minutes or until the syrup thickens again.

Put the fruit carefully into the warm sterilized jars and strain the syrup over the fruit while it is still hot. Seal with lids and caps while still warm. Let cool before labeling. Store in the dark for 1 month before opening. The fruit will keep until next year's crop is ready to harvest.

PICKLED RASPBERRIES

MAKES 14 OUNCES (400 ML)

4 tablespoons white wine vinegar

½ cup (125 g) granulated sugar

Small piece of fresh ginger root

Pinch of ground mixed pickling spice

Small piece of cinnamon stick

4 cups (500 g) firm ripe raspberries

EQUIPMENT

Preserving jars with lids and caps, washed and sterilized (see page 204); size of your choice

I never thought of pickling raspberries until one day when I happened to be passing my local grocery store. The shelf outside was stacked with plump, ruby-red raspberries still covered in that just-picked, early morning bloom. I could not resist and inevitably they ended up in the saucepan to be preserved. They are exquisite! Use this recipe to pickle blackberries too. Serve with Lady Llanover's Duck (see page 25).

Put the preserving jars to warm in a preheated low oven at 225 F (110 C).

Put the vinegar, sugar and spices in a heavy-based saucepan and set over low heat, stirring from time to time until the sugar has dissolved, then bring to a simmer. Carefully tip the raspberries into the syrup and leave for a few seconds until they are coated, then carefully transfer to the warm sterilized jars using a slotted spoon.

Boil the syrup until reduced by half or thick and sticky and pour over the raspberries. (As the syrup is very hot and the jars may have cooled a little by this time, put a teaspoon or narrow metal object into each jar as you pour in the boiling liquid to conduct the heat away from the glass and prevent the jars from cracking.)

Seal with lids and caps while still warm and let cool before labeling. Store in the dark for at least a month before opening. The fruit will keep for at least 1 year.

GREEN TOMATO PICKLES

MAKES 32 OUNCES (1 LITER)

2¼ pounds (1 kg) green tomatoes, thinly sliced

2 medium onions, thinly sliced

2 tablespoons fine sea salt

½ teaspoon whole cloves

½ teaspoon whole allspice

1 teaspoon white peppercorns

½ tablespoon black mustard seeds

1 tablespoon yellow mustard seeds

1 cup (250 ml) cider vinegar

1 cup (250 g) light brown sugar

EQUIPMENT

Preserving jars with lids and caps, washed and sterilized (see page 204) size of your choice

I particularly like making green tomato pickles this way because the tomato slices retain their shape and color and look nice on the plate or in a sandwich. Delicious with cold meats, particularly ham (see page 26), cheeses, eggs and English breakfast.

Layer the sliced tomatoes and onions in a large bowl with the salt, cover with a clean dish towel, and let stand in a cool place overnight.

The following day, drain off the salt water and carefully rinse the tomatoes in fresh water. Let drain well, then transfer to a stainless steel saucepan. Tie up the spices in a piece of cheesecloth and put in the pan. Add the cider vinegar and sugar.

Set the pan over medium heat and bring gently to simmering point, stirring regularly until the sugar has dissolved. Continue to simmer for 45 to 60 minutes until the vegetables are tender but still intact and the vinegar has become syrupy. Do not leave the pickles unattended, as it is essential to stir regularly, otherwise it will stick to the pan and burn.

Put the preserving jars to warm in a preheated low oven at 225 F (110 C).

Leave the pickles to rest for about 20 minutes before potting. Spoon into the warm sterilized jars and seal with lids and caps. Let cool before labeling. Store in the dark for at least a month before opening. The pickles will keep for at least 1 year.

SWEET TOMATO JAM

MAKES 30 TO 42 OUNCES (900 ML TO 1.2 LITERS)

4½ pounds (2 kg) ripe tomatoes, skinned

6 red chilies, deseeded and finely chopped

1 large piece of fresh ginger root, peeled and finely chopped

1 head of garlic, finely chopped

Finely grated zest and juice of 3 lemons

4 cups (1 kg) granulated sugar

EQUIPMENT

Preserving jars with lids and caps, washed and sterilized (see page 204); size of your choice

❧ **NOTE** It is not essential, but I like to skim off at least half the seeds as they float to the surface.

❧ **VARIATION** For chili jam, simply increase the quantity of chilies according to your personal taste.

This spiced tomato jam is perfect for any type of cure, from stridently spicy to delicate. It is a beautiful tomato-red color and so delicious that I would also recommend spreading it on crusty bread with ricotta cheese for breakfast.

Chop the skinned tomatoes and transfer them and all the juices to a stainless steel saucepan. Add the remaining ingredients to the pan, set over medium heat, and stir until the sugar has dissolved. When the tomato mixture starts to simmer, increase the heat to high until the water content of the tomatoes evaporates and the tomato jam becomes thick and translucent. This can take up to 2 hours, depending on the water content. As the tomatoes boil down they are liable to stick to the bottom of the pan, so it is essential to stir the mixture regularly, and towards the end of the cooking time it will be necessary to stir constantly to avoid burning the jam.

Put the preserving jars to warm in a preheated low oven at 225 F (110 C).

Leave the jam to rest for 20 minutes before potting. Stir the jam well and transfer to a large pitcher. Pour into the warm sterilized jars and seal with lids and caps while still hot. Let cool before labeling. Store in the dark for a month before opening. The jam will keep for at least 1 year.

PICKLED CABBAGE

MAKES 16 OUNCES (500 ML)

1 pound (500 g) red or green cabbage

2 heaping tablespoons (50 g) fine sea salt

4 cups (1 liter) spiced vinegar (see page 243)

EQUIPMENT

Preserving jars with lids and caps, washed and sterilized (see page 204); size of your choice

This is not the classic sauerkraut, which is left to ferment and very much more complicated to make, but a simple pickled vegetable that will keep in the refrigerator for a couple of months. It is delicious with sausages, gammon slices and bacon chops—in fact, anything salty and savory. Use straight from the jar or sautéed with onions. Serve with Rillons of Pork (see page 185).

Wash and drain the cabbage and discard the outer leaves. Shred the cabbage and put in a bowl. Sprinkle with salt. Cover with a clean dish towel and let stand in a cool place for 24 hours.

Put the preserving jar to warm in a preheated low oven at 225 F (110 C).

When the cabbage is ready for bottling, rinse the cabbage and drain well, then transfer to the warm sterilized jar. Top up with the cooled spiced vinegar and seal with lids and caps. Let cool before labeling. The cabbage will keep for at least 2 months.

PICKLED CABBAGE. 1. Spiced vinegar. 2. Topping up with spiced vinegar.
3. The filled jar. 4. Sealed pickled cabbage.

PICCALILLI

MAKES 28 TO 32 OUNCES (800 ML TO 1 LITER)

1 small cauliflower

1 small cucumber

Handful of green beans

11 ounces (300 g) shallots, peeled

1 large zucchini

Fine sea salt as desired

1 teaspoon dry mustard powder (you may like more)

1 teaspoon ground ginger

1 tablespoon turmeric

1 tablespoon all-purpose flour

3 cups (750 ml) white malt vinegar

2 tablespoons sugar

1 heaping tablespoon whole allspice

EQUIPMENT

Preserving jars with lids and caps, washed and sterilized (see page 204); size of your choice

Piccalilli is a distinctive name for a distinctive pickle. You can personalize it according to the vegetables you have available and the spices you like. As it is quite chunky, large jars are more suitable than small ones. If preferred, the vegetables can be left raw and simply stirred into the piccalilli sauce before potting.

Cut all the vegetables into small bite-size pieces and then weigh them. Layer in a large bowl with ½ cup (100 g) salt for every 2 pounds (1 kg) of vegetables. Cover with a clean dish towel and let stand in a cool place overnight. Rinse and drain well.

Put the mustard powder, ground spices and flour in a bowl and add approximately 2 tablespoons vinegar to make a paste.

Put the remaining vinegar in a large saucepan, add the sugar and allspice and boil for 5 minutes, then strain.

Add the spiced vinegar to the paste a little at a time. When all the vinegar has been added, return to the pan and slowly bring to a boil, then simmer for 15 minutes. Stir in the chopped vegetables and simmer for 5 minutes, stirring as you do so.

Put the preserving jars to warm in a preheated low oven at 225 F (110 C). Leave the piccalilli to rest for about 20 minutes before potting. Spoon into the warm sterilized jars and seal with lids and caps. Let cool before labeling. Store in the dark for at least a month before opening. It will keep for 1 year.

GIARDINIERA IN AGRODOLCE

ITALIAN SWEET AND SOUR GARDENER'S PICKLE

MAKES 16 TO 32 OUNCES (500 ML TO 1 LITERS)

2 teaspoons sunflower oil

2 teaspoons white wine vinegar

½ tablespoon sugar

½ tablespoon fine sea salt

Small piece of red chili

1 small carrot, finely chopped

1 celery stalk, finely chopped

Handful of green beans, cut into bite-size pieces

1 large red bell pepper, cut into bite-size pieces

1 medium zucchini, cut into bite-size pieces

3½ ounces (100 g) shallots, cut into bite-size pieces

EQUIPMENT

Preserving jars with lids and caps, washed and sterilized (see page 204); size of your choice

Giardiniera is the Italian equivalent to piccalilli. Agrodolce *means "sweet and sour," and although we tend to associate sweet and sour with Asian food, it is also very popular in Italian cooking, especially in some of the northern regions. Every household has its family recipe and they vary hugely. Use the vegetables you have available and add your favorite spices. You may like to add garlic or cook the vegetables in a tomato sauce strengthened with the pickling vinegar before potting. Serve as part of an antipasto misto.*

Put the preserving jars to warm in a preheated low oven at 225 F (110 C).

Gently heat the oil, white wine vinegar, sugar, salt and chili in a large saucepan for 5 minutes. Add the finely chopped carrot and celery and simmer over low heat until soft, taking care not to color it. Add the other vegetables and cook for 10 minutes.

Let rest for a few minutes, then pack the vegetables into the warm sterilized jar/s and top up with the remaining liquid. Cover with lids and caps and seal. Let cool before labeling. Store in the dark for at least a month before opening. The pickle will keep for a few months.

A COLLECTION OF PICKLES. 1. Piccalilli. **2.** Giardiniera in agrodolce.
3. Tsukemono (see page 242). **4.** Pickled onions (see page 242).

TSUKEMONO

JAPANESE CURED VEGETABLES

MAKES 8 OUNCES (250 ML)

1 large carrot or 2 small white turnips

6 scallions

½ cucumber

1 teaspoon fine sea salt

⅔ cup (150 ml) rice vinegar

5 tablespoons mirin (sweet rice wine)

Thumbnail-size piece of fresh ginger root, peeled

EQUIPMENT

Preserving jars with lids and caps, washed and sterilized (see page 204); size of your choice

The Japanese tradition for pickled vegetables is world famous, which is not surprising, as the preparation allows the vegetable to retain its integrity. But what few people realize is quite how easy Japanese pickles are to prepare. Try eggplant, cabbage, radish, cucumber, seaweed, scallion, carrot, turnip and, of course, fresh ginger root, the latter cut into paper-thin slices. Serve with Shimi Saba (see page 222).

Slice the vegetables (or those of your own choice) and lightly salt each layer. Cover and place a weight on top, then leave in the refrigerator overnight.

Put the preserving jar to warm in a preheated low oven at 225 F (110 C).

Drain off the liquid. Rinse the vegetables and pat dry.

Pack the vegetables into the sterilized jar, top with a mixture of two parts rice vinegar and one part mirin, and add the piece of ginger root. Seal with lids and caps, label and store for 1 month before opening. The vegetables will keep for 1 year.

PICKLED ONIONS

MAKES 16 OUNCES (500 ML)

2 tablespoons salt

2¼ pounds (1 kg) small pickling onions

4 cups (1 liter) sweet Spiced Vinegar (see opposite)

EQUIPMENT

Preserving jars with lids and caps, washed and sterilized (see page 204); size of your choice;

Growing up in the country I remember larder shelves stacked with huge green glass jars filled with onions floating in vinegar, tied up with crisp white greaseproof paper. A good old-fashioned pickled onion is preserved in 100 percent malt vinegar but for modern taste this can seem very harsh. Therefore, you may like to experiment with other vinegars such as red or white wine, cider or sherry. You might even pickle the onions in half wine vinegar and half wine for an altogether more mellow pickle.

Put the salt in a pan and add 4 cups (1 liter) of water, bring to a boil, stir to dissolve the salt and then let cool.

Put the onions in a large bowl, cover with boiling water and let stand for a few minutes and drain. Make yourself comfortable and start peeling; it's a slow old job.

Put the peeled onions in a bowl, cover with the cooled brine, and let stand for 24 hours covered with a clean dish towel. After this time, rinse in cold water and pat dry carefully.

Put the preserving jars to warm in a preheated low oven at 225 F (110 C).

Pack the onions into sterilized jars and top up with the sweet Spiced Vinegar. Seal with lids and caps and label.

Store in the dark for at least a month before opening. The pickled onions will keep for 12 months.

PICKLED WALNUTS

MAKES 64 OUNCES (2 LITERS)

1 pound (500 g) sea salt

8½ pints (4 liters) water

4½ pounds (2 kg) unripe green walnuts

Spiced Vinegar (see below)

EQUIPMENT

Preserving jars with lids and caps, washed and sterilized (see page 204); size of your choice

These are a classic, synonymous with English country food. The very words are uttered with reverence and their mere mention is guaranteed to bring a sigh of nostalgia to devotees. But for the uninitiated, a jar of pickled walnuts is not a pretty sight. Black, plum-like pickles float around in equally black fluid akin to squid ink. Their mystique is due to the fact that the whole walnut must be picked, outer casing and all, before the shell inside turns hard, around midsummer in the northern hemisphere. These unripe or "wet" walnuts are not easy to come by unless you have access to a walnut tree. I planted one specifically for pickling, and although it is said that it takes years for a tree to fruit, I have picked walnuts in our garden since year one.

To test for readiness, simply pick a walnut and plunge a bodkin or hefty needle into the center. If there is no resistance, the walnut is ripe for pickling. It is essential to wear plastic gloves to protect your hands from the black stain that the walnut emits.

Pickled walnuts are perfect for Christmas with cold meats and as an accompaniment to the Little Potted Venison Pies (see page 183).

Put the salt and water in a large saucepan and bring to a boil, then simmer until the salt has dissolved. Let cool.

Prick the whole walnuts with a needle or silver fork; if any are resistant, discard them. Trim the walnut's top and bottom. Put them in a large, noncorrosive bowl, cover with the cold brine, and let soak at room temperature for 3 to 4 days.

After this time, drain the walnuts and spread on trays exposed to the air for about 24 hours or until they turn black.

Put the preserving jars to warm in a preheated low oven at 225 F (110 C).

Pack the walnuts into the cooled sterilized jars and top up with the cold Spiced Vinegar. Seal with lids and caps, then label. Store in the dark for at least a month before opening. The pickled walnuts will keep for at least 1 year.

SPICED VINEGAR

MAKES 4 CUPS (1 LITER)

4 cups (1 liter) white malt or white wine vinegar

1 tablespoon whole mixed pickling spice (or mix 1 small piece of cinnamon stick with 1 teaspoon each of chili, coriander seeds, whole cloves, whole allspice, blade of mace, white peppercorns and a pinch of cayenne)

In the past, vinegar alone was used to preserve all kinds of fruit, vegetables, fish and meat and we were accustomed to its taste. However, it is not as palatable to modern taste and more often than not today's pickles are sweetened with sugar, honey or syrup or tempered with 50 percent white wine or water, creating a milder, sweeter pickle than the sour pickles of the past.

Put the vinegar (and sugar if using) and spices in a large noncorrosive bowl, stand the bowl in a saucepan of water, and bring to a boil. Remove from the heat and let stand for 2 hours or overnight to infuse.

❀ **VARIATION** For a sweeter pickle add ½ cup (100 g) soft brown sugar.

PICKLED CUCUMBERS OR GHERKINS

MAKES 64 OUNCES (2 LITERS)

8 cups (2 liters) water

¾ cup (200 g) coarse sea salt

12 small ridged cucumbers or gherkins (make sure that the cucumbers are freshly picked and firm)

1 large bunch of fresh dill or freshly picked dill heads

1 head of garlic, separated into cloves and peeled

1 (or more) red chilies

2 tablespoons whole mixed pickling spice

5 cups (1.2 liters) white malt or white wine vinegar

¾ cup (200 ml) extra virgin olive oil

EQUIPMENT

Preserving jars with lids and caps, washed and sterilized (see page 204); size of your choice

Use this recipe to pickle either whole or sliced cucumbers and serve with Salt Beef (see page 45), Pastrami (see page 72), or on their own with olives and other nibbles. It is not easy sourcing good, crisp small cucumbers unless you grow your own and therefore I only recommend pickling if you grow your own.

Put the water and salt in a saucepan and bring to a boil, then simmer until the salt has dissolved. Let cool.

Scrub the cucumbers and either leave whole, if using small cucumbers, or cut into ¼-inch (½-cm) slices, if using large cucumbers. If leaving whole, pierce the cucumbers with a needle at regular intervals.

Put the prepared cucumbers in a large bowl and pour the cooled brine over them. Cover with a clean dish towel and let stand in a cool place overnight.

Put the preserving jars to warm in a preheated low oven at 225 F (110 C).

Pack the cucumbers into the sterilized jars, dividing the dill, garlic, chilies and pickling spice between the jars, if using more than one. Fill the jars five-sixths with vinegar and one-sixth with extra virgin olive oil. Seal with lids and caps and label. Store in the dark for at least a month before opening. The pickled cucumbers will keep for up to 1 year.

PICKLED GINGER

MAKES 4 OUNCES (125 ML)

2 ounces (60 g) fresh ginger root

Pinch of sea salt

Scant 3 tablespoons rice vinegar

4 teaspoons mirin (sweet rice wine)

EQUIPMENT

Preserving jars with lids and caps, washed and sterilized (see page 204); size of your choice

This is a simple way of using up leftover ginger root. Delicious to serve with Shimi Saba (see page 222) or sushi but handy also to chop up and use in cooking. Don't throw away the ginger peelings—they make delicious stomach-soothing tea.

Peel the ginger root and slice as near to paper thin as you possibly can. Layer the slices with a little salt in a bowl. Place a weight on top and leave in the refrigerator overnight. Drain off the liquid, rinse the ginger and pat dry.

Put the preserving jar to warm in a preheated low oven at 225 F (110 C).

Pack the ginger into the sterilized jar and pour a mixture of two parts rice vinegar and one part mirin over the ginger until it is covered completely. Seal with lids and caps and label. The pickled ginger can be eaten straight away, or it will keep for several months.

❀ **VARIATION** If you like a sweet pickle, mix in ½ teaspoon of liquid honey per small jar.

opposite **Pickled cucumbers or gherkins**

PRESERVING FRUIT IN ALCOHOL

Preserving soft fruit in alcohol is a very simple and satisfying pastime. If you are preserving fruit for home consumption you can make a *rumtopf* using a large 16 or 32-ounce (1 or 2-liter) jar as the fruit season progresses. Make a layer of strawberries, add sugar and enough spirit to cover, and then seal the jar. Then when raspberries come into season, open the jar and add a layer of these. You can go on adding other fruit such as black currants, blueberries, purple plums, blackberries, black grapes and so forth. It is best not to mix red and green fruits as the juices from the berries bleed into the light-colored fruit. You can do another pot with gooseberries, grapes and greengages.

Choose top-quality fruit that is blemish-free and firm. Fruit with thick skins such as pears will need peeling and mandarins will need peeling and the pith cut off with a very sharp knife. Grapes and peaches can be preserved skin on or skin off. Large fruit such as peaches and pears may be preserved whole or cut in half. Oranges are best segmented and the pith cut away.

Recipes can be adapted to use your alcohol of choice: gin, vodka, rum, brandy or grappa. You decide. Flavor alcohol with whole spices such as vanilla, mace, cloves, star anise and cinnamon sticks and leave them in the jar.

PEACHES IN BRANDY SYRUP

MAKES 32 OUNCES (1 LITER)

8 peaches

8 cloves

SYRUP 1 FOR MARINATING

3 cups (750 ml) water

1 cup (250 g) superfine sugar

SYRUP 2 FOR PRESERVING

Scant ½ cup (100 ml) water

⅔ cup (150 g) superfine sugar

1¼ to 2 cups (300 to 500 ml) brandy

EQUIPMENT

Preserving jars with lids and caps, washed and sterilized (see page 204); size of your choice

It is not always easy to find a suitable jar in which to preserve whole peaches, so it may be necessary to cut them in half. In which case, simply put one clove for each peach into the syrup.

Make the first syrup by putting the water and sugar in a pan and bring gently to simmering point. Stir to dissolve the sugar and then simmer for 10 minutes.

Pierce the peaches to the pit, here and there, with a long needle. Put in a dish in a single layer and cover with the hot syrup and let stand for 24 hours.

Make the second syrup, dissolving the sugar in the water over low heat and simmering for 10 minutes. Measure and add two parts brandy, then let cool.

When the peaches have been in the marinade for 24 hours, stick a clove into each peach where the stem would have been, transfer the peaches to a sterilized jar, cover with the cooled brandy syrup, and seal with lids and caps. Leave for a month before opening. They will keep for at least a year.

❧ **VARIATION** Experiment with cherries, plums, mandarins and so on.

BLACK CHERRIES IN VODKA

MAKES 16 OUNCES (500 ML)

1 pound (500 g) firm cherries, stems on

1 tablespoon superfine sugar

Vodka

EQUIPMENT

Preserving jars with lids and caps, washed and sterilized (see page 204); size of your choice

This way of preserving fruit is for anyone who loves fine spirits, as it has the flavor of fruit and the alcohol you use. Serve in a shot glass after a meal instead of a liqueur.

Rinse the cherries and lay out on a cloth to dry for 24 hours.

Layer the cherries in a sterilized jar with sugar. Top the jar with vodka and seal with lids and caps. Keep for 2 months at least before opening, shaking gently from time to time to dissolve the sugar. They will keep for at least a year.

❧ **VARIATIONS**

❧ To make Mandarins in White Rum, slice off the top and bottom of the mandarins, cutting through both rind and pith. Slice off the remaining rind and pith, cutting in strips from top to bottom. The mandarins should have no white pith left attached. Transfer the mandarins to a washed and sterilized jar (see page 204)—for every 1 pound 500 g) of fruit use a 16-ounce (500-ml) jar—and add 1 tablespoon of superfine sugar for every 1 pound (500 g) of mandarins and top up the jar with white rum. Add half a vanilla bean and seal the jar.

❧ To make Spiced Grapes in Grappa, choose large, firm, fleshy grapes. Using scissors cut off the grapes, leaving a short stem attached to each one. Mix 1½ tablespoons of superfine sugar with 1¼ cups (300 ml) of grappa, stirring well to dissolve; add a blade of mace, 1 star anise, 1 cinnamon stick, and a few coriander seeds and let infuse for an hour. Put the grapes in a washed and sterilized jar (see page 204)—for every 1 pound (500 g) of fruit use a 16-ounce (500-ml) jar—top up with the spiced alcohol, and seal the jar.

Fillet of lamb rolled in a spice rub and wrapped, frozen, and ready for searing (see page 262)

⁊ RAW

Sliced seared fillet of beef (see page 266)

IN THE RAW

Italian crudi, South American ceviche and Japanese sashimi are all lightly marinated raw fish dishes that have become a feature of menus around the globe. But the origins of these meals are surprisingly humble. Fishermen, having no means to cook their fresh catch on deck, filleted the fish and ate it raw with a squeeze of lemon juice. There is no such unifying factor in the tradition of eating raw meat. Carpaccio is an Italian invention that has lent its name to raw fish dishes as well. The French specialty Steak Tartare's history is lost in the mists of time (see page 280).

Traditional curing methods were developed to prolong the life of meat and fish in order to ward off starvation in lean times and to provide victuals for armies and expeditions dispatched around the globe. However, we no longer cure food for the original purpose of preserving, but rather to create a new gastronomic experience—for the pleasure of eating something different. The modern processes of lightly salting, smoking, drying, pickling, and spicing fish and meat adopted by many chefs alter both the flavor and texture of the foods, but only preserve them short term. Nevertheless, this limited extension of their shelf life is a quality that many chefs value.

Although not curing in the traditional sense, marinating raw meat and fish deserves a place here as much as the classic curing ingredients—the natural antiseptics of citrus juices, wines, vinegars, spices, herbs and salt—change base texture and taste. Adding a light marinade to fresh fish gives the flesh a silky, melt-in-the-mouth quality. What happens is this: The acids in the citrus juice, vinegar and wine denature the proteins in the same way that heat does (see page 273).

Crudo has been elevated to all kinds of sophisticated levels by today's chefs. They heap herbs, spices and flavorings, vinegars and oils, salads, vegetables, mushrooms, cheeses and truffles on top of thin slices of meat and fish according to the season. But the truth is, the simpler the better. If the fish is freshly caught, it needs very little adornment. Crudo of fish is most often associated with the larger species, tuna and swordfish, but sea bass and sea bream make great crudo too, as do most white fish. Most oily fish and shellfish can also be served raw. My very favorite of all raw seafood is the jumbo shrimp. The flesh is sensual—barely pink, transparent and glistening—and slightly resistant to the bite; the taste rich, sweet, moist and satiating.

The very best cuts of meat such as fillet, sirloin and loin are delicious raw—the meat should be the best quality, well hung and freshly butchered. Crudo are generally cut paper thin, and to achieve this, the fish and meat can be partially frozen first. Sometimes the meat or fish is frozen, rolled in crushed spices and fried in hot oil to make a crust on the outside, leaving the flesh inside rare (a seared crudo or carpaccio). It is then sliced thinly and served straight away with a dressing poured over it. To my mind, portions should be kept at around 2 to 3 ounces (60 to 75 g) per serving for fish and 3 to 4 ounces (75 to 100 g) per serving for meat, unless you are an ardent crudo lover.

REGIONAL TRADITIONS

Sicily, Sardinia and Puglia in southeast Italy are my favorite places to eat carpaccio of fish, where I know it has come straight out of the sea. The fishermen of Pescara in the Abruzzo region of Italy make a traditional dish known as *crudo di calamaretti ai marinai pescaresi*, featuring baby calamari. They are simply dressed with good-quality wine vinegar and olive oil, and flavored with chopped chili and very thinly sliced onion, which is as much adornment as any fish crudo needs.

In sleepy Sant'Antioco in southwest Sardinia, the chefs are so proud of the quality and freshness of their fish and seafood that they use olive oil rather than extra virgin olive oil, as they believe it enhances its flavor where extra virgin oil masks it. Although I could understand this principle, I did not entirely agree with it until chef Roberto Floris insisted on doing a blind tasting with tuna crudo, and I have to say there was no argument. He was so right, and I have now re-evaluated my own recipes accordingly. Roberto's popular no-frills seafront trattoria is also renowned for that other popular "crudo," the sea urchin.

Since ancient times, Japan has been a voracious fish-eating nation, relying heavily on fish for its diet and taking advantage of the rich pickings from its seas. This has lead to an ever-increasing strain on its natural seafood resources, and today large quantities of fish are flown in from around the world to be sold at Tsukiji fish market in Tokyo. Much of the fish is eaten raw in sushi and as sashimi, lightly dabbed with soy sauce and piquant avocado-green wasabi, and consumed with palate-cleansing sliced pickled ginger. Fish for sashimi has to be ultra fresh. Japanese fish buyers travel the world's tuna migratory paths to buy the very best fish and have them flown home by Japan Air in containers of seawater and ice to Tsukiji market. Because of the presence of parasites in some wild fish, all fish destined to be served raw must now be pre-frozen for 48 hours. Salmon, tuna, eel, halibut, scallops, jumbo shrimps, crab, yellowtail, red snapper, cockles, clams, octopus and squid are all good sashimi fish. Citrus, vinegar and olive oil used in the Mediterranean to make carpaccios are replaced in Japan by rice vinegar, sake, mirin (sweet rice wine) and soy sauce to make sashimi.

Ceviche has its origins in the South American Indian words *cebo itche*, meaning "trawling for bait." This would seem to indicate that it came about much as crudo did in the Mediterranean, as a convenient way for fishermen to eat on board ships where no cooking facilities were available, simply catching and gutting the fish, slicing it thinly and then dressing it. While we probably have the Incas to thank for the tradition of ceviche, both Ecuador and Peru vie for the title of originator. In fact, each South American country has its own traditions, but essentially it is fish marinated until "cooked" in citrus juice and served with chili and coriander. In Peru it is served with cold potato or sweet corn, in Ecuador with popcorn, and in Mexico (*seviche*) with tortillas.

CONTEMPORARY FUSION

The age-old traditions of ceviche, carpaccio or crudo, and sashimi rooted in South America, Italy and Japan respectively have spawned a trend that has caught on everywhere. Young chefs all over the world have taken the concept of "in the raw" and flown with it. New York City's trendy midtown fish place, Esca, serves what glib New Yorkers like to call "Italian sashimi," while hip new eateries are mushrooming up around San Francisco serving what they choose to term "crudo." Across the pond, Alan Murchison in his L'ortolan restaurant in Berkshire, England, likes to have sashimi on the menu in summer. His favorite combination is an elegant offering of scallops rubbed with wasabi, salt and lime juice, seared tuna, and slow-marinated salmon.

This is invigorating and nutritious food that lends itself to experimentation and fusion, so why not explore its culinary potential in your own kitchen.

**Slicing raw tuna loin
(see page 258)**

SALMON CARPACCIO WITH AVOCADO

SERVES 4

11 ounces (300 g) skinned salmon fillet

1 teaspoon sea salt crystals

½ teaspoon freshly ground black pepper

2 avocados

DRESSING

Juice of 1 lemon

2 tablespoons olive oil

2 tablespoons finely chopped fennel fronds, plus extra fronds to garnish

Simple to make; delicious to eat! Prepare in advance and serve as a starter.

Freeze the salmon for 2 days, then let partially defrost in the refrigerator. Cut the salmon diagonally into paper-thin slices. Arrange the slices on a large platter. Sprinkle with the salt and the pepper.

Combine the ingredients for the dressing and pour half over the salmon. Cover and refrigerate for 2 hours or until required.

When ready to serve, halve the avocados and remove the stones. Peel and slice, then serve with the salmon, drizzled with the remaining dressing and garnished with the extra fennel fronds.

❧ **VARIATION** Blend the avocado with enough lemon juice to make a thick-pouring consistency and serve as a sauce with the salmon, adding seasoning to taste.

❧ **TOP TIPS FOR PERFECT CRUDO OR CARPACCIO OF FISH**

❧ Use a trusted fishmonger and ask if the fish is fresh enough to eat raw.

❧ Allow 2 to 3 ounces (60 to 75 g) fish per portion.

❧ You can freeze the fish for 90 minutes making it easier to slice. If you have previously frozen the fish, slice it while it is still partly frozen.

❧ Use a knife with a long, thin blade and sharpen it before you start.

❧ For D-cut, choose a thick fillet and slice straight down though the fish at right-angles to the skin creating D-shaped slices.

❧ If the slices are a bit thicker than you intended, lay them on a board and carefully stretch them by running the blade of the knife gently, firmly and closely along the fish slices.

❧ Make sure you use plenty of zingy citrus juice and sea salt crystals along with the other ingredients; raw fish needs more salt than you would expect.

❧ Marinate anywhere from a few seconds to 1 or 2 hours, according to taste.

❧ Serve with crusty bread and butter.

below **Tuna loin**
opposite **Carpaccio of tuna**

TUNA CARPACCIO WITH GINGER

SERVES 4

2 tablespoons light soy sauce

2 tablespoons mirin (sweet rice wine)

2-inch (5-cm) piece of fresh ginger root, peeled

11 ounces (300 g) tuna shoulder or loin

½ cucumber

This Asian-inspired combination of ginger, soy sauce and mirin creates an intense flavor that sets the palate tingling.

Put the soy sauce and mirin in a small bowl. Grate the ginger finely with a grater, allowing the juices to fall into the sauce. Scrape up any ginger on the blade and add to the sauce.

Cut the tuna into very thin slices, discarding the skin. Arrange on a plate. Cut the cucumber in half lengthwise, then cut it diagonally into thin slices 2 inches (5 cm) long. Arrange across the center of the tuna.

Drizzle the soy dressing over the tuna and cucumber and serve.

HALIBUT AND SCALLOP CARPACCIO

SERVES 4

12 large scallops without corals, shelled and cleaned

7 ounces (200 g) halibut fillet on the skin

2 garlic cloves, halved

Thyme leaves

4 tablespoons olive oil

Juice of 1 lemon

Sea salt crystals and freshly ground black pepper as desired

Fresh scallops and halibut are some of my favorite seafoods. Both have silky-soft flesh and lend themselves perfectly to being served raw.

Partially freeze the scallops before cutting into thin rounds. D-cut the halibut into thin slices (see page 254), discarding the skin. Rub four serving plates with the cut garlic.

Arrange the slices of halibut and scallop rings in alternate rows on the plates. Place a single thyme leaf in the center of each scallop round.

Crush a little salt between your fingers and scatter lightly over the halibut and scallop slices. Drizzle with the olive oil and lemon juice, add a grinding of black pepper, and serve at once.

❧ **VARIATION** For an Asian scallop and halibut platter, dress with Japanese rice vinegar, finely grated fresh ginger root and sea salt crystals.

CARPACCIO FACTS

"Carpaccio" was the name originally given to a plate of very thinly carved raw fillet steak dressed with a light mayonnaise sauce, made famous by Giuseppe Cipriani, the founder of Harry's Bar in Venice, and his son, Arrigo, in the mid-20th century. There was an exhibition of paintings in Venice at the time by the Venetian painter Vittore Carpaccio, and a poster advertising it on the wall opposite the bar provided the inspiration. The dish soon gained popularity in Italy and versions were made with veal and other meats. Raw fish dishes that had previously been called "crudi" subsequently also became known as "carpacci."

Halibut and scallop carpaccio platter

❊ CARPACCIO OF BEEF—THE RAW DEAL

❊ Ask your butcher to cut paper-thin slices of lean beef, such as fillet, or buy a piece of meat, partially freeze for 90 minutes, and slice with a long-bladed, sharp knife. To make the slices thinner, lay on a board and stretch them by firmly running a knife blade across them.

❊ Arrange the meat on a large platter and add lemon juice, olive oil, and plenty of sea salt and black pepper; you can also add Worcestershire or Tabasco sauce.

❊ Serve at once, or leave the meat to marinate for 10 minutes or so to "cook" it a little.

❊ Add Parmigiano Reggiano shavings or arugula as desired before serving the carpaccio.

❊ You might like to try thinly sliced truffle and ground pink peppercorns instead of Parmesan in autumn or thinly sliced artichoke in summer.

1

2

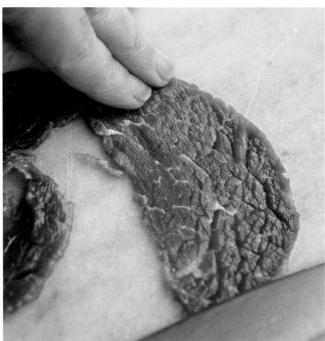

CARPACCIO OF BEEF. 1. Slicing raw lean beef for carpaccio.
2. Stretching the meat slices to get paper-thin slices.

SEARED CARPACCIO

Seared carpaccios are easy to make and fun to experiment with. Use neck fillet of lamb, loin of rabbit, fillet steak, tuna, salmon, or basically any premium cut of fish and meat that can be rolled into a sausage shape and frozen. Pork tenderloin may also be used, but I personally do not like pink pork; it tastes of pig rather than pork to me. However, many people do enjoy it and it does work well.

Whichever meat or fish you choose, you can roll it in just about any combination of ground spices, finely chopped herbs, sun-dried tomatoes, garlic, capers or ground nuts. The choice is yours!

SERVES 4 AS A STARTER

1 heaping tablespoon fresh rosemary

3 garlic cloves

1-inch (3-cm) piece of red chili

1 to 2 teaspoons coarsely ground black pepper

½ teaspoon sea salt crystals, plus extra to serve as desired

1 neck fillet of lamb, trimmed of any fat or skin and shaped into an even sausage

1 lemon

Olive oil, for frying

Neck fillet of lamb is a delicious tender cut of meat that is greatly undervalued. It does have quite a bit of fat running through it but do not let this put you off. Searing the meat seals the juices in, serving it raw enhances its richness and flavor. This is excellent when served with pickled fruit such as Pickled Mirabelles (see page 233) or Pickled Damsons (see page 235) or jellies such as Forager's Jelly (see page 228) or crab apple jelly.

Finely chop the rosemary, garlic and chili together, then mix in the black pepper and salt. Level the seasoning out on a chopping board and roll the lamb in it until completely and evenly coated. Cover with plastic wrap and freeze for a couple of hours or overnight.

When ready to serve, heat a skillet large enough to contain the neck fillet over high heat. Add enough olive oil to cover the base of the skillet and put the meat in the skillet. Reduce the heat to medium and fry until golden all over. This should take about 5 to 10 minutes, depending on how frozen the meat is.

Transfer the meat to a chopping board and cut into thin slices. Arrange on plates and squeeze the juice of the lemon all over. Collect up any of the bits of crust that may have fallen off the lamb and scatter these over the meat, adding a sprinkling of sea salt crystals.

Rolling the lamb in the seasoning

Pressing the seasoning in with the fingertips

SEARED CARPACCIO OF RABBIT LOIN

SERVES 4 AS STARTER

1 small bunch of flatleaf parsley, finely chopped

½ teaspoon sea salt crystals

4 teaspoons coriander seeds, crushed

4 rabbit loins, cut from 2 jointed rabbits (see below)

The loin is the crème de la crème of the rabbit meat. A truly delicate and dainty dish.

Mix the finely chopped parsley, salt, and crushed coriander seeds together and proceed as for the Seared Carpaccio of Lamb (see page 263). Cook the rabbit loins until golden, but this will only take a minute or two, as they are very tender.

Cut the loins into slices 1 inch (2 cm) thick and garnish with purple radish sprouts and arugula. Serve with Piccalilli (see page 240) as desired.

1 2
4 5

3
6

JOINTING A RABBIT LOIN. 1. Run a sharp, short-bladed knife close to and along the length of the spine. 2. Pull the loin away from the spine. 3. Run the blade under the loin, cutting it free of the bone. 4. The first loin is now detached from the bone. 5. Repeat on the other side. 6. The two loins detached from the bone.

INSALATA DI MANZO E RADICCHIO

VENETIAN CARPACCIO OF ROAST FILLET OF BEEF WITH RADICCHIO

SERVES 6 TO 8 AS A STARTER

1 pound (500 g) fillet steak

5 ounces (150 g) radicchio

8 to 10 radishes, sliced lengthwise into sections towards but not through the base and immersed in iced water to open out into "flowers"

7 ounces (200 g) cherry tomatoes

Scant ½ cup (100 ml) olive oil, plus 3 tablespoons for frying the beef

Juice of 1 lemon

⅓ cup (80 g) butter, softened

Sea salt crystals and freshly ground black pepper as desired

Frozen fillet of beef is fried in very hot olive oil and butter until golden all over, with the meat inside remaining raw. It is then thinly sliced and served with a citrus dressing. The vibrant shades of red of the raw beef, radicchio and tomatoes in this dish summon up the rich hues of Venice.

Cover the steak tightly in plastic wrap and freeze for several hours.

Shred the radicchio and arrange on the side of a large serving plate. Drain the radish flowers. Cut the cherry tomatoes in half and reserve.

Put the olive oil, lemon juice, and salt and pepper to taste together in a bowl and mix well with a fork.

Unwrap the steak and smother with the butter. Heat a skillet over high heat, and when hot, add the 3 tablespoons of olive oil. Add the fillet steak and brown quickly all over in the hot fat. Should the skillet get too hot, reduce the heat to medium after a while. When the meat is golden all over, transfer to a carving dish and slice thinly.

Arrange the beef on the plate and decorate with the tomatoes and radish flowers. Drizzle with the dressing and serve at once.

SEARED CARPACCIO OF SALMON

SERVES 4 AS A STARTER

3 teaspoons freshly ground black pepper

1 large bunch of dill, finely chopped, plus extra to serve

½ teaspoon sea salt crystals

1 pound (500 g) thick salmon fillet, cut down the centre into 2 pieces and rolled into 2 sausage shapes

1 white turnip, cut into julienne

Rice vinegar, for drizzling

Olive oil, for frying

❊ **NOTE** It is recommended that wild fish should be frozen for 48 hours to kill parasites that may be present prior to eating raw or cured.

I have used dill and black pepper to sear in the salmon but you can vary herbs and spices to suit your taste. Try juniper and parsley. Experiment with other types of fish too.

Combine the pepper, dill and salt and proceed as for the Seared Carpaccio of Lamb (see page 263), cooking for just 5 minutes.

Cut into slices ½ inch (1 cm) thick and serve with the julienne of white turnips drizzled with rice vinegar.

Venetian carpaccio of roast fillet of beef with radicchio

Salmon ceviche with roots and ginger

CEVICHE TABLE

Ryan Hattingh and Martin Williams have been perfecting the art of ceviche at the South American specialist restaurant Gaucho in London, and I was fortunate enough to be invited along to take part in a masterclass that set my taste buds dancing.

They do not believe in the long marinating of the fish, as is traditional, but rather dressing the fish and eating it straight away. First, the fish is salted to draw out the moisture, leaving it on just long enough to trigger the process of osmosis. The citrus juice is then added

and sucked back in to trigger the curing process. The fish becomes opaque after about another 15 to 30 seconds. After pouring off and discarding the excess liquid, the other herbs, spices and ingredients are added to create exotic starter salads or served with cold potatoes or tortillas for a main meal.

The following recipes are based on the Gaucho ceviche menu of the masterclass. Do not stint on the salt, as it is surprising how much is needed to enhance raw fish.

SERVES 1

½ teaspoon wasabi paste

4 teaspoons mirin (sweet rice wine)

Few drops of soy sauce

½ tablespoon olive oil

2 teaspoons stem ginger syrup

2½ ounces (75 g) salmon, salmon trout or salmon fillet, D-cut into thin slices (see page 254)

1 teaspoon sea salt crystals

½ lime

⅛ cup (10 g) candied ginger, chopped

1 ounce (30 g) kohlrabi, mouli or white turnip, cut into julienne

1 tablespoon cilantro leaves

As this "instant" ceviche (and the one below) requires last-minute preparation, I would suggest bringing the ingredients for each guest ready prepared in bowls to the table and leaving everyone to make their own, with a little direction from the host of course! Hence, the ingredients specified are per person.

Mix the wasabi, mirin, soy sauce and olive oil with the stem ginger syrup in a small pitcher.

Take all the prepared ingredients to the table. Give each of your guests a small bowl and plate to make their own ceviche.

Put the salmon slices on a plate and sprinkle the salt on top, crushing the crystals between your fingers. After 30 seconds, squeeze the lime over the fish and let cure for 15 to 30 seconds until the salmon starts to look opaque. Pour away the excess liquid into the small bowl and top the salmon with the chopped stem ginger.

Tip the julienne of kohlrabi, mouli or white turnip over the fish, scatter with the cilantro leaves and drizzle with the wasabi dressing.

CLASSIC SCALLOP CEVICHE

SERVES 1

2½ ounces (75 g) shelled and cleaned queen scallops, roe removed

½ teaspoon sea salt crystals

½ lime

1 small orange, peeled, pith and seeds removed and cut into segments

½ red chili, finely chopped

⅓ cup (30 g) red onion, very finely sliced

½ tablespoon cilantro sprouts mixed with 1 tablespoon chopped cilantro

Juice of ½ lemon, ½ orange and ¼ lime, combined

1 teaspoon chili paste

½ cup (20 g) carrots, cut into julienne, fried and salted in advance

This classic scallop ceviche can also be served as suggested in the recipe above.

Take all the prepared ingredients to the table. Give each of your guests two small bowls and a plate to make their own ceviche.

Put the scallops in one bowl and sprinkle the salt on top, crushing the crystals between your fingers. After 30 seconds, squeeze the lime over the scallops and let cure for 15 to 30 seconds until the scallops start to look opaque. Pour away the excess liquid into the other bowl, add the orange segments to the scallops and turn once.

Add the finely chopped chili, sliced onion and cilantro sprouts with the citrus juices, chili paste and salted julienne of carrots and toss lightly. Turn again and taste. Add extra salt and a squeeze of lime as desired.

below Classic scallop ceviche once cured *opposite* Ceviche once dressed

Ecuadorian prawn ceviche

ECUADORIAN SHRIMP CEVICHE

SERVES 4

5 ounces (125 g) raw jumbo shrimp, peeled and intestinal threads removed

Juice of ½ lemon

Pinch of chili flakes

Pinch of sea salt crystals

Juice of ½ lime

1 portion Ecuadorian Chili Tomato Sauce (see below)

⅛ cup (10 g) red onion, very finely sliced

¼ cup (30 g) avocado, thinly sliced and tossed in lemon juice

2 tablespoons cooked salted popcorn

1 tablespoon toasted pumpkin seeds

1 teaspoon cilantro leaves

The addition of savory popcorn to this ceviche adds an unusual element to the dish which I have since used in other salads. Make the chili tomato sauce in advance to serve with the shrimp. I like to make a double quantity.

Poach the shrimp in a saucepan of simmering salted water flavored with the lemon juice and chili flakes for 10 seconds or just enough to make the skin slightly pink. Drain the shrimp, put in a bowl, and let cool.

Sprinkle the salt on top of the shrimp, crushing the crystals between your fingers. After 30 seconds, squeeze the lime over them and let cure for 15 to 30 seconds until the shrimp start to look opaque. Pour away the excess liquid and toss the shrimp lightly in the tomato sauce.

Layer the prawns with the sliced onion and avocado, then scatter with the popcorn, toasted pumpkin seeds and cilantro leaves.

❧ **VARIATION** Instead of jumbo shrimp, you can use the same weight of shelled, cleaned scallops. Simply slice them into two rings, with or without corals.

ECUADORIAN CHILI TOMATO SAUCE

SERVES 4

½ to 1 ounce (10 to 30 g) whole red chilies, stems trimmed

½ cup (50 g) red bell pepper

1 medium Spanish onion, peeled and thickly sliced

½ cup (50 g) plum tomatoes

1 small garlic clove, peeled

½ orange

½ lemon

½ lime

1 teaspoon Tabasco sauce

⅓ cup (75 g) tomato purée

1 tablespoon extra virgin olive oil

Sea salt as desired

Preheat the oven to 350 F (180 C).

Put the chilies and red bell pepper in a roasting pan with the onion, tomatoes and garlic. Roast in the preheated oven for 20 to 30 minutes until tender.

Transfer to a blender, add all the remaining ingredients, and blend to a purée.

Cook the sauce on the stovetop over medium heat until smooth and creamy.

Freeze what sauce you don't use for next time around.

IN THE RAW OR IS IT?

Robert L. Wolke, a professor of chemistry at the University of Pittsburg and the author of *What Einstein Told his Cook*, explains: The citric acid in limes, lemons and other citrus fruits changes the proteins in fish in a process called denaturation. The normally twisted and folded protein molecules are unraveled or unfolded into less convoluted shapes. They lose their original nature or become denatured.

Heat denatures proteins; we call it cooking. High concentrations of salt denatures proteins too; we call that salting. Acetic acid in vinegar denatures proteins and we call that pickling. The acidity in wine denatures proteins, which we call marinating. Citrus juice denatures fish—we call this ceviche. The lime's acidity is more than strong enough to prevent bacterial growth in the fish.

above Marinating shrimp
opposite Marinated
swordfish and shrimp

IL PESCE SPADA E GAMBERETTI MARINATI

MARINATED SWORDFISH AND SHRIMP

SERVES 4

Scant ½ cup (100 ml) extra virgin olive oil

Handful of fennel fronds, finely chopped, plus extra fronds to serve

1 garlic clove, cut into slivers

Juice of 1 lemon

7 ounces (200 g) swordfish, cut into 8 paper-thin slices

12 large raw shrimp, peeled but heads left on and intestinal threads removed

1 large fennel bulb, cut into paper-thin slices

This recipe originates from Andrea's, a restaurant in the historic town of Palazzolo Acreide in the Iblea mountains in Sicily. The food here, say proprietors Andrea and Lucia Alì, "is inspired by the mountains" and by the rich heritage of the local gastronomy, but at the same time it has a contemporary edge. The restaurant has been awarded with a Slow Food Snail for the quality, authenticity and seasonality of the food supply in Sicily, along with only eight other restaurants on the island.

Put the extra virgin olive oil in a heatproof bowl and add the chopped fennel fronds and garlic slivers. Cover with plastic wrap and set over a saucepan of gently boiling water. When the plastic wrap lifts, the infusion is ready. Strain the oil, then whisk in the lemon juice.

Arrange the swordfish on a platter and put the shrimp in a noncorrosive dish. Drizzle both with half the fennel oil infusion, cover, and leave in a cool place for 1 hour.

When ready to serve, divide the swordfish and shrimp among four plates, adding the sliced fennel. Drizzle with the remaining dressing and top with a fennel frond.

JAPANESE SASHIMI SALAD

SERVES 4

3½ ounces (100 g) thick-cut salmon or salmon trout

3½ ounces (100 g) thick-cut tuna or swordfish

3½ ounces (100 g) thick-cut monkfish or other firm-fleshed white fish

3½ ounces (100 g) tiny cleaned scallops, raw peeled shrimp or small cleaned squid, cut into rings

1 tablespoon sesame seeds

3 tablespoons light soy sauce, plus extra to serve

½ to 1 teaspoon wasabi paste, plus extra to serve

½ cucumber, halved lengthwise and diagonally cut into long, thin slices

1 shallot, thinly sliced

2 small white turnips, cut into julienne

4 scallions, cut into julienne

1 to 2 sheets of nori (dried seaweed)

Good handful of purple radish sprouts

Inspired by the classic Japanese sashimi salad, this recipe would traditionally also contain boiled rice.

Freeze the salmon, tuna and monkfish for 2 days, then let partially defrost in the refrigerator. Cut it into equal-size pieces, about ¾ inch by 1 inch (2 cm by 3 cm) and 2 inches (5 mm) thick. Add scallops, cover and place in the refrigerator.

Put the sesame seeds in a hot, dry pan and stir until golden all over. Transfer to a baking sheet to cool.

Mix the soy sauce with the wasabi.

Combine the salad ingredients in a single-serving bowl or divide among four individual bowls. Shred the nori and toss it into the salad. Arrange the prepared fish on top, drizzle with the soy and wasabi dressing, and sprinkle with the toasted sesame seeds and a few pruple radish sprouts.

Serve with small dipping bowls of wasabi, light soy sauce and Pickled Ginger (see page 245).

Japanese sashimi salad

SEA BASS WITH ORANGE AND CORIANDER

SERVES 4

4 sea bass fillets

1 heaping teaspoon sea salt crystals

Juice and finely grated zest of 3 large oranges

Good pinch of chili flakes

2 tablespoons chopped cilantro, plus extra cilantro leaves to serve

This recipe uses the classic ceviche combination of orange juice, chili and cilantro to marinate sea bass. If you prefer, you can lightly steam the fish for four minutes before marinating.

Arrange the sea bass fillets in a shallow, noncorrosive dish and sprinkle generously with the salt, crushing the crystals between your fingers. Add the juice and zest of two oranges and the chili flakes, cover, and leave in a cool place for 2 hours.

After this time, pour off the marinade and either leave whole or cut each fillet into three or five pieces. Arrange the fish on serving plates.

Mix the chopped cilantro with the orange zest and juice of the third orange and drizzle over the fish. Top each serving with a cilantro leaf and serve.

SCALLOP AND CAVIAR SHOTS

SERVES 4

12 shelled and cleaned queen scallops or large scallops, diced

Few mint leaves, plus extra tiny sprigs or small leaves to serve

Juice and finely grated zest of ½ lime

Pinch of chili flakes

Good pinch of sea salt crystals

1 tablespoon finely chopped cilantro

1 to 2 tablespoons grapeseed oil

¼ cup (50 g) lumpfish roe or caviar

⅓ cup (50 g) red onion, finely chopped

EQUIPMENT

4 shot glasses

This is a simple and fun way to serve raw fish as there is no paper-thin slicing involved. Simply marinate the scallops and transfer to glasses when required.

Put the scallops in a small noncorrosive bowl. Add the mint leaves, lime juice, chili flakes and sea salt crystals and mix together. Cover and leave in a cool place for at least an hour.

Put the lime zest in a small bowl and mix in the chopped cilantro and the grapeseed oil. Mix together the lumpfish roe and the finely chopped onion. After an hour, pour off the excess marinade from the scallops, discard the mint, and add the lime zest, cilantro and oil mixture.

Divide the scallops among four shot glasses and top with a little of the roe mixture and a tiny sprig or small mint leaf.

LOST IN THE MISTS OF TIME

The preparation and serving of raw meat also has its distinct traditions. Steak tartare, or *biftek à l'Américaine* as it is sometimes known, is regarded as a quintessentially French dish of very finely chopped raw best beef or horse steak, seasoned with salt, pepper, finely chopped onion and parsley, and enriched with a raw egg, sometimes with the addition of Tabasco, Worcestershire sauce or capers for extra piquancy. There is, however, a great deal of fascinating mythology connecting steak tartare to the Tartar people, though there is no documentation to suggest that they actually ate raw meat. It was certainly a popular dish in Germany in the Middle Ages and was introduced by German immigrants to the USA, along with hamburgers, delicatessens and many other specialties that have now become irreversibly identified with North America.

above **Steak tartare ready to serve** *opposite* **Steak tartare once mixed**

STEAK TARTARE

SERVES 4

1¾ cups (400 g) ground or very finely chopped sirloin or fillet of beef or horse steak

1 onion, finely chopped

4 teaspoons olive oil

½ teaspoon Tabasco sauce

1 teaspoon Worcestershire sauce

3 tablespoons finely chopped flat-leaf parsley

4 free-range egg yolks

4 cocktail gherkins, finely chopped

2 tablespoon salted capers, rinsed, drained and chopped

4 tablespoons mayonnaise

Sea salt and freshly ground black pepper as desired

Do you like your steak ground or finely chopped? Steak tartare is another of those ritualistic dishes that gets talked about in hallowed tones and excites passionate argument over how it should be made. Some would say the simpler the better; others say it should contain 21 ingredients.

I would, however, as a starting point, like to quote the New Larousse Gastronomique *on the subject: "á la tartare is the name given to ground beef steak seasoned with salt and pepper reshaped into a steak and served uncooked with a raw egg on top and on the side capers, chopped onion and parsley."*

Whatever you do, don't put the steak in a blender to chop it! If you don't have a grinder, ask your butcher to grind it for you, or use your very best knife (don't forget to sharpen it first) and chopping skills, because the meat must be very finely chopped.

Put the meat in a bowl, add the onion, olive oil, Tabasco and Worcestershire sauces and parsley and season with salt and pepper. Using your hands, mix together well.

Take approximately a quarter of the seasoned meat, about 7 ounces (200 g), form into a ball and then place it to the side of a serving plate, pressing lightly on the meat to gently flatten it. Repeat three more times. Make an indentation in the top of each tartare with the back of a spoon and add an egg yolk.

Divide the remaining ingredients between the plates, arranging them in small piles around the tartare.

Serve at once with French fries, if desired.

TUNA TARTARE AND TOMATO JEWEL TIAN

SERVES 4

9 ounces (250 g) tuna loin, diced into tiny pieces

Handful of flat-leaf parsley, finely chopped, plus extra leaves to serve

1 tablespoon salted capers rinsed, squeezed dry and finely chopped

Juice of 1 lemon

4 to 6 tablespoons olive oil

2 to 3 large firm tomatoes, skinned, seeded, drained on paper towels and diced into concassé (tomato jewels), plus extra to serve

Sea salt crystals (optional) and freshly ground black pepper

EQUIPMENT

4 tian rings

Best cuts, such as loin of tuna, also make utterly delicious tartare. The longer you leave the lemon juice marinade on the tuna, the more the tuna "cooks." This recipe has a very refreshing and reviving quality.

Put the diced tuna in a noncorrosive bowl with the finely chopped parsley, capers, lemon juice and extra virgin olive oil. Season with pepper. Mix well and taste, only adding salt if necessary. Cover and refrigerate for 1 hour.

When ready to serve, stir in the tomato concassé.

Put a tian ring on each of four serving plates and divide the tartare mixture between the tians. Slide off the rings and top the tartare with a few tomato jewels and a leaf of parsley. Serve with hunks of hot baguette and butter, if desired.

Tuna tartare and tomato jewel tian

THE DIRECTORY

Whether we live in a country village, market town or city, I believe we have a duty to support our community wherever possible. Local butchers, bakers, grocers, greengrocers, fishmongers, corner shops, delis and markets suffered massive closures with the advent of the supermarkets. However, over the past decade or so with the resurgence of interest in food and how it is produced such specialist businesses are thriving again but without continuing support they could disappear once more. Much of the food in this book is specialist and therefore may not be available either in your local specialist shops or favorite supermarket and this is why I have compiled this directory but please check out your regular suppliers first.

U.S. SUPPLIERS

ORGANIC FOOD

County Market
Organic food and products
1819 Philo Rd.
Urbana, IL 61802
Phone: 217-337-0210

For the Good of It
Organic food and products
3135 West Jefferson St.
Joliet, IL 60435
Tel: 815-744-7659
www.ftgoi.com

Naturally Yours Grocery
Organic food and products
4700 North University
Peoria, IL 61614
Tel: 309-692-4448
www.naturallyyoursgrocery.com

The Old Country Store
Organic food and products
455 Broadway
Hot Springs, AR 71901
Tel: 501-624-1172

Rising Tide Market
Organic food and products
42 Forest Ave.
Glen Cove, NY
Tel: 516-676-7895

Harvest Market
Organic food and products
7417 Lancaster Pike
Hockessin, DE
Tel: 302-234-6779
www.harvestmarketnaturalfoods.com

Vim N Vigor
Organic food and products
98-1247 Kaahumanu Street
Aiea, HI 96701
Tel: 808-484-4787
www.vimnvigor.com

Natural Foods Co-Op
Organic food and products
745 Francis St.
San Luis Obispo, CA
Tel: 805-544-7928
www.coopdirectory.com

Food For Thought, Inc
Organic food and products
2929 E. Central
Wichita, KS
Tel: 316-683-6078
www.foodsforthoughtkitchens.com

The Source
Organic food and products
32 Kainehe St
Kailua, HI
Tel: 808-262-5604

Freddie's Market
Organic food and products
9052 Big Bend Boulevard
Saint Louis, MO 63119
Tel: 314-968-1914
www.freddiesmarket.com

Amelia's Garden
Organic food and products
305 S. Main Street
Snowflake, AZ 85937
Tel: 928-536-2046
www.ameliasgardenhealth.com

Tommy K Vitamins
Organic food and products
54 Research Drive
Stamford, CT 06906
Phone: 203-325-9544
www.tommykvitamins.com

La Buena Salud
Organic food and products
917-A Locust Street
St. Louis, MO 63101
Tel: 314-283-9016
www.labuenasaludllc.com

Winslow's Farm, Home and Kitchen
Organic food and products
7213 Delmar Boulevard
St. Louis, MO 63130
Tel: 314-725-7550
www.winslowshome.com

Local Harvest Grocery
Organic food and products
3148 Morgan Ford Road
St. Louis, MO 63116
Tel: 314-865-5260
www.localharvestgrocery.com

Bagliani's Italian Market
Organic food and products
417 E. 12th St.
Hammonton, NJ 08037
Tel: 609-561-0693
www.baglianis.com

Savenor's Market
Organic food and products
92 Kirkland Street
Cambridge, MA 02138
Tel: 617-576-6328
www.savenorsmarket.com

Savenor's Market
Organic Food and products
160 Charles Street
Boston, MA 02114
Tel: 617-723-6328
www.savenorsmarket.com

Pasta Nostra
Organic food and products
116 Washington St
Norwalk, CT 06854
Tel: 203-854-9700
www.pastanostra.com

Ringside Steakhouse
Organic food and products
2165 West Burnside
Portland, OR
Tel: 503-223-1513
www.ringsidesteakhouse.com

Diamond Organics, Inc.
All organic products
1272 Highway 1
Moss Landing, California, 95039
Tel: 888-674-2642
www.diamondorganics.com

Whole Foods Market
www.wholefoodsmarket.com

Trader Joe's
www.traderjoes.com

MEAT AND FISH SUPPLIERS

Lava Lake Land & Livestock, L.L.C.
Lamb products
P.O. Box 2249
Hailey, Idaho 83333
Tel: 888-52-5253
Fax: 208-788-1264

Texas Heritage Beef
Grass-fed beef
Fort Worth, Texas
Tel: 817-690-7327
Email: info@texasheritagebeef.com
www.texasheritagebeef.com

Organic Prairie
Grass-fed beef, organic pork and chicken
1 Organic Way
La Farge, WI 54639
Tel: 877-662-6328
Email: consumerrelations@organicprairie.com
www.organicprairie.com

LINDNER BISON™
Grass-fed beef
Valencia, CA 91355
Tel: 661-254-0200
Fax: 661-254-0224
Email: klindner@lindnerbison.com

Peninsula Processing & Smokehouse
Sustainable seafood
720 Kalifonsky Beach Road
Soldotna, Alaska, 99669
Tel: 866-262-8846
Fax: 907-262-0827
www.great-alaska-seafood.com

Willowfield Enterprises Ltd.
Sustainable seafood
117-15272 Croydon Drive
Surrey, B.C.
V3S 0Z5 Canada
Tel: 877-588-1227
Fax: 604-531-1255
Email: info@willowfield.net
www.willowfield.net

Llano Seco™ California's Organic Pork
Tel: 530- 342-0839
www.llanoseco.com

SMOKEHOUSES

Homestead Harvest
Smokehouses
P.O. Box 31125
Bellingham, WA 98228
Tel: 877-300-3427
www.homesteadharvest.com

Mid-Western Research & Supply
Smokehouses and supplies
430 N. Mosley St.
Wichita, KS 67202-2814
Tel: 800-835-2832
Fax: 316-522-5136
Email: sales@midwesternresearch.com
www.midwesternresearch.com

The Sausage Maker, Inc.
500 Clinton St. Bldg. 123
Buffalo, NY 14206-3099
Tel: 888-490-8525
Fax: 716-824-6465
www.sausagemaker.com

Highland Brands, LLC
19 North 100 West
Hyrum, UT 84319
Tel: 800-285-9044
www.canningpantry.com

Do Right Services, Inc.
Smoking and meat processing supplies
10312 Highway 28 West
Boyce, LA 71409
Tel: 888-588-7267
Fax: 318-793-5573
www.sausage-stuffer.com

INTERNATIONAL SUPPLIERS

WHEN IN THE CITY CHECK OUT:

BERLIN (GERMANY)

KaDeWe Feinschmecker-Etage
The gourmet fifth floor at KaDeWe department store boasts 1200 sausage and ham specialities

BAD KISSINGEN (GERMANY)

Faber Feinkost
Sausage and ham makers for four generations
www.faber-feinkost.de

LONDON (U.K.)

Harrods Food Hall
What don't they sell?

Selfridges Food Hall
And the salt beef bar

Fortnam and Mason
Amazing selection of jams, jellies and chutneys and biltong.

Fatboys Diner
For pastrami on rye
Trinity Bouy Wharf, 64 Orchard Place, London, E14 OJW
Tel: +44 (0) 20 7987 4334
hello@fatboysdiner.co.uk

The Bagel Factory
For salt beef on rye
155 Brick Lane, Shoreditch, London E1 6SB

Scotts Sandwich Bar
10 New Row, Covent Garden, London, WC2N 4LH
Tel: +44 (0) 20 7240 0340

The Salt Beef Bar
2 Finchley Road, Golders Green, London
Tel: +44 (0) 208 7317375

MILAN

Peck
Salumeria and style since 1883
Via Spadari 9
Milano
www.peck.it

NEW YORK

Dean and Deluca
'Where the big is pig'
www.deandeluca.com

Katz Deli
Best pastrami and corned beef sandwiches

205 East Houston Street
New York, NY10002
www.katzdeli.com

PARIS

Bellota Bellota
Ham specialist – whole pigs and deli
18 Rue Jean Nicot, Paris, 75007
www.bellota-bellota.com

La Crémerie
Taste the best charcuterie with organic wines
9 Rue des Quatre Vents, Paris, 75006
www.lacremerie.fr

EQUIPMENT AND SUNDRIES

Tim Weschenfelder & Son
Sausage making supplies
Domestic and commercial meat slicers; vacpac and sausage machines; curing salts that give perfect results; fab pastrami; sausage skins; and dried pig's blood
Tel: 01642 247524
www.weschenfelder.co.uk

Sausage making supplies
(including saltpeter and much more)
www.sausagemaking.org

Grakka Ltd
Bradley Smoker
www.bradleysmoker.com
UK distributor:
www.grakka.com

King Coops of Long Island New York
For information on Southern 'Barbeque' style pits and smokers
www.kingcookers.com
commoninterest.blogspot.com
all you ever needed to know about Southern States 'barbeque'

SMOKERIES AND SMOKEHOUSES

Foreman and Field: mail order
(Oldest smokers of salmon in the UK.) For world famous smoked food and many other cured specialities plus everything you always wanted to eat but never got round to making.
Stour Road, Fish Island, London E3 2NT
Tel: +44 (0) 208 5252352
www.formanandfield.com

Inverawe: mail order
Traditional smoked Scottish salmon and much more smoked in Scotland in a traditional smokebox environment
Taynuilt, Argyll, PA35 1HU
Scotland
Tel: +44 (0) 844 8475490
www.smokedsalmon.co.uk

The Organic Smokehouse: mail order
The only dedicated organic smokehouse in the world
Michael and Debbie Leviseur
Oak Meadow Bacheldre Church
Stoke Montgomary SY15 6TE
Tel: +44 (0) 1588 660206
www.organicsmokehouse.com

SALT COD

Valvona and Crolla: mail order and personal shoppers
Ham; salami; sausages including salsiccia lucanica; salt cod
19 Elm Road, Edinburgh
Tel: +44 (0) 1315566066
www.valvonacrolla.co.uk

Robson & Sons Ltd: mail order
Kippers, smoked haddock and smoked salmon
Craster, Northumberland, NE66 3TR
Tel: +44 (0) 1665 576223
enquiry@kipper.co.uk
www.kipper.co.uk

BOTTARGA

La Fromargerie
Shops at Highbury Park and Moxon Street, London
www.lafromagerie.co.uk

Solky – antioco.fois@tiscali.it
E.Salis – ef.salis@tiscali.it

U.K. PROVISIONERS

Lishman's of Ilkley – mail order
Sausages, bacon and hams from rare breed pigs
25 Leeds Rd, Ilkley, W. Yorkshire LS29 8DP
Tel: +44 (0) 1943 603809
www.lishmansofilkley.co.uk

Trealy Farm for stockists and farmers markets
Bacon sausages and hams also continental charcuterie all from local free ranging pigs
Trealy Farm, Monmouthshire, Wales
www.trealyfarm.com

CHINESE SPECIALITIES

The Asian Cookshop: mail order
Dried shrimp and everything you will ever need for making Japanese food at home
www.theasiancookshop.co.uk

FRENCH CHARCUTERIE AND DELI

La Fromagerie: personal shoppers only
Jambon persillé; goose rilettes; chorizo di Pate Negra; Saucissons; Toulouse sausages; Bayonne and auvergne hams;
Shops at Highbury Park and Moxon Street, London
www.lafromagerie.co.uk

GERMAN SPECIALITIES

German Deli: mail order and personal shoppers
Air-dried Westphalian ham; Black Forest ham; German sausages; Bismarck herring; roll mops; traditional breads and pumperkickel canapé bases
www.germandeli.co.uk

ITALIAN SALUMERIA

Fratelli Camisa: mail order and personal shoppers
Marinated anchovy and octopus; wild boar and cacciatore salamis; onions in balsamic vinegar; pickled fruits and vegetables
Old Compton Street, London, W1
Tel: +44 (0) 1992763076
www.camisa.co.uk

JAPANESE SPECIALITIES

The Asian Cookshop: mail order
Dried shrimp and everything you need for making oriental food
www.theasiancookshop.co.uk

SCANDINAVIAN CURED FISH AND OTHER SMORGASBORD SPECIALITIES

Ikea: personal shoppers only after the checkout and before the exit
Branches everywhere

SPANISH TAPAS, HAMS, SALCHICHÓNS ETC

Brindisa: Spanish ham delivery and personal shoppers
Hams; salchichón; chorizo; morcilla; cecina; smoked paprika and membrillo
Borough Market
Tel: +44 (0) 208 7721600
sales@brindisa.com
www.brindisa.com

Orce Serrano Hams: mail order
Everything for Spanish tapas from Bellota to Serrano ham; from salt cod to cured tuna loin; La Carniceria de Julian chorizo sausages to paella pans and spices
Fuente Nueva, 93, 18858 Orce
Granada, Spain
Tel: 0034 958 065170
www.orceserranohams.com

PICKLES, FRUIT IN SPIRIT, JELLIES AND SAUCES

Hawkeshead Relish Company Ltd
The Square, Hawkeshead, Cumbria, LA22 ONZ
www.hawksheadrelish.com/shop

The English Provender Company: mail order
Piccalilli; apple chutney; sweet tomato and chili chutney
www.englishprovender.com

INDEX

ACKNOWLEDGMENTS

My thanks to all who have helped in some way to make this the book it is:

Master smokers Michael and Debbie Leviseur of The Organic Smokehouse, Shropshire; Lance Forman of Forman and Son, London; Neil and Rosie Robson of Robson and Sons Ltd., Craster; and Richard Cook of the Severn and Wye.

The Chef/patrons Shaun Hill now of the Walnut Tree and his head chef Roger Brook; Alan Murchison, chef patron L'Ortolan, Reading and his satellite star Will Holland, head chef of La Bécasse in Ludlow; Ryan Hattingh and Martin Williams of Gaucho, London; Henry Herbert, head chef of the Coach and Horses pub, Clerkenwell, London; Steve Robbins, head chef, Prego, Monmouth; and retired Michelin-starred chef Rinaldo Dalsasso from the Trentino region of Italy.

Alessandra Smith and the Italian State tourist office ENIT in London. To Mario Corongiu, town mayor, Comune di Sant'Antioco, my guide Chicco and all the delightful people who were happy to talk about bottarga and other curing traditions. Antioco Fernandeo de Fois of Sulkey; Mario and Anna Maria of Salis, producers of Bottarga. To chef patrons Stefano Cannas of Golfo di Cannas restaurant; to Paola and Roberto chef proprietors of Del Passeggero.

Cherry Haigh of the Dialogue Agency; The Parma Ham Festival in Parma; Fabrizio Raimondi and Elke Fernandez of the Parma Ham Consortium; Stefano Borchini of Slega Parma Ham.

Francesco and Ide Bagliardi of Masticabrodo; Rowley Leigh, food writer and proprietor of Le Cafe' Anglais, Porchester Gardens, London; and chef/ food writer Alex Mackay for their contributions. Gabriella Bruschi journalist from Milano and Mirca Bolognese, ENIT Parma.

The southern region of Puglia, the region of Gargano and the town of Vieste; Antonio Calabresi; innovative young chef patron, Andrea Ali of 'da Andrea' in Palazzolo Acreidi in the hills near Syracuse in Sicily.

To Mario Stoppani who gave me carte blanche to roam amid the forest of hams, salamis and other fine comestibles in the Peck SpA, Milano. Journalist Mariella Belloni.

The Terra Madre pavilion of the Salone del Gusto is a worldwide culinary melting pot where local traditions can be exchanged from one side of the globe to the other: stock fish from Norway; bottarga made by Imraguen women in Mauritania; fish smoking on Robinson Crusoe Island, Chile; salting greens in Japan.

Joed Hansen, Alvestad Slow food presidium coordinator; Birgit Aarones of Seafood Norway; *agriturismo* Casale Cjanor – Friuli; Giacomo Mosso, Ceresole d' Alba, Turin; Sunday and Pietro Bologna of the Organic small holding Serpepe *agriturismo* near Viterbo.

James Swift and Graham Waddington of Trealy Farm Charcuterie, Wales.

Chris Callwood and his team of Callwood & sons family butchers, Ross-on-Wye, Herefordshire; David Lishman butcher of Ilkley Yorkshire; Mark Bruce of Hanson's Salt Beef; Sammy Minzly of Brick Lane Bagel Factory; Rachel Revell of Epping for lending me her wonderful brawn recipe.

Andre Pope, Senior Judge, South Carolina Barbeque Association and Lake E. High, President, South Carolina Barbeque Association; Jens Degn Andersen, Greenland; Robert L.Wolke Professor of Chemistry at the University of Pittsberg; Birit Lyregård food journalist, based in Stockholm; Iain Macdonald and Gayle Hartley; La Carniceria de Julian, Orce Andalusia; Annegret Schrick, Germany; Martha Eike Norway; Susanne Sherwood Rogers, Sweden; Christian Allison, Holland; Tony Maslin, Scotland.

Ann and Franco Taruschio.

John Watkins, Grakka Ltd; Tim Weschenfelder, Weschenfelder and Son.

To our good humored and hard working team: food stylist Monaz Dumasia, assistants Sandra Stafford and Lin Bridges; Lawrence Morton and Simon Wheeler, book designer and photographer, who doubled cheerfully as delivery boys, furniture removers and general dogs bodies; Jacqui 'of all trades' Small, publisher and assistant extraordinaire; Kerenza Swift and Abi Waters for suffering the thankless task of editing.

All photography by Simon Wheeler excluding Parma ham image on page 111 from the Consorzio del Prosciutto di Parma by photographer Steve Lee.